*"NORTHERN LIBERTIES SIXTH LARGEST
AMERICAN TOWN IN 1800"*

PEGG'S RUN IN NORTHERN LIBERTIES.

Happenings
in
Ye Olde
Philadelphia
1680–1900

Rudolph J. Walther

Heritage Books
2025

HERITAGE BOOKS

AN IMPRINT OF HERITAGE BOOKS, INC.

Books, CDs, and more—Worldwide

For our listing of thousands of titles see our website
at
www.HeritageBooks.com

A Facsimile Reprint
Published 2025 by
HERITAGE BOOKS, INC.
Publishing Division
5810 Ruatan Street
Berwyn Heights, MD 20740

Originally published by:
Walther Printing House
Third Street and Girard Avenue
Philadelphia
1925

Republished by:
Adams Apple Press
PO Box E, Bedminster, PA 18910
1994

International Standard Book Number
Paperbound: 978-0-7884-4101-1

HAPPENINGS

IN YE OLDE

PHILADELPHIA
1680 - - - 1900

BY RUDOLPH J. WALTHER
1925

WALTHER PRINTING HOUSE
THIRD STREET AND GIRARD AVENUE
PHILADELPHIA

REPUBLISHED BY
ADAMS APPLE PRESS
PO BOX E, BEDMINSTER, PA 18910
1994

Penn's Treaty with the Indians.

"Fair Philadelphia next is rising seen,
Between two rivers plac'd, two miles between;
The Delaware and Schulkil, new to fame
Both ancient streams, yet of a modern name.
The city form'd upon a beauteous plan,
Has many houses built, tho' late began;
Rectangular the streets, direct and fair;
And rectilinear all the ranges are."

THOMAS MANKIN, 1729.

TO THOSE WHO LOVE THE OLD
ASSOCIATIONS AND DELIGHT IN
TALKING ABOUT THE GOOD OLD
DAYS, THIS LITTLE BOOK IS
SYMPATHETICALLY DEDICATED.

PREFACE

An examination of American cities a century ago presents many curiosities. In 1800, not New York, but Philadelphia, was our largest city, a pre-eminence it held until 1830. After Philadelphia, New York, Baltimore and Boston, Charleston, S.C., was the largest American city. But I defy any one to give the name of the sixth largest American town in 1800. It was Northern Liberties. How many Americans today ever heard of this metropolis? An antiquarian research discloses that it is now part of Philadelphia. After Northern Liberties, our biggest city was Southwark, Pa, also a part of the present Philadelphia; then came Salem, Mass. Such were the places, a hundred years ago, which were entered in the competition for primacy.

FROM WORLD'S WORK.

THE above article appeared a few years ago in a magazine published in Chicago. Being proud of the "sixth largest town," the place of my birth, my swimmin' holes, my sport on the river, my home for more than half a century, and my business location since its beginning in 1869, the reading of the article prompted me to compile some items of interest of the old days of this section as well as of some of the other sections that finally formed this great city of Brotherly Love, and print them in book form for private distribution.

They, no doubt, will prove of interest to many, especially to those of the older generation, who will recall many of the happenings mentioned in the Chronology. The various articles and items were gleaned from old publications, "History of Philadelphia," by Scharff & Westcott, the "Public Ledger," "The Evening Bulletin" and "The Philadelphia Inquirer," as well as from personal observations and recollections.

The wandering singer was received with joy among all early peoples, not so much for his music as because he brought news from afar and fascinating stories of distant, unknown countries to which few of those who listened could ever hope to go; it was with this thought that I compiled this book.

RUDOLPH J. WALTHER.

WILLIAM PENN.

PENN'S HOUSE.

CONTENTS

PENNSYLVANIA

PENNSYLVANIA was settled as early as 1630 by Dutch pioneers who came up the Delaware Bay and River and settled at Gloucester point.

Captain Kornelius Jacobus Mey, a Dutchman, is regarded as the first explorer of our bay and river, after whom Cape May was named.

These pioneers eventually drifted over to Pennsylvania. They designed to raise tobacco and grain. A few scattered and settled in Bucks County, other settlers having made New York, which they named New Amsterdam, their objective point.

Swedes began to arrive about 1631, as related by their historian Campanius. Their first landing was at New Castle, which they named Stockholm.

King Charles II, in 1664, whose claim to New England gave him power to claim to the southward, being unwilling to sanction the prosperity of the Dutch, as a separate community, granted a patent to his brother James, Duke of York and Albany, of lands in America, including all that the Dutch then held as their New Netherlands. The Dutch reluctantly submitted, New York being named after the conquering duke.

The Duke of York, possessed of the Jerseys, granted same to Sir George Carteret, who came from the Isle of Jersey. His intention was to call same in honor of his family, Nova Caesaria, but the people preferred to call it by a name they could better understand, to-wit the Jerseys. (The Indian name of the Jerseys was *Scheyichbi.*)

In 1675 the west part of Jersey was sold to one Edward Byllinge of the Society of Friends, to whom William Penn, soon afterwards, became a trustee. Penn, in his efforts to settle the estate of Byllinge, became so well acquainted with the region of Pennsylvania and colonial settlements, as to be afterwards induced to purchase that for himself, by receiving it as an equivalent for claims due his father, Admiral Penn.

MICHAEL SCHLATTER'S DESCRIPTION OF PENNSYLVANIA
WRITTEN AT AMSTERDAM, JUNE, 1751

"Pennsylvania, lying in the northern part of America, is a country of no small compass. It lies in a healthy climate; it is not merely inhabitable, but very much inhabited, not only by the ancient dwellers in the land, but also by thousands who have emigrated thither from Europe and still arrive every year. It extends toward the north to the five largest inland seas known in the world, along the course of which it is not difficult to reach the celebrated Mississippi River, down which one can sail to the Gulf of Mexico.

"Since the time when the English have taken possession of Pennsylvania, and the country has been peopled from various European nations, it has been divided into nine cantons, these called counties. The most important towns, as they have been built successively, are:

"1. Philadelphia, consisting at present of 2,800 houses, mostly of stone.

"2. New Castle, consisting at present of 240 houses, mostly of stone, and lying from Philadelphia distant 40 miles.

"3. Chester, consisting of 120 houses, lying 10 miles distant from New Castle.

"4. Germantown, consisting of 260 houses, lying 6 miles from Philadelphia.

"5. Lancaster, consisting of 600 houses, lying from Germantown 63 miles.

1

"6. York, consisting of 190 houses, lying from Lancaster 23 miles.

"7. Reading, lately built, consisting of 60 houses, lying 60 miles from York.

"In the whole of Pennsylvania, according to estimation, there are 190,000 souls, in which the pagan inhabitants are not included. Of these, it is estimated 90,000 are Germans; . . . These are scattered through all the cantons or counties; still they have more especially settled down in the counties of Philadelphia, Bucks, Lancaster, York, and Chester."

In this same document Schlatter solicited contributions for educational and religious work among the Pennsylvania Germans from charitable persons in Holland, Switzerland and England, stating that "a yearly salary of forty or fifty Belgic florins . . . would be sufficient (for the yearly salary of a clergyman) in Pennsylvania, a very fertile province, where the cost of living is generally low."

As a result of Schlatter's appeal $60,000—an enormous sum for those days—was contributed by the people of Holland for educational purposes in Pennsylvania in 1762. He also caused nearly $100,000 to be raised in England. An interesting feature of this was the application of some of this money that "four or six young persons of talent from these free schools (at York, Lancaster, Reading, New Hanover, Skippack and Goshenhoppen) should have the privilege of going to the University of Oxford, there to study and afterwards to serve their Fatherland."

The first English colony that came out under the sale to Byllinge went into Salem Creek, which they so named, and there began the present existing town of Salem. The neighborhood had been previously settled by the Swedes, who had near there a fort which they called Elsinburgh. In fact the Swedes built numbers of forts, or rather block houses, at the entrance of creeks in the bay and river.

In 1677 the ship Kent arrived with 230 passengers, mostly Friends, with good estates. They landed at Raccoon Creek, where they found some Swedish houses, but not being well accommodated, they, with the commissioners who came in the ship, went up to Chygoe's Island (now Burlington) called after the Indian Sachem who then dwelt there. The town plot was purchased and called New Beverly. Shortly thereafter another band of settlers came from Wiccacoa.

The first ship that ever visited Burlington was the Shield of Stockton, from Hull, in 1678. Then the site of the present Philadelphia was a bold and high shore called Coaquanock. The ship in veering there, chanced to strike the trees with her sails and spars. It was then observed that the passengers often exclaimed "what a fine place for a town."

Other vessels continued to follow to Jersey. In 1682, as many as 360 passengers came out in one vessel.

Burlington and the adjacent county settled very rapidly.

Some Friends settled on the western side of the Delaware before Philadelphia was laid out, notably at Shackamaxon, now called Kensington.

The founding of Pennsylvania, about 40,000 square miles, was confirmed to William Penn under the Great Seal on the 6th of January, 1681. Thereupon Penn induced people to emigrate, the terms being 40 shillings per 100 acres, and "shares" of 5,000 acres for £100. These generous terms induced many to set out for the new world.

The town of Philadelphia was located in 1682, "having a high and dry land next to the water, with a shore ornamented with a fine view of pine trees growing upon it."

The first adventurers made their settlements in this way, to dig caves or shelter in which to place their families or effects, then to get warrants of survey, and to wander about for their choice of localities.

William Penn set sail from England in August, 1682, with Captain Greenway, in the ship Welcome. The ship was filled with additional passengers, mostly Friends. They arrived at New Castle on October 27th, 1682, the next day arriving at Philadelphia. Penn and his friends came up from Chester in an open boat and landed on the low and sandy beach at Dock Creek. Penn at that time was 38 years of age.

In the year 1683-4, emigration increased. Pioneers came from England, Ireland, Wales, Holland and Germany.

King Charles the Second owed Admiral Penn, the father of William Penn, a large debt, and to cancel same, the claim being the main part of William's inheritance, he merrily gave a large tract of wilderness to Penn in cancellation of the debt.

Penn with broad ideas and unarmed, as was natural for a Quaker, came and made the famous treaty with the Indians, "as long as water flows and the sun shines and grass grows." A treaty which was not sworn to and yet never broken.

A plain and simple monument stands in Shackamaxon, at Penn Treaty Park, in Kensington, a modest memorial of a momentous act, the spot where was signed an unbroken treaty; probably the only treaty of the world's which was not broken.

PHILADELPHIA

THE city of Philadelphia, as laid out by William Penn, comprised only that portion of the present city situated between South and Vine Streets and the Delaware and Schuylkill Rivers. In fact, the city proper was that portion between High (Market) Street and Dock Creek. Here is where the pioneers dug caves in the banks of the Delaware or built huts on the land higher up. Meanwhile, the women equally busy in their sphere, had lighted their fire on the bare earth, and having "their kettle slung between two poles upon a stick transverse," thus prepared the meal of homely and frugal fare for the repast of the diligent builders.

Indians were more or less present, either as spectators of the improvements then progressing, or, as venders of their game and venison from the neighboring wilds. The Swedes and Dutch, who were the earliest settlers, as neighbors, brought their productions to market as a matter of course.

Settlements were made, however, outside of these boundaries, and in the course of time they became separately incorporated and had separate governments, making a congeries of towns and districts, the whole group being known abroad simply as Philadelphia. Several of these were situated immediately contiguous to the "city proper"— viz., Southwark and Moyamensing in the south, and Northern Liberties, Kensington, Spring Garden and Penn District to the north, and West Philadelphia to the west—all of which were practically one town continuously built up. Besides these, there were a number of other outlying townships, villages and settlements near the built-up town, though detached from it. Among these were Bridesburg, Frankford, Harrowgate, Holmesburg, the unincorporated Northern Liberties, Port Richmond, Nicetown, Rising Sun, Fox Chase, Germantown, Roxborough, Falls of Schuylkill, unincorporated Penn Township, Francisville, Hamilton Village, Mantua, Blockley, Kingsessing and Passyunk. Some of these also became absorbed in the extending streets of the congeries of towns of which Philadelphia was composed, and in 1854 they were all consolidated under one municipal government, the boundaries of which are coincident with those of the old county of Philadelphia. In the earlier times some of the districts mentioned had marked characteristics, but these have mostly passed away.

Southwark, immediately on the river front, was marked by great wood-yards for supplying fuel before the days of anthracite coal, also by the sheds and yards of boat-builders and mast-makers, and by ship-builders' yards down to the site of the United States Navy Yard. A great many of the Southwark dwellings were inhabited by sea captains and seafaring men, and down to quite a recent period a considerable portion of its inhabitants were the families of seagoing people and "watermen." The wood-yards, mast and shipyards have gone to other localities, and their old sites are now occupied by commercial warehouses, extensive sugar refineries, the wharves and depots of the sugar, molasses and West Indies trade, the great grain warehouses, elevators and shipping-piers of the Pennsylvania R. R. Co., the wharves and depots of the American and Red Star lines of ocean steamships. The district was also characterized by the extensive machine-shops and iron-works of Merricks, Morris & Tasker, Savery and others, as well as by the mechanical work promoted by the navy yard, which was situated at the foot of Federal Street, previous to removing to League Island.

HAPPENINGS IN YE OLDE PHILADELPHIA

The Northern Liberties also had its great cord-wood wharves and yards along the river front, and extensive lumber-yards. The wood-yards have mostly disappeared, and have given place to large markets for farm-produce, commercial warehouses, railroad landings, depots and shipping wharves. Some of the lumber-yards remain, however. This district was also characterized, particularly along Second Street, by its farmers' market-yards for the wholesale trade in butter, eggs, poultry, meats, vegetables and other products of the farms of the adjacent country. Some of the fine old market-taverns and produce-yards still remain, but their marked characteristics have become obscured by the spread of the great city. Long before the consolidation of the Northern Liberties into the city Second Street was famous for its fine retail shops, and Third Street was the site of a large wholesale trade in groceries, provisions and leather. Second Street is now lined by a double row of retail stores along nearly its entire length, not only in the old Northern Liberties, but for miles below and above. Pegg's Run and Cohocksink Creek, which flowed through the Northern Liberties, were the sites of numerous extensive tanyards. One of the pioneer mills in Philadelphia's great industries, the Old Globe Mill, was near the line of the Northern Liberties, Germantown Avenue below Girard Avenue. The Northern Liberties embraced what are now the Eleventh, Twelfth and part of the Sixteenth Wards of the city.

Kensington was a ship- and boat-building district, and another considerable portion of its old time inhabitants were fishermen engaged in supplying the Philadelphia markets. Kensington, however, soon got into the iron and steel manufacture, and the building of steam-engines and machinery, the outcropping of which may be seen in the large works now in operation there and on the river front above. Kensington embraced part of the present Sixteenth, Seventeenth and Eighteenth Wards.

Spring Garden District, which is now characterized by extensive manufacturing establishments of nearly all descriptions—among them the great Baldwin Locomotive Works and Powers & Weightman's chemical laboratory—and for its masses of handsome dwellings, was, in the old time, one of the most pleasant suburbs of Philadelphia and the principal dwelling-place of the Ancient and Honorable Fraternity of Butchers or Victuallers.

Port Richmond, occupying the Delaware River front to the north and northeast of Old Kensington, was brought into prominence by the establishment at that point of the tidewater terminus of the Reading R. R. Co. for its immense coal traffic by sea. This at once began to improve the unproductive land in the vicinity; for the shipping-piers, the coal-depots, the engine-houses, workshops, offices, etc., were accompanied and followed by a large increase of population the erection of dwellings, great activity and rapid progress in all respects. The coal trade built it up in the first place, but the district is now the centre of a manufacturing trade that has but few superiors in the United States.

The other districts and villages now incorporated in the city have been built up so that they are now in fact, as in name, the city itself.

INCORPORATED DISTRICTS, BOROUGHS AND TOWNSHIPS IN THE COUNTY OF PHILADELPHIA, 1854

ARAMINGO.—A borough created out of the township of Northern Liberties, incorporated April 11, 1850. Bounded on the northeast by a portion of the borough of Bridesburg and Frankford Creek, which divided it from a portion of Oxford township and Frankford; on the northwest the unincorporated Northern Liberties, and the District of Northern Liberties were boundaries, the latter partly on the southwest; and Richmond district on the southeast and southwest. The name is an abbreviation and alteration from the Indian name of the stream adjacent, called by the Swedes and English, Gunner's Run. The original name was Tumanaranaming, the meaning of which is not known. By cutting off a portion of the head, and omitting two letters in the centre and adding an o, the word "Aramingo" was coined.

BELMONT.—A district created by act of April 14, 1853. It embraced that part of Blockley township which lay along the River Schuylkill from the northern boundary-line of West Philadelphia to the northern boundary-line between Philadelphia and Montgomery counties, and had also its western boundary on that line. This district had scarcely time to be organized before the Act of Consolidation of February 2, 1854, put an end to its franchises. The name was derived from Belmont, the county seat of the Peters family, which is now a portion of Fairmount Park. The mansion was erected by William Peters about 1743, and the name was descriptive of the fine position of the property and suggestive of the beautiful views of the river and valley of the Schuylkill. The property became the estate of Judge Richard Peters, of the United States District Court; he lived there until his death, August 22, 1828.

BLOCKLEY.—A township on the west side of the Schuylkill River, north of Kingsessing township; bounded on the east by the river; extending south from the county line, opposite to, but a little below, the mouth of the Wissahickon, down to the Nanganesy or Mill Creek, below the Woodlands; thence by the same creek up to Chadd's Ford Turnpike, known in later years as the Baltimore Pike; along the same to Cobb's Creek; thence by the courses of the same to the county line adjoining Lower Merion township, Montgomery county, and along the same to the River Delaware. It was traversed by the Darby Road, Chadd's Ford, or Baltimore Pike, the road to West Chester, to Haverford and to Lancaster. Within its boundaries were the villages of Hamilton, Mantua, West Philadelphia, Hestonville and Haddington. The greatest length, 4 miles; the greatest breadth, 5 miles; area, 7,580 acres. The name is supposed to have been derived from Blockley, a parish in England in the county of Worcester.

BRIDESBURG.—A village south of Frankford Creek and upon a tract of land formerly belonging to Point-no-Point. It took its name from Joseph Kirkbride, who for many years was land-owner there and proprietor of a ferry over Frankford Creek, and to whom the Legislature gave a right to build a bridge and receive toll for passage over the same by act of March 20, 1811. On April 1, 1833, the County of Philadelphia bought the Kirkbride bridge and two and a half acres of land annexed for $5,500. Kirkbridesburg was considered too long a name for convenient use, and the shorter one was adopted. Bridesburg was incorporated as a borough on April 1, 1848.

BRISTOL.—A township at the north end of the county, at the intersection of the angle which runs down from the extreme point of the city boundary and

Montgomery county. It was of irregular form, and was bounded on the northwest by a portion of Springfield township, Montgomery county; on the northeast by Cheltenham, Montgomery county. It extended along the latter to Oxford township, but was bounded mainly on the east by Tacony Creek, on the south partly by the Wingohocking and the township of the Northern Liberties, and on the west and southwest by Germantown township. The Old York Road ran through it to Branchtown and Milestown (now Oak Lane), and thence to Bucks county. Greatest length, $5^{1}/_{2}$ miles; greatest breadth, 3 miles; area, 5,650 acres. The name is derived from the city of Bristol in England.

BYBERRY.—A township in the extreme northeastern part of the county of Philadelphia; bounded on the east and northeast by Poquessing Creek and Bucks county; on the northwest by Montgomery county; and on the west and southwest by the township of Moreland.

Its greatest length was estimated at 5 miles; its greatest breadth, $2^{1}/_{2}$ miles; area, 4,700 acres. It was settled by a few Swedes previous to the year 1675, and in that year by four brothers—Nathaniel, Thomas, Daniel and William Walton—who were all young and single men. They had arrived at Newcastle from England early in that year, and, having prospected the land in the neighborhood of the Delaware, chose the country near Poquessing Creek, and settled there. They gave to it the name Byberry, in honor of their native town, near Bristol, in England. They were joined after the arrival of the ship Welcome in 1682, by Giles and Joseph Knight, John Carver, John Heart, Richard Collett and their families, and others.

The township of Byberry was established at a very early date after the coming of Penn. It contained very few villages at the time of consolidation, and was the most rural of all the townships of Philadelphia county. Byberry Crossroads, once called Plumbsock, and Knightsville, were the principal villages.

DELAWARE.—A township formed out of a portion of Dublin township in 1853. Its inhabitants voted at one general election. Its officers were superseded in the next year by consolidation:

DUBLIN.—Commonly called Lower Dublin, a township in the upper part of the county, adjoining Moreland and Byberry on the south, extending southeast nearly in parallel line to Poquessing Creek and the Delaware River. Bustleton, Fox Chase and Holmesburg were in this township. It was 5 miles at its greatest length; 3 miles in breadth; area, 9,500 acres. This township was formerly called Lower Dublin to distinguish it from another Dublin township, formerly in Philadelphia county, but now in Montgomery county, and there called Upper Dublin. This township was one of the first created in Philadelphia county, but the date is not known.

FRANKFORD.—Situate on Tacony, since called Frankford Creek, in the lower part of the township of Oxford. The name of the village was very likely derived from the title of the Franckfort Company, which took up ground there. This village was incorporated into a borough by act of March 2, 1800. By act of April 4, 1881, the boundaries of the borough were extended.

GERMAN TOWNSHIP.—Afterward called Germantown township, was laid out by virtue of three warrants: October 12, 1683, for 6,000 acres, to Francis Daniel Pastorius, for the German and Dutch purchasers; February 13, 1683, to Francis Daniel Pastorius for 200 acres; April 25, 1684, to Jurian Hartsfelder, for 150 acres. The first purchasers of Frankfurt in Germany were Jacobus van der Walle, Johann Jacob Schutz, Johann Wilhelm Ueberfeld, Daniel Behagel, George Strauss, Jan Leureiss, Abram Hasevoet. Among them were divided 2,675 acres. The same quantity was divided among the first purchasers of Crevelt in Germany, namely, Jacob Felner, Jan Strepers, Dirk Sipman, Ganert Reniks, Lenard Artes, Jacob Isaacs. The township was divided into settlements, called Germantown, Cresheim, Sommerhausen and Crevelt. These Germans were from the palatinates of Cresheim and Crevelt, many of them having become Friends through the preaching of William Penn in Germany. The greatest length of the German township was 5½ miles; the greatest breadth, 2 miles; area, 7,040 acres. The township was bounded on the northwest and northeast by Springfield township, Montgomery county; on the northeast partly by Bristol township; on the southeast by Penn township and Roxborough. Within the German township were the settlements known as Germantown, Cresheim (afterward Mount Airy), Sommerhausen (later called Chestnut Hill) and Crevelt, a rural section north of Chestnut Hill.

GERMANTOWN.—A settlement in the German township, which was commenced by Pastorius, October 21, 1685. On August 12, 1689, William Penn at London signed a charter constituting some of the inhabitants a corporation by the name of "the bailiff, burgesses and commonalty of German towne, in the county of Philadelphia, in the province of Pennsylvania." Francis Daniel Pastorius was the first bailiff. Jacob Telner, Dirck Isaacs Opdagraaf, Herman Isaacs Opdegraaf and Tennis Coender were burgesses, besides six committeemen. They had authority to hold "the general court of the corporation of Germantowne," to make laws for the government of the settlement, and to hold a court of record. This court went into operation in 1690, and continued its services for sixteen years. Sometimes, to distinguish Germantown from the upper portion of German township, outside the borough, the township portion was called Upper Germantown.

KENSINGTON.—That part of the township of the Northern Liberties which lay between Cohocksink Creek and Gunner's Run, in the neighborhood of the road to Frankford, and between that road and the Delaware River. It was originally known as Shakamaxon, an Indian village. It was a tract of land lying on the River Delaware above Hartsfield, subsequently a part of Northern Liberties, lying north of Peg's Run. Shakamaxon was known as a town before November 12, 1678, when Lawrence Cock made a grant of 300 acres there. In the deed it is stated that the whole tract of land surveyed at Shakamaxon was 1800 acres, of which Lawrence Cock, Moens Cock, Gunner Rambo and Michael Neilson were owners. It began to grow into a settlement soon after the village of the Northern Liberties felt an increase of population. Kensington was a straggling, scattered region of streets running parallel with the Delaware from southwest to northeast, and crossed by others from southeast to northwest. It was inhabited principally by fishermen and ship-carpenters. On March 6, 1820, the Legislature created a new corporation, called the "commissioners and inhabitants of the Kensington district of the Northern Liberties." Their jurisdiction extended over the ground which commenced at the mouth of Cohocksink Creek (Brown Street) and the Northern Liberties line, along the River Delaware to the south line of Gibson's land, and thence along that line to Gunner's Creek, and across to the south line of the land of the Norris estate, then along the same crossing Frankford Road, to the Germantown Road, down the eastwardly side of the latter to the middle of Sixth Street, and then down said street to the line of the Northern Liberties, which touched Sixth Street at

Cohocksink Creek, and then along that creek to the place of beginning. The name is derived from Kensington town and parish of Middlesex, England, and a western suburb of the city of London.

The town-hall, or rather Commissioners' hall was in the centre of a plot of ground extending from Frankford Avenue to Front Street, from Master Street northward. From the consolidation of the city in 1854 and for a long period afterwards it was used as a police station.

KINGSESSING.—A township in the extreme southwestern portion of the city, bounded on the north by Blockley; on the east by Mill Creek and Schuylkill River; on the south by Delaware River and Bow Creek; and on the west by Darby Creek and Cobb's Creek; shaped irregularly. It embraces the site of the old village of Kingsessing, but no settlement of any size except Maylandville. It was traversed principally by the Darby Road and the road to Lazaretto. Its greatest length, 5 miles; greatest breadth, 21,4 miles; area, 6,800 acres. This was the oldest settled portion of the county of Philadelphia.

KINGSESSING, or Chinsessing (a place where there is a meadow), was the name of a place lying on the west side of the Schuylkill River, below the western abutment of Penrose Ferry Bridge, and not far distant therefrom.

Kingsessing became the name of the township in which the original Indian and Swedish village stood. The Kingsessing settlement was called a town by the Swedes, and was the first village entitled to that appellation made by white men within the territory of Philadelphia. The township of Kingsessing was created at a very early date after the settlement by William Penn.

MANAYUNK.—An Indian name which means "our place for drinking" and applied to the Schuylkill River, was a borough situate near the Schuylkill, south of the Wissahickon. The original name was Flat Rock, from a peculiar flat rock lying on the lower side of the bridge, which was subsequently called Flat Rock Bridge. The settlement had its origin from the construction of the dam, canal and locks there by the Schuylkill Navigation Company. These works were finished about the end of the year 1818, and, the water-power being extensive, the Navigation Company sought for lessees of the power for use in mills and factories. Capt. John Towers was the first lessee of the water-power, one hundred inches, April 10, 1819, and he built a mill at Flat Rock. About the same time Silas Levering built the first hotel there. In 1820, Charles V. Hagner was the second person who bought a water right and erected an oil-mill. After that purchasers of water-power and the erection of mills and factories increased greatly, and the place became famous as a manufacturing village. After a time the inhabitants became dissatisfied with the name Flat Rock, and held meetings on the subject. On such an occasion, in 1824, it was resolved to adopt for the place one of the names of the River Schuylkill, and from that time the village was known as Manayunk. The borough of Manayunk was incorporated June 11, 1840.

MORELAND.—A manor of 9,815 acres on a branch of Poquessing Creek. It was in the most northern portion of the county of Philadelphia, in the neighborhood of the Delaware, and lay to the westward of Byberry township. It extended over into Bucks county, and was divided into two townships, one in each county and each called Moreland. The size of Moreland township in Philadelphia county was 5 miles, its greatest length; 2 miles in width; area, 3,720 acres. The principal village was Smithfield or Pleasantville, afterward called Somerton, which was partly in Moreland and partly in Byberry.

MOYAMENSING.—Originally a tract of ground on the fast land of the Neck, lying between Passyunk and Wicaco. It was granted by the Dutch governor Alexander d'Hinoyossa, to Martin Clensmith, William Stille and Lawrence Andries. The title was confirmed in 1684 by William Penn to Lassey Andrews, William Stille, Andrew Bankson and John Matson. Moyamensing township included this ground and Wicaco, except such parts of the latter as were included in Southwark. It extended from about Schuylkill Sixth (Seventeenth Street) and South Street over to the Passyunk Road, and down the same to the Buck Road, and over to the Delaware below the built parts of Southwark. In 1816 the greatest length of Moyamensing was estimated to be 3 miles; the greatest breadth, 2 miles; area, 2,560 acres. By act of March 24, 1812, the inhabitants of Moyamensing were incorporated by the style of "the commissioners and inhabitants of the township of Moyamensing." By act of April 4, 1831, the township was divided into East and West Moyamensing. The township was one of the earliest created after the settlement of Pennsylvania.

NORTHERN LIBERTIES TOWNSHIP.—The Liberties was a term applied by William Penn to a certain tract of land lying north and west of the city. It contained what was called "the liberty land or free lots" because the proprietaries gave to the first purchaser of ground in the colony, according to the extent of their purchase, a portion of the land within those limits free of price. The original idea of Penn was to lay out a great town of 10,000 acres; but when the commissioners came to survey this space of ground it was found somewhat difficult, and when Penn arrived in 1682 he determined to divide the great town into two parts, one to be called the city and the other the Liberties. The city contained about 1,820 acres. The Liberties extended north of Vine Street to the mouth of Cohoquinoque Creek or Pegg's Run, and up the same so as to go round the lands of Jurian Hartsfelder, which had already been granted away before Penn came to the colony. There were also Swedish, Dutch and English grants of land made before Penn came to be the proprietary that had to be respected, so that the liberty lands were very irregular in their boundaries, and ran by various courses along the Cohocksink, Wissinoming, Tacony, Wingohocking and other streams, and Germantown and Bristol townships, to the Schuylkill, and over the same and out to Cobb's Creek, and down the same and along the west side of the Schuylkill to a point opposite Vine Street, at the north city line, and along the same to the place of beginning. This survey was made in 1682, and the Liberties contained on the east side of the Schuylkill, 9, 161 acres; west side, 7,074 acres; total, 16,235 acres. These liberty lands on the east side of the Schuylkill became a township nearly from the time of survey, and were called the Northern Liberties, while the western Liberties, beyond the Schuylkill, became a portion of the township of Blockley. The territory between the Delaware and Schuylkill was subsequently divided; the western part was called Penn Township, and the eastern part was sometimes called the Unincorporated Northern Liberties. Whenever so spoken of, the reference was to that portion of the township which had not been taken up by the formation of districts, and by the time of consolidation the area of the township was very small, the districts of Northern Liberties, Spring Garden, Kensington, Penn, Richmond, and the township of Penn and the boroughs of Aramingo and Bridesburg, having been carved out of it. In 1854 the township or Unincorporated Northern Liberties was the space of land north of Kensington, west of Richmond and Aramingo, and a portion of Frankford, south of a portion of Oxford and Bristol townships, and east of Penn township. A part of it was west of the Frankford Road, and all of it was east of the Germantown Road.

NORTHERN LIBERTIES District.—A portion of the township of the Northern Liberties, was first the object of particular care by Act of Assembly of March 9, 1771, which provided for the appointment of persons to regulate streets, direction of buildings, etc. By act of March 30, 1791, the inhabitants of that portion of the Northern Liberties between Vine Street and Pegg's Run and the middle of Fourth Street and the Delaware River were empowered to elect three commissioners to lay taxes for the purpose of lighting, watching and establishing pumps within those bounds. On March 28, 1803, the Legislature passed an act to incorporate that part of the township of the Northern Liberties lying between the west side of Sixth Street and the Delaware River and between Vine Street and Cohocksink Creek. Under the Consolidation law this district ceased to exist in 1854, and became a part of Philadelphia. The Northern Liberties was principally composed of a tract of land originally called Hartsfield. This was a title given in a patent to the ground granted March 25, 1676, before the arrival of William Penn, to Jurian Hartsfelder. It included all the ground bounded by the River Delaware between Coakquenauque (Pegg's Run) and the Cohocksink Creeks, and extended westward about as far as the line of Ridge Road. In the tract was nearly the whole of the ground afterward the Northern Liberties, and a portion of Spring Garden and Penn Districts. Hartsfelder sold a portion of this property in 1679-80 to Hannah Salter, and another portion to Daniel Pegg in 1683-89, he having previously bought Hannah Salter's interest. William Penn patented the whole Hartsfelder tract to Daniel Pegg in 1689.

OXFORD.—A township running from the county line in a southeast direction to the Delaware River, and along the same southwest to Frankford Creek, and up the same northwestwardly to Tacony Creek, which it followed until it reached the county line near where the northwestern boundary joined it. Frankford, White Hall, Fox Chase, Cedar Grove and Volunteer Town were in this township, and it also took in the former township of Tacony. Greatest length, 3 miles; greatest breadth, 4 miles; area, 7,680 acres. It was one of the earliest townships established. The township was surrounded by the waters of the Delaware and Frankford Creek on two sides, and was traversed by the Little Tacony and Sissamocksink (Wissinoming) or Little Wahauk Creeks.

PASSYUNK, spelled in old deeds and records Perslajingh, Passayunk, Passyonck, Passajon, Passajungh, Passaming and Paisajungh, the name of an Indian village, and afterward of a tract of land computed at 1,000 acres, was originally given by Queen Christina, August 20, 1653, to Lieut. Swen Schute in consideration of important services rendered to the King of Sweden by the said gallant lieutenant. On January 1, 1667-68, Governor Richard Nichols, of New York, granted Passyunk to Robert Ashman, John Ashman, Thomas Jacob, Dunkin Williams, Francis Walker, and others, at a quit-rent of ten bushels of wheat per year. Passyunk was the first tract of land above the marsh-land in the Neck, which latter has since become fast land. It fronted on the Schuylkill River from Point Breeze up to a little stream called Pinney's Creek. From the head of Pinney's Creek the boundary extended in a straight line towards the southeast, to a point which formed the boundary of Moyamensing, thence south by west to the limit of the fast-land, and over in irregular shape to the Schuylkill. The northeastern boundary was about on the parallel of Twelfth Street.

Passyunk occupied something more than a full quarter of the fast-land south of the city. It became a township at a very early period. The limit of the township was extended from the South Street city line along the Schuylkill and the Delaware and Back Channel to a point beyond the eastern end of League Island, whence it ran north by west and struck the city line at South Street between Schuylkill Fifth (Eighteenth) and Sixth (Seventeenth) Streets. The township was estimated to be in its greatest length 3³/₄ miles; greatest breadth, 3 miles; area, 5,110 acres. There were no villages in this township, but it was at one time a favorite place for country-seats. It was traversed by the Federal Road, afterwards called Federal Street, from the Delaware to Grays Ferry, by a portion of Moyamensing Road across to Greenwich Island, Passyunk Road, Long Lane and the Irish Tract Lane.

PENN DISTRICT, that portion of the township of Penn which lay north of the north boundary-line of Spring Garden between Delaware, Sixth Street and the River Schuylkill and between a line parallel with Hickory Lane (formerly Coates Street, now Fairmount Avenue), west of Sixth Street as far as Broad Street, and then due west to the Schuylkill, and along the same to a line parallel with, and at a distance of one hundred feet north of Susquehanna Avenue, and thence to the middle of Sixth Street. It was created a district by Act of February 26, 1844, as "the Commissioners and Inhabitants of the district of Penn."

PENN TOWNSHIP was formed from the western portion of the township of the Northern Liberties by order of the Court of Quarter Sessions in the year 1807. It was north of Vine Street, bounded on the east by Sixth Street to the intersection of the road to Germantown; thence by the same north by west to the foot of Logan's Hill; southwest to the Township Line Road; along the same to a point a short distance above Manheim Lane; then over in a southwest direction to the Schuylkill, and down the same to Vine Street. Its greatest length was four miles; its greatest width three miles; area, 7680 acres. The districts of Spring Garden and Penn were created out of this township, and it included portions of Rising Sun and Nicetown and Fort St. Davids, afterward called Falls Village. It was traversed in a northwestern direction by the Ridge Avenue, from Ninth and Vine Streets, and northeastwardly from the Schuylkill, between Fairmount and Lemon Hill, by Farmers' Road below the Falls, and over to Nicetown, Germantown and beyond.

PORT RICHMOND, originally the name of a tract of land in the township of Northern Liberties, adjoining the Delaware north of Ball Town and south of Point-No-Point. It was incorporated as a district on February 27, 1847. It extended along the Delaware River to a point some distance northwest of the upper end of Petty's Island; then northwest nearly to the point where Frankford Creek makes its most southerly bend; thence southwest to Westmoreland Street; northwest along the same to Emerald Street; southwest along the latter to a lane running from Frankford Turnpike to Nicetown Lane; along Frankford Turnpike to the north boundary of Kensington, and down the same to Gunners' Run, and along that stream to the Delaware River. The area was 1163 acres.

SOUTHWARK was the oldest district in the county of Philadelphia. It began to grow much earlier than the northern portions of the county beyond the city limits. In this increase the section was very much aided by the Swedish settlements of Wicaco and Moyamensing. This region was the first which required the attention of the General Assembly. By agreement the inhabitants had continued some of the principal streets of the city running north and south through their territory. In regard to the cross streets there was not always as much unanimity, and for the want of such regulations the inhabitants applied to the Assembly by petition. On May 14, 1762, an Act was passed to create a municipality in the southern suburbs to be called the district of Southwark. The bounds commenced on Cedar (South) Street and the River Delaware, and proceeded thence west to Passyunk Road; along the latter to Moyamensing Road; thence by Keeler's Lane to Greenwich Road; thence to the River Delaware, and along the several courses of the same to the place of beginning. The greatest dimensions were $1^{1}/4$ miles in length by $1^{1}/4$ miles in breath; area 760 acres. The name was adopted, partly, in allusion to the situation of the district south of the city of Philadelphia, but it was also adopted from the name of a borough in the county of Surrey, England, immediately opposite the city of London.

SPRING GARDEN appears in Varie's map of 1796 as a small settlement between Vine Street and Buttonwood Lane and a point on a line with Seventh Street, and extending as far west as Ridge Road. There was a street (now known as Franklin Street) which ran north from Vine Street across Callowhill, and stopped opposite a house halfway between Callowhill Street and Buttonwood Lane. The street now known as Eighth Street (then called Garden Street) ran through the centre of the district, and the street now called Darien, formerly Garden Street (then known as Spring Street) ran from Vine to Buttonwood. The district was incorporated March 22, 1813, as "the Commissioners and Inhabitants of the district of Spring Garden." The original boundaries were Vine Street on the south; the middle of Hickory Lane (afterwards Coates Street, now Fairmount Avenue) on the north; Broad Street on the west, and the middle of Sixth Street on the east. On March 21, 1827, the district was enlarged by adding that part of Penn township beginning at the middle of Sixth Street to a point 210 feet north of the north side of Poplar Lane; thence northwest, parallel to the lane, at a distance of 200 feet from the latter, to the middle of Broad Street, thence parallel with Vine Street to the River Schuylkill. The meaning of this was, that whilst the upper boundary of the district took a course from Sixth Street west by north to Broad Street, the line beyond the latter ran due east and west to the Schuylkill. It extended by the course of that river to Vine Street, and along the latter to Broad, where it met the old district line. By this addition the size of Spring Garden was more than doubled. At the time of consolidation the area of the district was estimated to be 1100 acres.

TACONY, Toaconing or Toaconick, a small township situate in the bend between the River Delaware, Wissinoming Creek on the northeast and Frankford Creek and Little Tacony Creek on the south and west. It lay east of the town of Frankford, and at an early date was incorporated in Oxford Township.

WEST PHILADELPHIA, in the township of Blockley and west of the Schuylkill River, was created a borough on February 17, 1844, and embraced Hamilton and Mantua villages and the ground between. On April 3, 1853, its title was changed to the district of West Philadelphia, and its boundaries considerably enlarged.

WHITE HALL, northwest of Bridesburg, extending from the United States Arsenal (Frankford Arsenal) westward, contained in the bend made by Frankford Creek and Little Tacony, and adjoining Frankford. It was situate in the old township of Tacony and the later township of the Northern Liberties. It was incorporated into a borough on April 9, 1849.

CONSOLIDATION OF THE CITY, 1854

The movement in favor of the consolidation of the city and districts had been agitated. A committee appointed by a town meeting drafted a bill to be laid before the Legislature, fixing the details of the measure, was adopted by the General Assembly on February 2, 1854.

The bill provided that the city of Philadelphia, as limited by the charter of 1789, should be enlarged by taking in all the territory comprised within the county of Philadelphia. The incorporated districts were abolished. Southwark, Northern Liberties, Kensington, Spring Garden, Moyamensing, Penn, Richmond, West Philadelphia, and Belmont ceased to have corporate existence. The boroughs of Frankford, Germantown, Manayunk, Whitehall, Bridesburg and Aramingo were deprived of their franchises. The townships of Passyunk, Blockley, Kingsessing, Roxborough, Germantown, Bristol, Oxford, Lower Dublin, Moreland, Northern Liberties (unincorporated), Byberry, Delaware, and Penn were abolished, and all the franchises and property of these governments transferred to the city of Philadelphia.

The enlarged territory thrown into the city was divided into twenty-four wards, twenty-three of which lay east of the Schuylkill. Beginning at League Island, the enumeration of the wards ran northward in tiers. The First Ward extended from the Delaware to the Schuylkill south of Wharton Street, Passyunk Road, Little Washington Street, and below South Street, west of Broad. The Second, Third, Fourth, Fifth and Sixth Wards lay adjoining the First Ward on the front as far north as Vine Street. The Seventh, Eighth, Ninth, and Tenth Wards, were on the east side of the Schuylkill. The Eleventh and Twelfth Wards (old Northern Liberties) extended as far north as Poplar Street. The Thirteenth, Fourteenth and Fifteenth, took in nearly the whole of Spring Garden. The Sixteenth, Seventeenth, Eighteenth and Nineteenth Wards were originally portions of Kensington and Richmond. The Twentieth Ward took up the district of North Penn and ground belonging to the unincorporated Northern Liberties. The Twenty-first Ward was above the Twentieth, on the east side of the Schuylkill, and included the township of Roxborough and the borough of Manayunk. The Twenty-second Ward included the borough and township of Germantown and the township of Bristol. All the rest of the county east of the Schuylkill was the Twenty-third Ward, including Frankford, Holmesburg, Bridesburg, Aramingo, Byberry, Moreland, and Lower Dublin townships. The Twenty-fourth Ward was composed of Blockley and Kingsessing.

The passage of the bill was the cause of great rejoicing.

The Governor and Legislature and the chief officers of the State were invited to participate in ceremonies arranged by a committee. The Board of Trade engaged the Robert F. Stockton for a ride on the river on March 11, 1854, with a banquet on board. In the evening the Consolidation Ball was held in the Museum building. The next day, March 12, 1854, a banquet was given the city's guests at Sansom Hall.

CHRONOLOGY

1646
First church built by the Swedes consecrated on Tinicum Island.

1677
Second Swedes Church dedicated, in Southwark, below the present Christian Street.

1681
March 4. Charter of Pennsylvania granted by Charles II.

1682
October 24. Landing of Wm. Penn at New Castle, Delaware.
November. Penn's Treaty with the Indians at Shackamaxon.

1684
August 12. Wm. Penn left Philadelphia, and returned to England.

1690
First paper mill established by William Rittenhouse, on Wissahickon Creek.

1698
Quaker Meeting House built, S.W. Corner Second and High (Market) Streets, which was pulled down in 1755, and another erected, which was demolished in 1808.
First school book published in America by Francis Pastorius.

1700
July 2. New Swedes Church consecrated on the ground formerly occupied by the Swedes Church, Southwark.
December 2. Wm. Penn arrived at Philadelphia.

1701
October 25. Charter granted to the city of Philadelphia by Wm. Penn.
November 1. Wm. Penn left Philadelphia for England.

1704
First Presbyterian Church built, High Street and White Horse Alley (Market and Bank Streets).

1710
Christ Church, Protestant Episcopal, built on Second Street, above Market; replaced by the present church in 1727.

1715

HAPPENINGS IN YE OLDE PHILADELPHIA

A club was formed called the Bachelors' Club, situate on the Delaware shore, above Gunners' Run. This was the first country club adjacent to the city. "Bachelors' Hall," as it was commonly called, was made notorious by its festivities.

1718

First American-made printing press, Adam Ramage.

1719

December 22. The American Weekly Mercury issued by Andrew Bradford. Price, ten shillings per annum. The first newspaper issued in Philadelphia.

1723

October. Benjamin Franklin arrived in Philadelphia and applied to Andrew Bradford, the printer, for employment. Employed as printer until he and his friend James Ralph, a merchant's clerk, in 1724 sailed together to London to "seek their fortunes." Franklin returned to Philadelphia October 11, 1726. In the winter of 1726-27, he founded the Junto.

1724

Founding of The Carpenter's Company.

1729

March 1. St. David's Day. Welsh citizens organize the "Society of Ancient Britons" at the Queen's Head Tavern in King Street (now Water Street.) Attend service in Christ Church, sermon preached in the original Cymric.

1731

July 1.—Philadelphia Library founded.
First Baptist Church built, Second Street below Arch.

1732

A fishing club was instituted under the title of "Colony of Schuylkill." This club, which is yet in existence on the Delaware, at Andalusia, is now known as the State in Schuylkill.

1733

St. Joseph's Catholic Church, in Willing's Alley, built.

1734

September 22. Arrival of the English ship *St. Andrew* with the first contingent of emigrants, followers of Caspar Schwenkfeld, a repressed sect in Silesia and Germany. On the next day (September 23d) all male persons over the age of sixteen years proceeded to the State House, and there subscribed a pledge of allegiance to George II, King of Great Britain, and his successors. They spent the 24th in thanksgiving to Almighty God for delivering them out of the hands of their persecutors, for raising up friends in the times of their greatest need, and for leading them into a land of freedom where they might worship Him unmolested by civil or ecclesiastical power. To this day the 24th of September is so observed by this sect.

The emigrants settled in Montgomery, Berks and Lehigh Counties.

1742

First Moravian Church built at the S.E. Cor. Race and Bread Streets.

First type made by Christopher Sauer, Germantown.

1743

First German Calvanistic Church built in Race Street below Fourth.

St. Michael's German Lutheran Church, corner of Fifth and Appletree Alley, built.

1753

The Philadelphia Contributionship. The first fire insurance company in America.

1754

April 15. The first theatrical performance given in Philadelphia, in a storehouse, Water Street, near Vine.

1755

May 28. Cornerstone of the Pennsylvania Hospital laid.

1761

Lottery schemes proposed and ran riot. Lottery held for disposing of 46 acres of land on Petty's Island, the property of Alexander Alexander. Other projects were for the paving of streets in Philadelphia, and for the benefit of various churches.

1762

May. District of Southwark created. Boundary, Delaware River, Cedar Street (South); thence west to the Passyunk Road, to the Moyamensing Road, by Keeler's Lane to the Greenwich Road to Delaware River.

November. Organization of the first medical college in Pennsylvania, by Dr. Wm. Shippen, Jr. Located on Fourth Street, below Arch.

1771

The Assembly this year resolved to provide the city a new jail, the one at southwest corner of Third and High (Market) Streets being confusedly and notoriously inefficient.

1773

October 21. The building of Walnut Street prison authorized by act of Assembly.

1774

September 5. Provincial Congress met at Carpenters' Hall.

1775

HAPPENINGS IN YE OLDE PHILADELPHIA

Continental Congress in session at Philadelphia elects Benjamin Franklin (Printer) first Postmaster General of the United Colonies.

(A Pony Express was established. In summer the mail left New York for Philadelphia twice a week and vice versa. In winter if mail came within two weeks, was considered good. Franklin, with his keen appreciation of all the advance of science, doubtless would be lost in admiration of those winged couriers of the skies who daily traverse the aerial paths from the Hudson to the Golden Gate and who now span the Continent in less time than it took in his day to transmit a letter from Boston to the Potomac.)

1776

July 4. The Declaration of Independence adopted.
July 8. The Declaration of Independence read to the people from the Observatory, State House Yard, by John Nixon.

1777

September 26. The British entered Philadelphia.
October 15. Battle of Germantown.
October 22. Battle of Red Bank.
November 15. Mud Fort evacuated, and taken by the British.

1778

June 18. The British evacuated Philadelphia.

1781

· May 26. Act of Congress passed, authorizing the establishment of the Bank of North America The bank opened January, 1783.

1782

First Hebrew Synagogue built, Cherry Street, above Third.

1784

January 14. Definitive treaty of peace with England ratified by Congress. Triumphal arch erected at "the upper end of High Street," then between Sixth and Seventh Streets.

1786

July 20. First skiff steamboat navigated on the Delaware River, by John Fitch.

1787

August 22. Steamboat forty-five feet long navigated on the Delaware River by John Fitch.

1788

July. Steamboat navigated from Philadelphia to Burlington, New Jersey, by John Fitch.

1789

March 11. Act to incorporate the city of Philadelphia passed by the Legislature.

October 12. David Cronan, Francis Burns, John Burnett, John Logan and John Ferguson hung at Centre Square for the murder of John McFarland.

First election of President of the United States.

1790

April 17. (Saturday evening.) Death of Benjamin Franklin. Buried in Christ Church burying ground, southeast corner of Fifth and Arch Sts.

In keeping with his wishes, the epitaph Franklin composed was not carved on his tombstone in Christ Church Cemetery, this city.

The autograph "copy" of the epitaph in the Library of Congress is dated 1784 and reads:

> THE BODY
> OF B. FRANKLIN, PRINTER
> (LIKE THE COVER OF AN OLD BOOK
> ITS CONTENTS TORN OUT
> AND STRIPPED OF ITS LETTERING AND GILDING)
> LIES HERE, FOOD FOR WORMS.
> BUT THE WORK SHALL NOT BE LOST,
> FOR IT WILL (AS HE BELIEV'D) APPEAR ONCE MORE
> IN A NEW AND MORE ELEGANT
> EDITION REVISED AND CORRECTED
> BY THE AUTHOR.

1791

The Bank of North America abandoned the old system of keeping its accounts in pounds, shillings and pence and adopted that of dollars and cents.

Yellow Fever. Deaths in August-November, 4,002.

1792

April 2. Act passed establishing United States Mint in Philadelphia. Mint erected on the east side of Seventh Street, above Sugar Alley (afterward known as Farmer Street, now Filbert Street).

1793

First Universalist Church built in Lombard Street, above Fourth.

March 23. The Assembly passed an act to extend the market house on High Street (Market) from Third to Fourth Street, and to extend it as occasion required, from street to street westward.

1794

April 18. District of Southwark incorporated.

Market house erected in the middle of Second Street to extend from Coates (Fairmount Avenue) to Poplar Street.

1795

The Philadelphia and Lancaster Turnpike, the first in the United States, opened.

April. Ordinance passed compelling the owners and occupants of houses in the city to provide and keep in repair any number of leathern buckets not exceeding six for each building, to be used in extinguishing fires.

1797
Yellow Fever. Deaths, August-November, 1,292.

1798
Yellow Fever. Deaths, August-November, 3,637.

March. An act was passed by the Legislature chartering "The Germantown and Reading Turnpike Road," said turnpike to commence at the intersection of Front Street with the Germantown Road, thence through Germantown to the top of Chestnut Hill and thence through Hickorytown, the Trappe, and Pottstown to Reading.

August 18. Arrival of General Thaddeus Kosciusko, the Polish Patriot. Received by a large gathering of citizens.

September 2. Bank of Pennsylvania entered at night and robbed of $162,821.61. Other banks becoming alarmed, transferred to Germantown. The streets at night being deserted due to the prevailing fever.

1799
May 2. Work upon the Schuylkill Water Works, at Chestnut Street wharf and Centre Square commenced. First water thrown into the city January 21, 1801.

1800
March 7. The town of Frankford incorporated as a borough.
Yellow Fever. Deaths, August-November, 1,015.
Schuylkill Arsenal, near Gray's Ferry, built.

1801
United States Navy Yard (foot of Federal Street, Delaware River) established.

February 12. Incorporation of the Germantown and Perkiomen Turnpike Company. The road to begin at the corner of Third and Vine Streets.

1802
Yellow Fever. Deaths, August-November, 835.

1803
District of Northern Liberties incorporated.

March 24. The Cheltenham and Willow Grove Turnpike Company incorporated. Their route was "from the Rising Sun Tavern through Shoemakertown (Ogontz) to the Red Lion Inn (Willow Grove), on the Old York Road."

On the same day another company was incorporated to build a turnpike "from Front Street through Frankford and Bustleton to the Morrisville Ferry, Bucks County."

1804

Manufacturing enterprises continued to be established. The largest of the year was the Seth Craige cotton mill (later the old Globe Mill), bordering on the Cohocksink Creek, Germantown Ave. below Franklin Ave. (Girard Ave.). This formerly was "the Governor's grist mill." This cotton mill became later on an extensive concern, manufacturing cotton and woolen fabrics.

1807

Arch Street prison built.
Spark's Shot Tower, Southwark, built.
Beck's Shot Tower, near the Schuylkill River, above Arch Street, built.

1808

Race course established in the Northern Liberties, on the Old York Road at the corner of Nicetown Lane. Afterwards known as Hunting Park. Later on purchased by some public spirited citizens and presented to the city for a public park.

1809

Olympic Theatre built, N.E. Cor. Ninth and Walnut Streets.

1810

The first steam ferry boat used to convey passengers from Philadelphia to Camden. "Camden" Captain Zeiba Kellam. Course, lower side of Market Street to Cooper Street.

1812

March 24. District of Moyamensing incorporated.

1813

March 22. District of Spring Garden incorporated.

1814

Anthracite coal introduced in Philadelphia. In "History of the Falls of Schuylkill," Chas. V. Hagner describes the introduction of anthracite coal as follows: "White & Hazard were using in their rolling mill, bituminous coal. They knew of the large body of anthracite at the head of the Schuylkill, and early commenced making experiments with it. They had some brought down in wagons, at an expense of one dollar per bushel—twenty-eight dollars per ton—expended a considerable sum of money in experimenting but could not succeed in making it burn. The hands working in the mill got heartily sick and tired of it, and it was about being abandoned. But, on a certain occasion, after they had been trying for a long time to make it burn without success, they became exasperated, threw a large quantity of the 'black stones' as they called them, into the furnace, shut the doors, and left the mill. It so happened that one of them had left his jacket in the mill, and in going there for it some time afterwards he discovered a tremendous fire in the furnace, the doors red with heat. He immediately called all hands and they ran through the rolls three separate heats of iron with that one fire. Here was an important discovery, and it was the first practically successful use of our anthracite coal, now so common. The important discovery was the simple fact that all that was wanted to ignite it was time, and to be 'let alone.' All this may appear strange now, but the men employed in that mill—and everyone else who used the bituminous coal— were accustomed to see it blaze up the moment they threw it on the fire, and because the anthracite would not do so they could not understand it, and the more they scratched and poked at it—an operation necessary with the bituminous coal—the worse it was with the anthracite. Upon making this discovery, Josiah White immediately began to make experiments in contriving various kinds of grates to make the anthracite applicable for domestic use, in which he finally succeeded to admiration."

This coal was sent down from the Lehigh; it cost delivered in Philadelphia about fourteen dollars a ton.

1815

February 13. News received of the signing of a treaty of peace with England. Grand illumination in the evening. Grand Ball given at Vauxhall Garden, northeast corner of Broad and Walnut Streets.

A grand Te Deum, in honor of the event, sung at St. Augustine's Church on February 26th.

December 29. Launching of the new steamboat Baltimore at the shipyard of Vaughn & Bowers, Kensington.

1816

Gas as an illuminant introduced. The first private residence in the United States lighted by gas was that of William Henry, coppersmith, at No. 200 Lombard Street, near Seventh.

1818

In November, 1815, the County Commissioners proposed a plan of education to the City Councils, which led, in January, 1816, to the appointment of a committee to consult with the commissioners of Southwark and of the Northern Liberties. But it was not until 1818 that the details were sanctioned by the Legislature, when an act was passed providing for the education of poor children at the public expense in the city and county of Philadelphia, forming the "First School District of Pennsylvania."

The School Controllers established two schools in Southwark, two in Moyamensing, two in Northern Liberties and two in Penn Township. A model school was erected on the side of Chester Street, above Race. The first Superintendent of Schools was Joseph Lancaster.

The team boat Peacock ran from Market Street Ferry to the Mineral Springs on the Rancocas. The team boat Phoenix ran between Greenwich Point and Gloucester, propelled by the action of eight horses.

The Legislature passed an act dividing the Northern Liberties into seven wards. The boundaries were as follows: First Ward, Vine Street to Willow, from the Delaware River to Third Street; the Second Ward, from Third Street to Sixth, and from Vine to Willow; Third Ward, from Third Street to the Delaware, between Willow and Green Streets, and Well's Alley, commonly called Whitehall Street; the Fourth Ward, from Third Street to Sixth, between Willow and Green; Fifth Ward, from Third Street to the Delaware River, between Green Street and Poplar Lane, and that part of Cohocksink Creek called the Canal; Sixth Ward, from Third Street to Sixth, between Green Street and Poplar Lane; Seventh Ward bounded by Cohocksink Creek on the north and east, Poplar Street to the south, and Sixth Street on the west. "There are now in the city and liberties thirty-four engines and fifteen thousand feet of hose, under the direction of forty-nine companies. These companies are all willing to receive new members."

In order to prevent danger as much as possible it was directed that the manner in which powder should be transported from vessels in the Delaware River to the magazine on the Grays Ferry Road should be by landing at Conoroe & Co.'s Wharf, in the village of Richmond; thence up Ann Street west to Frankford Road; down that road to the Black Horse and Mud Lane (Montgomery Avenue); thence to Sixth Street; down the latter to Hickory Lane (Coates Street, now Fairmount Avenue); thence west crossing the Ridge Road, to Broad Street, and to the Callowhill turnpike road; thence west to Schuylkill Front Street (Twenty-second); down the same, and by way of the Grays Ferry Road to the destination. The intention was that the powder should be carried at a distance from the built-up portions of the city.

1819

March 9. Masonic Hall, Chestnut Street between Seventh and Eighth Streets, burned.

April 19. Work commenced on Fairmount Water Works. Completed 1822.

In the United States Gazette appeared an advertisement, Orders for Lehigh Coal will be received at 172 Arch Street "in quantities not less than one ton, at thirty cents per bushel of eighty pounds." The coal may be seen burning at the above place.

September 8. Vauxhall Garden, N.E. Cor. Broad and Walnut Streets, destroyed by a mob.

1820

March 6. District of Kensington incorporated.

April 2. Chestnut Street Theatre burned.

Yellow Fever. Deaths, September, 67.

1821

May 9. South Street Theatre (below Fifth Street) burned.

Coal was being extensively consumed. In this year the Lehigh Coal and Navigation Company delivered three hundred and sixty-five tons of coal to Philadelphia.

March 20. The Legislature passed an act to provide a State penitentiary within the city and county of Philadelphia. The Cherry Hill farm property on the north side of Francis Lane (later on Coates Street, now Fairmount Avenue) west of the Ridge Road (Corinthian Ave. and Fairmount Ave.). Cornerstone laid on May 22d.

Incorporation of Apprentices Library.

1822

January 24. Orphans' Asylum, corner Eighteenth and Cherry Streets, burned. Twenty-three children perished.

1823

May 31. Turner Camac conveys to the Bible Christian Society a lot of ground on the west side of Third Street above Girard Avenue, sixty feet front and two hundred feet deep to a twenty feet wide alley. On this plot was erected a church, later on sold to Louis and William Burk. The bricks forming the sidewalk fronting this church were studded with nails.

1824

March 31. Legislature incorporated a company to construct a railroad from Philadelphia to Columbia, in Lancaster County; the company to be called "The President, Directors and Company of the Pennsylvania Railroad Company."

During the year Schuylkill water was introduced into 3,954 private houses, and 185 manufactories.

May 9. Fire in the Northern Liberties, Third Street near Brown. About thirty houses destroyed.

September 27. Arrival of Gen. Lafayette in Philadelphia stopping and sleeping at the Frankford Arsenal.

Grand procession on the 28th. Reception in Independence Hall.

A census taken in 1824 showed that the city contained fifty-five printing offices, one hundred and fifty printers.

1827

Penn Treaty monument erected upon the spot where Wm. Penn made his treaty with the Indians.

1828

August. Stephen Heimer, a watchman, set upon and killed at corner of Third and George Streets. This precipitated a riot among the weavers residing in this neighborhood.

October 1. Arch Street Theatre opened, Arch Street above Sixth.

December 6. The Reading mail coach which left the city with nine passengers, held up by three men on the Ridge Road and Turner's Lane (Oxford Street). James Porter, George Wilson and John Poteet afterwards arrested and convicted. Poteet turned State's evidence. Porter executed at Bush Hill on July 2, 1830.

1829

July 4. Cornerstone laid of United States Mint, S.W. Cor. Chestnut and Juniper Streets.

1831

December 26. Stephen Girard, a native of France but for many years an active merchant and citizen of Philadelphia, died in his house, Water Street above Market. He was buried on the 30th of December at the Roman Catholic Church of the Holy Trinity, Sixth and Spruce Streets. The remains were transferred in 1850 to the sarcophagus in Girard College, under the control of members of the Masonic order. At his death the value of his estate was appraised at $7,500,000.

1832

February 22. Cornerstone of the Merchants' Exchange laid.
April 2. Cornerstone of the Moyamensing Prison laid.

June 6. The Philadelphia and Norristown Railroad opened to Germantown.

July 5. Cholera commenced. Ended October 4. Deaths, 935.

August 10-12. Race riots between whites and blacks at and adjacent to a flying horse exhibition (carousel) South Street above Seventh. Three hundred special constables sworn in to quell the nightly riots.

September 13. West Chester Railroad opened to the intersection of Columbia Railroad.

1833

February 22. Cornerstone of Washington Monument laid, in Washington Square.

April 8. Cornerstone of St. Michael's R. C. Church laid at the southeast corner of Second and Jefferson Streets.

1834

March 4. Wm. Penn steamboat burned below the Navy Yard.

September 28. St. Michael's R. C. Church consecrated.

October 14. Political riot in Moyamensing. Robb's Row, Christian Street above Ninth, burned.

1835

July 12. Riots. Houses inhabited by negroes, in the neighborhood of Shippen (Bainbridge) and Eighth Streets, sacked.

1 6

February 8. Philadelphia Gas Works went into operation.

February 22. An ox roasted on the ice of the Delaware River, near Smith's Island (in the Delaware, opposite Chestnut Street).

1837

Banks suspended specie payments. The city of Philadelphia issued "shin plasters."

1838

March 15. The Commissioners passed an ordinance establishing the Northern Liberties Gas Works. Capital, $200,000.

April 1. Upper Ferry Bridge burned.

May 14. Pennsylvania Hall, corner Sixth and Haines (Cresson) Streets, attacked by a mob.

May 17. Pennsylvania Hall burned.

May 18. Shelter for Colored Orphans, Thirteenth Street, above Callowhill, burned by a mob.

October 4. Great fire on Chestnut Street Wharf, Delaware.

December 17. Schuylkill Bank failed.

1840

Riots in Kensington. The Philadelphia and Trenton Railroad torn up on Front Street, and Emery's tavern burned.

HAPPENINGS IN YE OLDE PHILADELPHIA

1841

January 15. The banks resumed specie payments.

February 4. Bank of the United States failed and other banks suspended specie payments.

1842

January 20. Celebration of the opening of the Reading and Pottsville Railroad.

August 1. Abolition Riots. African Presbyterian Church, St. Mary's Street, and Smith's Hall, Lombard Street, burned.

August 26. Reading Railroad bridge and the old bridge at the Falls of Schuylkill destroyed by fire.

Ground purchased at the southeast corner of Fifth Street and Franklin Avenue (Girard Avenue) for the erection of a German Catholic Church. Purchase price $11,700.

1843

January 11. Weavers' Riots in Kensington, (Germantown Avenue and Master Street).

Rioters assemble at "The Nanny Goat" Market, Washington (American) Street north of Master. Sheriff's posse assailed and beaten. Rioters later dispersed by General Cadwalader's brigade.

August 15. Cornerstone laid of Roman Catholic Church of St. Peter, Fifth Street and Franklin Avenue (Girard Avenue). Solemnly consecrated February 14, 1847. In 1853 the Christian Brothers took charge of the boys' school.

1844

May 6. Riots in Kensington. Several killed.

May 7. Riots renewed in Kensington. More people killed.

May 8. Riots continued. St. Michael's Church (Second and Jefferson Streets) with the Female Seminary adjoining, burned in the afternoon. St. Augustine's Church (Fourth and New Streets) burned in the evening. All of above buildings totally destroyed.

July 7. (Sunday). Riots in Southwark; Church of St. Philip de Neri attacked. Fight at night between the military and the rioters; several persons killed.

July 24. This is considered as the foundation date of the establishing of Fairmount Park. On this date the city purchased from the assignees of the defunct Bank of the United States the estate known as Lemon Hill, formerly the estate of Henry Pratt, fifty-two acres for $75,000. Lemon Hill Park dedicated for public use September 18, 1855. Sedgely, north of Lemon Hill, was acquired in 1856. The Landsdown property, on the west side of the Schuylkill, was acquired in 1866.

1845

April 12. By act of Assembly, the city of Philadelphia and the incorp-orated districts of Spring Garden, Northern Liberties and Penn, and the town-ship of Moyamensing are required to establish and maintain police forces of "not less than one able-bodied man for one hundred and fifty taxable inhabitants" for the prevention of riots and the preservation of the public peace.

July 4. Cornerstone of St. Anne's R. C. Church laid at Memphis Street and

Lehigh Avenue.

December 29. St. Peter's R. C. Church dedicated.

1846

May 11. Congress of the United States declared that war existed by the act of the republic of Mexico. Ten million dollars appropriated, and the President authorized to call out fifty thousand volunteers.

May 13. The journeymen printers met at Keystone Hall and resolved that they would take up their shooting sticks in their country's cause.

August 24. Cornerstone laid of the new St. Michael's R. C. Church, to replace the one destroyed by fire in 1844.

September 17. Odd Fellows' Hall, Sixth and Haines (Cresson) Streets, dedicated.

November 5. St. Anne's R. C. Church dedicated.

1847

February 7. Dedication of the new St. Michael's R. C. Church.

February 14. St. Peter's R. C. Church consecrated.

April 15. Two elephants were drowned in the Delaware River in attempting to swim from Greenwich Point to Gloucester Point, New Jersey.

August 21. At the sugar refinery of George L. Broome & Co., Bread Street near Quarry, twenty-seven men struck down by falling walls. They were members of Fairmount Engine and Perseverance Hose Companies. Andrew Butler and Charles H. Hines, members of the Perseverance Hose Company, killed. They were buried at the same time, the funeral was attended by fifty-one fire companies, numbering over three thousand members. The line of march was estimated to be three miles long.

1848

February 27. Incorporation of the district of Richmond in the county of Philadelphia. Bounded on the east by the Delaware River, on the north by Westmoreland Street, along the same westward to the westward side of Emerald Street, along the same to the southerly side of Hart Lane, and along the latter to the northern boundary of Kensington district, and by the same to the Delaware River and place of beginning. March 25, 1848, the boundaries were extended to beginning at the river Delaware, on the west side of Westmoreland Street, and extending along the river to the north side of Tioga Street; thence along Tioga to the east side of the Point Road; along the Point Road to Westmoreland Street, and along the same to the place of beginning.

1849

May 30. Cholera commenced. Ended September 8th. Deaths, 1012.

October 8. Riot at Sixth and St. Mary Streets: "California House" destroyed.

1850

July 9. Great fire which commenced on Vine Street Wharf and destroyed three hundred and sixty-seven houses.

October 18 and 19. Jenny Lind, "the Nightingale," managed by P. T. Barnum, sang both evenings at Musical Fund Hall, on Locust Street. The two concerts netted $19,000, a sum unprecedented for such an entertainment.

HAPPENINGS IN YE OLDE PHILADELPHIA

1851

March 18. Assembly Building, S.W. Corner Tenth and Chestnut Streets, burned.

December 24. Public reception to Louis Kossuth, the Hungarian patriot.

December 26. Hart's Building and the Shakespeare Building at Sixth and Chestnut Streets burned.

December 30. Barnum's Museum, corner Seventh and Chestnut Streets, burned.

1852

May 22. The Diligent Engine played one hundred and eighty-nine feet perpendicular at Jayne's building, Chestnut Street, below Third.

1854

February 2. Consolidation Act passed.

July 5. Chinese Museum at Ninth and Sansom Streets, and National Theatre, Chestnut Street, below Ninth, burned.

1856

July 1. The long wharf of Merrick & Sons, at the foot of Reed Street, Delaware River, frequently used by the residents of the neighborhood as a recreation resort, caved in; ten persons drowned.

July 17. An excursion train on the North Pennsylvania Railroad leaving the Cohocksink depot, Germantown Avenue and Thompson Street, containing about six hundred children and young people of St. Michael's R. C. Church, on reaching Camp Hill, near Ambler, collided head-on with a train going southward. Fifty dead and one hundred injured.

September 21. Banks suspended.

October 12. The ship Cathedral drawing twenty-five feet four inches of water, being unable to get into New York, and cross the bar, came to Philadelphia up the Delaware without difficultly.

1857

January 18. Tremendous snowfall and gale. The thermometer touching zero. Numerous fire alarms to which the volunteer firemen gallantly responded.

Fire destroyed Tabernacle Methodist Church, Eleventh below Oxford Street.

February 26. Opening of the Academy of Music, Broad and Locust Streets. Production of Il Trovatore, with Brignold and Gazzaniga in the principal characters.

September 25. Financial panic of 1857 precipitated. Bank of Pennsylvania closed its doors. Other banks suspended specie payments.

November 2. Dedication of the new hall and parade of the American United Mechanics, Northeast corner of Fourth and George Streets.

1858

January 20. City passenger cars run for the first time in Philadelphia, over Fifth and Sixth Street Railway.

Introduction of steam fire engines.

September 1. Atlantic Telegraph celebration.

1859

January 4. Fire, factory, Lawrence Street above Brown. Loss, $35,000. Steam fire engines in efficient operation.

March 3. Great fire, Second Street below Dock. Seventeen families burned out.

March 14. Girard College Railroad goes into operation. (Ridge Avenue line).

March 24. Chestnut and Walnut Street Railway, act of legislature, approved by council and bill signed by mayor. Company agreed to pay $100,000 towards bridge over the Schuylkill.

March 27. Holy Trinity Church, Nineteenth and Walnut Streets, opened.

April 19. New Western Market, Sixteenth and Market Streets, opened.

May 30. Sunday cars run on Green and Coates Streets, (Fairmount Avenue) Railway.

June 23. Arch Street Railway to Fairmount commences operation.

July 17. (Sunday) Green and Coates Streets cars stopped by order of the Mayor.

July 21-23. Sunday car case argument on habeas corpus before Justice Thompson of Supreme Court.

July 23. Indignation meeting in Independence Square on Sunday cars.

August 15. Grand trial of steam fire engines at Fairmount on account of visit of City Council of Cincinnati.

August 20. Great fire. Stout's Planing Mill and Sewing Machine Factory, 18th Ward. Loss very heavy.

September 8. Great fire. Good Intent Mills, 24th Ward.

October 1. Fire. Hughes Hay Press, Jefferson Avenue and Marriott Street. No water to be had.

October 24. Chestnut and Walnut Streets cars commence running to Twenty-second Street.

November 21. Market sheds in Market Street between Front and Eighth, demolition commenced.

December 25. Dedication of Siloam Methodist Episcopal Church, Wood and Brown Streets (E. Susquehanna Avenue and Moyer Street).

December 28. Washington Street Wharf fixed upon as the Delaware terminus of Pennsylvania Railroad.

1860

January 5. Bishop John Nepomucene Neumann falls dead at Thirteenth and Vine Streets.

January 9. Obsequies of Bishop Neumann at St. John's Cathedral, Thirteenth Street above Chestnut. Buried at St. Peter's Church, Fifth Street and Girard Avenue.

February 13. Continental Hotel open for visitors, and open for guests February 16.

April 25. Public Building Commission holds its first meeting under act of legislature.

May 7. Fire, Tattersall's Stables, Filbert, below Thirteenth. 28 horses burned.

May 24. Fire. Richmond and Schuylkill River Railway (Girard Avenue line) Depot, Girard Avenue and Twenty-sixth Street.

May 24. Cornerstone of Episcopal Hospital, Lehigh Avenue and Front Street, laid.

July 6. Public Buildings Commissioners decide on Penn Square as the site of the court houses.

July 13. Fire. Kimball & Gorton's car factory, Fifteenth Ward.

July 22. Fire. Yard, Gilmore & Co.'s store, 40-42 North Third Street. Loss, $50,000.

July 26. Tremendous tornado at Camden, N. J. Factory blown down. Three men killed.

September 6. Plans for Public Buildings adopted.

September 20. Contracts for Public Buildings awarded to John McArthur, Jr.

October 9-11. Visit of Prince of Wales.

October 19. Fire. Franklin Building, Sixth Street, below Arch.

November 12. Sensation from threats of secession at the South. Great depression of stocks.

November 22. Philadelphia banks suspend specie payments.

November 23. Destructive fire, Twelfth and Willow Streets.

1861

January 3. Meeting of citizens at Board of Trade rooms, to take action concerning the peril of the Union.

January 7. Destructive fire, Maule & Bros., lumber-yard, Twenty-third and South Streets.

February 10. Ship John Trucks cut through by ice and sunk at Arch Street Wharf, Delaware River.

April. War excitement.

April 23. Whale caught in the Delaware opposite the city.

May 8. First Regiment Pennsylvania Volunteers march South.

July 4. Grand parade of Gray Reserves and Home Guards.

September 4. Seizure of property belonging to rebels.

September 10. Ferry boat Curlew with 142 head of cattle aboard, sunk in the Delaware. Most of the cattle escaped.

September 14. Fire in Continental Theatre, Walnut Street above Eighth. Fourteen ballet girls burned, nine of whom died.

October 19. Boiler explosion at I. P. Morris' machine works, Richmond. Two men killed.

October 30. Fire. Cotton and woolen mills, Twelfth Street and Washington Avenue. Loss $100,000.

November 5. Explosion at Bridesburg Arsenal. Two men killed.

1862

March 29. Explosion at cartridge factory of Prof. Jackson, Tenth Street near Moyamensing Avenue. Houses in vicinity shattered, seventeen persons died from injuries.

April 20. Cathedral of Sts. Peter and Paul, Logan Square, opened.

June 17. City Councils pass an ordinance appropriating $310,000 for purchase of League Island, to be presented to the United States as a naval station for construction of ironclads.

July 17. Gold eighteen and a half per cent. premium. Silver thirteen per cent. Great scarcity of specie and small change.

July 19. Postage stamps and car tickets put in circulation for small change.

September 5. Funeral of Col. John A. Koltes.

September 8. Independence Square made a recruiting camp.

September 12. Tremendous rains. Cohocksink Creek overflows. Several lives lost. Great damage in upper part of city.

October 16. Gold at thirty-seven per cent. premium.

October 18. Destructive fire at Ninth and Market Streets.

1863

February 25. Gold reaches seventy-two per cent. premium.

February 26. New post office building, Chestnut Street below Fifth (now eastern portion of Drexel Building) opened for business.

May 2. Fire. Car factory, Nineteenth and Market Streets. Loss, $100,000.

June 16. Mayor Henry issues a proclamation calling on the citizens to close their places of business and prepare to defend the State. State House bell tolled at 3 P. M. A large assembly convened in Independence Square.

June 29. A general mustering for defence of the advance of Lee. Earthworks constructed on roads leading to the city.

July 15. Draft commences in Fourth Congressional District.

August 24. Grand German festival at Washington Retreat. (Fairmount Park).

September 24. Grand review of colored troops at Chelten Hills. (Camp Wm. Penn).

October 3. Grand parade of colored troops.

November 7. Dummy engines commence running from the depot of the Fifth and Sixth Street Railway, Fourth and Berks Streets to Frankford. They proved very satisfactory.

December 18. Destructive fire in a petroleum warehouse, Delaware Avenue below Almond Street.

December 22. Cooper's Shop Soldiers' Home dedicated.

December 23. Grand military procession to receive 29th Regiment Pennsylvania Volunteers.

December 23. West end of Grays' Ferry bridge burned.

1864

March 1. Ringing of State House bell for ordinary fires forbidden by Mayor Henry.

March 5. Old Fish Market at foot of Market Street vacated.

March 27. Destructive fire at Ninth and Wallace Streets.

April 20. Grant's candle factory, Fifteenth Ward, burned. Loss, $75,000.

April 25. Boiler explosion, Cornelius & Baker's chandelier factory, Cherry Street above Eighth. Several killed and injured.

May 19. Coal Oil Refinery, Twenty-third and Arch Streets, burned.

May 24. Destructive fire, Twelfth and Willow Streets.

June 7. Opening of Great Central Fair, Logan Square. Receipts of Fair, over $1,000,000.

July 22. Simon's Wagon Works, Second and Huntingdon Streets, entirely destroyed by incendiary fire.

August 12. Grand reception Baxter's Fire Zouaves (72d Pennsylvania Volunteers).

September 24. Fall of iron rafters at the new depot, Philadelphia and Erie Railroad, Market and Sixteenth Streets; several persons killed, others injured.

Large unfinished building at northwest corner of Eighth and Vine Streets, falls down.

November 20. Cathedral of Sts. Peter and Paul, Logan Square, consecrated.

December 26. Serious riots among coal heavers, Port Richmond.

1865

January 28. Delaware River frozen over; people crossed over to New Jersey.

February 1. Passenger railway fares raised to 7 cents.

February 8. Disastrous conflagration at Ninth and Washington Streets. Fire originated in coal-oil establishment. Fifty dwelling houses burned. Several persons perished. Streets filled with snow, and banked up the burning coal-oil, forming a sea of fire.

February 23. Draft commences in First and Second Wards.

February 24. Draft in Third, Fourth and Seventh Wards.

February 27. Draft in Sixth and Ninth Wards.

March 14. Mrs. Rachel Hancock dies from effects of a shot which the provost Guard was firing at a deserter in Fourth Street, near Buttonwood.

March 22. Draft in Twenty-fifth Ward.

April 3. News of capture of Richmond, Va. Great rejoicing. State House bell rung. Blowing of steam whistles and ringing of hose carriage bells, and striking of gongs in front of Independence Hall. Parade of firemen. Mass meeting in front of Custom House. Illumination in evening.

April 9. News of surrender of Lee's Army. Illumination, blowing of steam whistles and ringing of fire bells. Firing of cannon.

April 15. News of assassination of President Lincoln at Ford's Theatre on the evening of Good Friday, April 14. General mourning throughout the city.

April 22. President Lincoln's body escorted to Independence Hall by a large military and civic procession.

May 14. New Union League House, Broad and Sansom Streets, opened.

May 17. Merrick's foundry partially destroyed by fire. Loss, $75,000.

June 10. Review of returned Philadelphia troops, General Meade commanding.

June 24. Reception of General Grant at Union League House.

June 27. Fire. Joseph B. Bussier & Co.'s fire works store, 108-110 South Delaware Avenue. Loss, $100,000.

June 28. Fire. C. J. Fell & Co.'s spice establishment, 120 South Front Street. Loss, $70,000.

July 1. Spire of German Reformed Church, Green above Fifteenth Street, blown down; no one hurt.

July 3. Mary Ridey kills, by stabbing, two brothers, Joseph and Isaac Sides, at 1170 North Third Street, a house known as "The New Idea."

August 10. Large sale of Government vessels at the Navy Yard.

August 12. St. George's M. E. Church, Fourth Street, below New, partially destroyed by fire.

August 28. Union and Cooper Shop Volunteer Refreshment Saloons closed. Imposing ceremonies at the Academy of Music.

October 3. Great fire. French, Richards & Co.'s drug establishment, Tenth and Market Streets. Loss, near $300,000.

October 8. Fire. Coal-oil sheds, Dickinson Street Wharf. Loss, $100,000.

October 16. Grand parade of Volunteer Firemen. In line 102 hose carriages, 57 steam fire engines, 11 hand engines, 12 hook and ladder trucks, 26 ambulances, including 30 companies from other cities.

November 29. Boiler explosion, Penn Treaty Iron Works, one man killed, three injured.

December 2. Landreth Public School partially destroyed by fire.

December 28. City Councils pass ordinance for the erection of a new court house on Sixth Street side of Independence Square.

1866

January 2. Great fire, 607 Chestnut Street. Loss, $150,000.

January 7. Coldest night known; thermometer 18 degrees below zero. Delaware and Schuylkill frozen over.

Centenary services of the Methodist Episcopal Church, held at St. George's Church, Fourth below New Street.

January 20. Fenian mass meeting at Sansom Street Hall.

January 30. Fire, Delaware Avenue below Vine Street. Loss, $100,000.

February 22. Firemen's procession on the return of Hibernian steam fire engine after four years' service at Fortress Monroe.

February 26. Great fire extending from George H. Roberts' hardware store, 235-237 North Third Street, James, Kent and Santee, wholesale dry goods house, 237 and 239, Smith & Shoemakers', wholesale drug house, and others. Loss, $800,000. One man killed and nine injured by falling wall.

April 11. Christopher Deering and family murdered by Antoine Probst, on a farm in the southern section of the city. Probst hung on June 8th.

May 13. Chestnut and Walnut Street Railway commenced west of new Chestnut Street Bridge.

June 9. Great fire at Dearie's Mill, Twenty-fifth and Callowhill Streets. Loss, $200,000.

June 23. Chestnut Street Bridge formally opened by the Mayor.

July 4. Grand parade. Representatives from over one hundred veteran regiments, and the orphan children of soldiers and sailors killed during the rebellion. State flags carried by the color-guards restored to the State. Ceremonies in Independence Square. Presentation made by Major General George G. Meade and flags received by Governor Andrew G. Curtin.

July 5. Fire, Baker & McFaddens planing-mill, Hillsdale Street below Race (east of Fourth Street). Loss, $100,000.

July 7. Fire, Fitler, Weaver & Co.'s rope factory, Germantown Avenue and Tenth Street (fronting this factory was the toll-gate, Germantown Pike). Loss, $130,000.

July 12. Great fire, Tacony Print Works, Frankford, belonging to A. S. Lippincott. Loss, $1,000,000.

July 26. Boiler explosion. Yewdalls Mills, Hestonville. Three persons killed.

July 27. Fire, Biddle & Co.'s hardware store, 509 Commerce Street. Loss, $150,000.

August 4. Moyamensing Hall, Christian Street above 9th, set on fire and totally destroyed. The deed was committed by persons opposed to the use of the hall as a cholera hospital, cholera prevailing at this time.

November 3. City ice-boat launched.

December 14. North Broad Street opened from Nicetown Lane to Fisher's Lane.

December 23. Fire. Gustav Bergner's malt-house, 31st and Thompson Streets; loss, $100,000.

1867

June 4. Cornerstone of the new hall, Improved Order of Red Men, S.W. Cor. Third and Brown Streets, laid.

June 6. Explosion at steam saw-mill of Geasy and Ward, Sansom Street, between 10th and 11th. Twenty-two persons killed (some being burned alive) and seven injured. A relief fund of $15,000 raised for the families of the sufferers.

June 19. American Theatre, Walnut between 8th and 9th, destroyed by fire. Ten persons killed by the falling of the front wall.

July 17. Grand parade of societies participating in Tenth General Saengerfest at Engel & Wolf's farm. (Fairmount Park, vicinity of Grant Monument.)

August 27. Cornerstone laid of the new Siloam Methodist Church, Wood Street above Duke (E. Susquehanna Avenue above Thompson Street).

September 14. American Theatre rebuilt and opened.

September 26. Grand reception of Gen. Philip H. Sheridan; great military and civic display.

November 28. Obsequies of David M. Lyle, Chief Engineer of Fire Department, who was found dead in his office November 25th.

Grand procession of military, firemen and citizens.

1868

January 8. Great Fenian demonstration and obsequies in honor of Allen, Larkin and O'Brien.

April 27. Boiler explosion, Penn Treaty Iron Works, Beach above Marlborough Street. Five persons killed.

July 17. Strike of firemen at Gas Works. City in total darkness. July 18th advance of wages granted, and work resumed.

July 30. Charles E. Becker, proprietor of a zoological garden, in the rear of his saloon, 441-443 North Ninth Street, bitten by a rattle-snake, and dies in twenty minutes.

Ice-house of Star Ice Company, on the Schuylkill above Girard Ave., falls, injuring 9 men and killing 3 horses.

August 4. Cotton and woolen mill of John Brown & Sons, Moyamensing Ave. and Moore Street, burned. Loss, $105,000.

August 11. Parade of Independent Order of Red Men, and dedication of the hall at S.W. Cor. Third and Brown Streets. Conflagration at Front and New Streets. Loss, $70,000.

September 28. Brig Sunny South, loaded with coal-oil, explodes near Chester; Capt. James R. Kelley, pilot, of Philadelphia, killed.

October 1. Mass Convention, "Boys in Blue," of the United States, being discharged soldiers of the U. S. Army.

October 2. Parade of "Boys in Blue."

October 17. George W. Childs, of Public Ledger, presents burial lot in Woodland Cemetery, valued at $8,000, to the Philadelphia Typographical Society.

October 22. Mrs. Mary E. Hill killed in her house, N.E. Cor. Tenth and Pine Streets. George S. Twitchell, Jr., and his wife, the daughter of Mrs. Hill, arrested on the charge of having committed the murder. Subsequently Twitchell was found guilty and sentenced to be hung. On April 8th, the day he was to be executed, committed suicide. Mrs. Twitchell acquitted.

November 25. City Museum Theatre, Callowhill Street between Fourth and Fifth, destroyed by fire. Rebuilt and opened as Concordia Theatre. Later bottling establishment of John F. Betz & Son.

December 3. Fire, 619-623 Market Street. Loss, $150,000.

December 4. Ferry boat Brooklyn, belonging to Gloucester Ferry Company, destroyed by fire. Loss, $30,000.

December 17. City Councils pass an ordinance for the erection of the public buildings on Independence Square.

December 23. John and Rebecca George present 83 acres of land, known as "George's Hill," to the city as an addition to Fairmount Park.

December 30. Depot of 2d and 3d Street Railroad destroyed by fire.

1869

January 7. The commission appointed to provide for the erection of new public buildings, meet and organize.

January 14. Jewelry establishment of J. E. Caldwell, Chestnut Street, above Ninth, destroyed by fire. Two clerks in Caldwell's store were burned to death.

February 21. Mrs. Lydia R. Bailey, a well-known printer, dies in her 91st year.

March 24. Joseph W. Smith, janitor of hall at Sixth Street and Girard Ave., found dead; Coroner's jury rendered a verdict that his death was caused by violence.

April 4. The Beneficial Saving Society robbed of $1,000,000 in bonds by burglars; bonds subsequently returned.

April 6. The new building of the Fidelity Insurance, Trust and Safe Deposit Company opened.

April 26. Grand parade of Odd Fellows on occasion of the semicentennial celebration.

April 28. Burning of the old depot of the Germantown and Norristown Railroad Co., Ninth and Green Streets.

April 29. Skating Rink, at 21st and Race Streets, burned.

May 3. The steam canal-barge Fulton sunk at the foot of Walnut Street. Two men drowned.

May 10. The cornerstone of Zion German Lutheran Church, Franklin Street below Vine, laid.

May 12. Parade of the Improved Order of Red Men. Imposing display.

May 17. John Dobson's blanket factory, Falls of Schuylkill, destroyed by fire.

Pennypacker & Sildey's panel factory, Willow Street above 11th, burned down.

May 31. The will of Dr. James Rush, bequeathing over $1,000,000 to the Philadelphia Library Company, admitted to probate.

June 20. The carriage of the West Philadelphia Hose Co. is thrown into the Schuylkill by a party of rowdies.

June 21. The Independent Order of Druids celebrate their twenty-fifth anniversary at Washington Retreat.

June 23. Vista drive at Fairmount Park, opened by Park Commissioners.

June 25. Destructive fire at Sixth Street and Columbia Ave. Loss, $250,000.

June 26. Cornerstone of First Reformed Church, Seventh Street below Oxford, laid.

June 30. Raid made on the unlicensed distilleries in the Twenty-fifth Ward.

Revenue officers accompanied by a corps of marines.

July 4. German Lutheran Church, Fourth and Carpenter Streets, consecrated.

July 5. Unveiling the statue of Washington Monument in front of Independence Hall. Dedicated by the school children.

July 13. The Third Reformed Church, Tenth and Filbert Streets, damaged by fire.

July 15. New building of the Mercantile Library, Tenth Street above Chestnut, inaugurated with appropriate ceremonies.

July 20. Cornerstone of the German Synagogue, "Rodef Sholem," laid.

August 4. Great conflagration of Col. W. C. Patterson's bonded warehouse, Front and Lombard Streets. Thousands of barrels of whiskey burnt. Loss over $2,000,000.

August 15. Destruction of the Boston Fish Company's building, Fifth Street and Columbia Avenue. Loss over $50,000.

August 16. Scarcity of water in the Schuylkill. Steam fire-engines used to pump water into Fairmount basin.

August 24. Large factory building, Ninth and Wallace Streeb, destroyed by fire. Loss, $100,000.

August 26. Additional steam fire-engines used to pump water into Fairmount basin.

August 28. The Tax Receiver's office at Sixth and Chestnut Streets entered and robbed of $28,000.

August 31. The art store of James S. Earle & Sons, Chestnut Street below Ninth, destroyed by fire. Loss over $100,000.

September 12. Burning of spice mills, 137 North Front Street. Loss, $40,000.

September 13. The Humboldt Centennial celebrated by a parade and laying the cornerstone of a monument in Fairmount Park.

September 16. Barrel manufactory of W. B. Thomas, 12th and Buttonwood Streets, destroyed by fire. Loss, $50,000.

October 3. The tide in the Delaware and Schuylkill Rivers overflow the wharves and fill cellars.

October 19. The stockholders of the Philadelphia Library Company vote in favor of accepting the legacy of Dr. Rush.

November 24. Centennial celebration at St. George's M. E. Church.

1870

February 3. Horace Binney, Jr., a noted lawyer, dies.

February 17. The cotton mill of J. P. Bruner & Sons, Twenty-fourth and Hamilton Streets, destroyed by fire. Loss, $200,000.

February 22. Parade of firemen and dedication of monument to the late Chief Engineer David M. Lyle.

March 8. Harmonie Hall, 717 Coates Street (later Mænnerchor Hall, Franklin and Fairmount Ave.), destroyed by fire.

April 23. Attempt to rob the Southwark National Bank; entrance effected through the roof.

April 26. Celebration of the ratification of the Fifteenth Amendment to the United States Constitution; long procession of colored people and mass meeting at Horticultural Hall.

May 1. The Mercantile Library Company opened to the public for the first time on Sunday.

May 8. Tremendous hailstorm; hail fell for twenty minutes, some of the hailstones larger than hen eggs; great destruction of windows.

June 13. Gaul's brewery, New Market and Callowhill Streets, destroyed by fire.

June 29. Robert J. Hemphill, secretary to the Board of School Controllers from 1849-1862, dies.

July 10. Flour-mill of Rowland & Ervien, Broad Street below Vine, destroyed by fire; rioting among firemen, and carriage of Goodwill Engine is thrown in the Schuylkill.

July 26. Sugar refinery of Newhall, Borie & Co., Crown (now Lawrence) and Race Streets, destroyed by fire; loss, $1,000,000; a number of firemen injured.

August 8. The large mill of Theodore Vetterlein, Twenty-second and Wood Streets, destroyed by fire.

August 14. Bergdoll & Psotta's Brewery destroyed by fire.

August 27. Coulson's planing mill, Twenty-fourth and Brown Streets, destroyed by fire.

September 6. Smith & Harper's saw-mill, Beach and Coates (Fairmount Ave.) Streets, destroyed by fire. A large quantity of lumber belonging to other parties also destroyed.

September 10. The carpet manufactory of Bromley & Brothers, Jasper and York Streets, destroyed by fire; loss over $75,000.

The new synagogue "Rodef Sholem" dedicated.

September 11. The cornerstone of the Church of the Immaculate Conception, Front and Canal (Allen) Streets, laid.

Zion German Lutheran Church, Franklin Street below Vine, dedicated.

September 17. The planing mill of N. F. Wood, Spruce Street Wharf, Schuylkill, destroyed by fire.

September 22. Race on the Schuylkill between the Nassau Boat Club, of New York, and a crew of Philadelphians, won by the New Yorkers.

October 11. Penn Square selected as the site for the Public Buildings by a vote of the people, the vote being 51,623 for Penn Square, and 32,825 for Washington Square.

October 20. The chair factory of George Fennen, 1730 North Fifth Street, destroyed by fire.

November 9. The schooner Harmonie capsized and sunk in the Delaware off South Street during a gale.

November 22. Steamboat City of Bridgeton burned while lying above Pier 7, North Wharves, on the Delaware. Loss about $70,000.

1871

January 3. The Board of Commissioners of the Paid Fire Department meet and organize.

January 10. Rudolph Stein, of the firm of Stein & Jones, a well-known printing firm, corner Hudson Alley and Chestnut Street, dies suddenly.

January 22. The cabinet works of P. P. Weiss & Co., 622 North Twenty-fourth Street, destroyed by fire.

February 2. The Kensington Bank, Beach Street, below Laurel, entered by pretended policemen, and its vault robbed of bonds and cash to the amount of $100,000.

March 3. Opening of the Northern Dispensary with appropriate ceremonies.

March 15. The Paid Fire Department of the city goes into operation.

March 24. Mass meeting of citizens at Academy of Music to advocate the abolishment of the Public Building Commission.

March 30. The soldiers and sailors (colored) hold a meeting and parade in honor of the anniversary of the ratification of the Fifteenth Amendment.

May 15. German peace celebration; procession nine miles long; various trades and occupations in line.

May 16. The German peace celebration continued. Picnic at the new Philadelphia Schuetzen Park, Indian Queen Lane.

May 27. Keystone Marble Works, Market Street near Twentieth, damaged by fire; loss, $65,000.

Warehouse of Malone & Co., 1126-28 Washington Ave., destroyed by fire.

June 5. Saw-mill of Stanley & Neber, Marshall Street, below Girard Avenue, destroyed by fire. Also about forty other buildings. Loss, $150,000.

June 15. Cornerstone of new building of University of Pennsylvania, Thirty-fourth and Locust Streets, laid with impressive ceremonies.

June 15. Dedication of the new Methodist Episcopal Home for the Aged and Infirm, Lehigh Ave. and 13th St.

June 23. Gillingham & Garrison's saw-mill, Richmond and Norris Streets, destroyed by fire. Loss, $40,000.

June 24. Monument to the memory of William B. Schneider, late Grand Tyler, Masonic fraternity, dedicated at Mt. Moriah Cemetery.

July 11. Pattern-shop of I. P. Morris & Co., Port Richmond, struck by lightning and destroyed by fire; loss, $55,000.

July 17. Three boys, Cornelius Ryan, Samuel Glass and William Galvin, drowned in a brick pond at Seventeenth and Reed Streets.

August 28. Celebration of the twenty-fifth anniversary of the Philadelphia Schuetzen-Verein (Rifle Club) at the park of the association, Indian Queen Lane.

Six hundred kegs of powder, found on board a canal-boat on the Delaware, seized.

September 22. Lincoln Monument at Fairmount Park unveiled and dedicated.

September 24. Cornerstone laid of the German Evangelical Lutheran Church of St. Michael, Trenton Ave. and Cumberland Street.

September 29. Jessup & Moore's paper warehouse, 524 North Street, destroyed by fire; loss, $200,000.

Jacob Schœnning's morocco factory, Randolph Street below Oxford, destroyed by fire; loss, $90,000.

October 10. An election riot occurs in the Fourth and Fifth Wards. Isaiah Chase and Octavius V. Catto, both colored, are shot and killed, and about seventeen men are wounded.

October 13. Mass meeting at National Hall to give expression to the feeling in regard to the murder of Major Octavius V. Catto, Principal of the Institute for Colored Youth.

October 15. Meetings held and collections taken up for the relief of the sufferers of the Chicago fire. Nearly $500,000 collected.

October 17. Old brick church building, Second Street above Poplar, used as an opera house by Samuel S. Sandford's Minstrels, destroyed by fire.

October 18. Parker & Macphilimy's planing-mill, Sixteenth and Fitzwater Streets, destroyed by fire.

October 20. Defalcation announced of City Treasurer, Joseph F. Marcer, in the sum of $478,000. This defalcation was caused by the failure of Chas. F. Yerkes, Jr., & Co., brokers, to whom the City Treasurer, contrary to law, had loaned the public money.

October 21. Planing-mill of Wm. Barth, Trenton Ave. and Adams Street, destroyed by fire; loss, $11,000.

October 28. Charles F. Yerkes, Jr., broker for the City Treasurer, held in $50,000 bail to answer the charge of embezzlement, and $30,000 on the charge of larceny as bailee.

November 1. The grand jury presents bills of indictment against Joseph F. Marcer, City Treasurer, and William F. Yerkes, Jr.

November 4. Phosphate works of Watson & Clark, near the Point Breeze Gas Works, destroyed by fire; loss, $150,000.

December 4. Reception of Grand Duke Alexis of Russia. Grand ball at the Academy of Music, in the evening.

December 5. Charles F. Yerkes, Jr., charged with embezzlement of funds belonging to the City of Philadelphia, sentenced to pay a fine of $500 and undergo an imprisonment in the Eastern Penitentiary of two years and nine months.

December 6. Joseph F. Marcer, City Treasurer, sentenced to an imprisonment of four years and nine months in the Eastern Penitentiary and to pay a fine of $300,000. Pardoned September 27, 1872.

December 19. Fourth National Bank, Arch Street below Fifth, stopped payment and failed.

December 25. Steam frigate Chattanooga sunk at League Island.

1872

January 1. Hon. William S. Stokley inaugurated as Mayor of the city.

January 21. The new Catholic Church of the Immaculate Conception at Front and Canal Streets opened with appropriate ceremonies.

Water pumped for the first time into the new reservoir of the Delaware Water Works at Sixth Street and Lehigh Avenue.

February 4. Central Presbyterian Church, corner of Franklin and Thompson Streets, dedicated.

February 17. The new Philadelphia Orthopœdic Hospital, Seventeenth and Summer Streets, formally opened.

Steam-propelled Claymont sinks at Girard Wharf, about Market Street.

February 22. Meeting of the surviving soldiers of the War of 1812.

March 4. Centennial Commission meets at Independence Hall.

New hall of the Philadelphia Rifle Club (Schuetzen Verein), North Third Street below Green, opened.

March 20. Simmons & Slocum's Opera House, 1005-07 Arch Street, burned.

March 25. The Pennsylvania Railroad Company commenced business at their new office, Fourth Street and Willings Alley.

April 2. Joseph Wittle, lion-tamer, mangled by a lion at "Porgey" O'Brien's menagerie, Frankford.

April 7. Trinity Reformed Church, Seventh Street below Oxford, dedicated.

April 17. The Public Buildings Commission annulled a former resolution directing that the buildings should be constructed upon the four Penn Squares, and ordering the erection of one building at the intersection of Broad and Market Streets.

HAPPENINGS IN YE OLDE PHILADELPHIA

May 5. Friends' Meeting House, northwest corner of Seventeenth Street and Girard Avenue, was opened for the first time for public worship.

May 27. Steam boiler explodes at the factory of Troth, Gordon & Co., Crease Street above Girard Avenue. Two persons killed and six injured.

June 1. The new Lincoln Market, corner of Broad and Coates (Fairmount Avenue) Streets, opened for business. (Later on site of the Hotel Lorraine).

June 13. National Amateur Regatta on the Schuylkill.

August 1. Spotted Tail, with eighteen other Indians and their wives, of the Upper Brule, Sioux tribe, arrived in this city, and the next day went upon an excursion to Cape May.

August 9. The Post Office Commission decided that the new post office should be placed on the lot northwest corner of Ninth and Chestnut Streets, containing 176 feet 9 inches on Chestnut Street and 378 feet 9 inches on Ninth Street.

The first stone of the foundation walls of the new Public Buildings at Broad and Market Streets was laid at the southwest corner of the southwest square.

August 15. The iron steamship Pennsylvania, the first vessel of the American Steamship Company of Philadelphia, launched at Cramps' shipyard, Beach and Norris Streets. The ship was 355 feet over all in length, with a beam of 45 feet, a depth of 43 feet and a capacity of 3016 tons.

September 21. International Cricket Match between the English gentlemen 12 and 22 Philadelphia picked cricketers on the grounds of the Germantown Club, closed September 24th with the following score: Philadelphia, 22, first inning, 63; second inning, 74. English 12—first inning, 105; second inning, 34, with four wickets to go down.

September 23. Cornerstone of the Roman Catholic Church of St. Elizabeth laid at the southeast corner of Twenty-third and Berks Streets.

September 28. Fall regatta of the Schuylkill Navy. Prize for single sculls won by Max Schmitt, three miles in 22m, 30s. Prize for six-oared gunwale barges won by the Ione of the Crescent Club, time, 21m, 34s. Prize for junior single sculls won by Frank Street of the Pennsylvania Club, time, 23m, 33s. Prize for four-oared gigs won by the Pennsylvania Club, time, 20m, 20s. Prize for double scull gigs won by the Ariel of the University Club, time, 24m.

September 30. Medicine Bear, Long Fox, Red Thunder and thirty-one others of the Teton and Grand River Sioux Indians arrived in the city in charge of the Indian agents.

October 5. The managers of the German Hospital took formal possession of their new hospital, corner of Girard Avenue and Corinthian Avenue. Removing from their old location at Twentieth and Norris Streets.

October 7. New depot of the Reading Railroad Company at Chelten Avenue, Germantown, opened.

October 9. Cornerstone laid of the Jewish Hospital, Olney Road, near the York Pike.

October 11. The new building of the University of Pennsylvania at Thirty-fourth and Locust Streets, was dedicated.

October 26. Big Mouth, Milky Way and forty-five other Indians of the Comanche, Kiowa, Arrapalio, Apache, Washita, Caddo, Delaware, Kihi and Tawa Earac tribes arrived from Washington and were taken to the Girard House (Hotel, N.E. corner Ninth and Chestnut Streets) .

October 28. The "epizooty," or horse disease, made its appearance in Philadelphia. It continued its ravages for about a month; during that time almost every horse in the city was affected. Two of the passenger railway companies during this period suspended the running of cars for six days; others suspended on Sundays, and ran but few cars on weekdays. The transportation of goods and other articles almost ceased for some days, and wagons and carts were drawn through the streets by men.

October 30. Cornerstone laid of the building of the Academy of Natural Science, S.W. corner Nineteenth and Race Streets.

The Ohio, the second iron steamship of the American Steamship Company, was launched at Cramps' Shipyard, Port Richmond.

November 11. Funeral of Major General George G. Meade, with impressive public ceremonies.

November 18. Meeting of committee of three hundred citizens appointed to obtain subscriptions to the stock of the corporation which is to manage the great Centennial Exposition of Industry of 1876.

November 20. The tercentenary of Presbyterianism was celebrated at the Penn Square Church, Broad Street above Chestnut.

November 27. City Councils fix the tax rate at $2.05, with ten cents public buildings tax.

November 28. Race on the Schuylkill between eight-oared English-built shells. Won by boat Longfellow of Crescent Club, over Leviathan of Undine Club. Course 2½ miles; time, 11.15m.

December 6. Fire at Warrington & Co.'s pen factory, northwest corner of Twelfth and Buttonwood Streets; loss, $25,000. .

December 12. Edwin Forrest, the tragedian, dies.

December 15. St. Bonifacius R. C. Church, corner Hancock and Diamond Streets, dedicated.

German Evangelical Lutheran Church of St. Peter, Forty-second and Myrtle Streets, West Philadelphia, dedicated.

Lehigh Avenue M. E. Church, Lehigh Avenue and Hancock Street, dedicated.

December 20. Fire at the stables of Forepaugh's circus and menagerie (winter quarters) Wister Street above Mill, Germantown; loss, $100,000.

December 22. German Methodist Episcopal Church, York Street above Frankford Avenue, dedicated.

St. Elizabeth's R. C. Church, Twenty-third and Berks Streets, dedicated.

Grace Mission Presbyterian Church, Twenty-second and Federal Streets, dedicated.

December 30. Protestant Episcopal church, St. James, Hestonville, consecrated.

December 31. Gottfried Kuehnle was killed at his residence and a journeyman under employ, tried for the crime, convicted and hung for the murder, January 20, 1875.

1873

January 22. The boiler of the locomotive Edge Hill exploded at American and Norris Streets, North Pennsylvania Railroad; one man killed, and several wounded.

February 6. City Councils pass an ordinance appropriating $500,000 in aid of the Centennial Exposition.

Wm. Siner, member of Common Council from the Sixteenth Ward, was impeached before Select Council upon the charge of keeping a gambling-house.

March 25. The Indiana, the third ship of the American Steamship Co.'s line, launched at the ship-yard of Wm. Cramp & Sons.

March 27. The Legislature of Pennsylvania passed a bill granting $1,000,000 to the Centennial Exposition, the same to be principally collected by a tax on the receipts of passenger railways.

April 13. Norris Square United Presbyterian Church, corner Hancock Street and Susquehanna Avenue, dedicated.

April 18. Explosion of a still filled with oil at the adamantine candle works of C. H. Grant & Co., southwest corner of Twenty-third and Hamilton Streets. Alexander Wilson and Samuel Walker, employes, burned, and lost their lives.

April 24. Cornerstone laid of the Cumberland M. E. Church, southwest corner Coral and Cumberland Streets.

April 27. Park Avenue M. E. Church, corner Park Avenue and Norris Street, dedicated.

May 18. German Evangelical Reformed Church, Thirty-eighth and Baring Streets, dedicated.

June 7. The steamship Illinois, the fourth vessel of the American Steamship Company, launched from the ship-yard of Wm. Cramp & Sons.

June 14. Regatta of the Schuylkill Navy. Prize for four-oared shells won by the Vesper, of the Vesper Club, in nineteen minutes and twenty-four seconds; course, three miles. Prize for six-oar gun-wale barges won by the Falcon, of the Pennsylvania Club; time, twenty-one minutes. Prize for four-oared gigs won by the Phantom, the Pennsylvania Club, in twenty minutes and four and a half seconds.

June 22. Broad and Diamond Street Presbyterian Chapel, dedicated.

June 29. Cornerstone laid of the Lutheran church at Roxborough.

June 30. Cornerstone laid of the Protestant Episcopal church, St. Peter's, corner of Wayne Avenue and Harvey Street, Germantown.

July 4. The Commissioners of Fairmount Park formally conveyed to the U.S. Commissioners of the Centennial Exposition, and to the Centennial Board of Finance, at Lansdowne, in Fairmount Park, four hundred and fifty acres of land, for building and other purposes connected with the Centennial Exposition of 1876.

Meeting of veterans of the war of 1812 at Independence Hall.

July 13. Services in commemoration of the hundredth anniversary of the meeting of the first Annual Conference of the Methodist Episcopal Church in Philadelphia, held in the Methodist churches.

July 31. Cornerstone laid of the Harriet Holland Mission (Presbyterian), Broad and Federal Streets.

August 6. Justice Beuislay ascended from Smith's Island (in the center of the Delaware River, opposite Chestnut Street) on a trapeze attached to a balloon expanded with hot air, which fell into the river Delaware shortly afterward, being carried a considerable distance before Beuislay was rescued from the water.

August 12. Very heavy rain fell continuing until next day. The rainfall being seven and thirty-two hundredths inches. Great damage and loss, especi-ally in the district east of Fifth Street, between Poplar and Oxford Streets.

August 17. Cornerstone laid of the chapel of Eighteenth Street M. E. Church, corner of Wharton Street and Herman Avenue.

August 20. Cornerstone laid of M. E. Mariners' Bethel Church, northwest corner of Moyamensing and Washington Avenue..

September 7. Chapel of the North Star Mission (Baptist), Seventh Street and Susquehanna Avenue, dedicated.

Cornerstone laid of the Church of the United Brethren at Mount Airy.

September 9. Cornerstone laid of Second Baptist Church, Seventh Street below Girard Avenue.

September 14. The Jewish Hospital, Nineteenth Street and Olney Road, was dedicated.

Church of the Brethren (Dunkards), Marshall Street below Girard Avenue, dedicated.

Cornerstone laid of the First Presbyterian Church of Mantua, Thirty-fifth and Baring Streets.

September 16. Celebration of the twenty-fifth anniversary of the Aztec Club, formed in the city of Mexico during the Mexican War by officers of the U. S. Army, held at the residence of Gen. Robert Patterson. Generals Grant, Hooker and many other officers being present.

September 18. The banking firms of Jay Cooke & Co., and E. W. Clarke & Co. suspended payment, which announcement was followed by great excitement. A run was commenced upon the Fidelity Safe Deposit and Trust Company, which was sustained during the day.

September 19. The financial panic continued. Great run upon the Fidelity Trust Company and Union Banking Company; both sustained demands. During the day several prominent brokers failed.

Great excitement throughout the United States in consequence of the failure of Jay Cooke & Co. In New York and other Atlantic cities there was a panic. Banks, trust companies and individuals failed, and a panic and business revulsion commenced throughout the country.

September 25. Commencement of the ceremonies of dedication of the new Masonic Temple, Broad and Filbert Streets. Grand tournoi of Knights Templar at Academy of Music and Horticultural Hall.

Gethsemane Baptist Church, corner of Eighteenth Street and Columbia Avenue, dedicated.

September 26. Great parade of the Masonic Order for the dedication of the new hall. The Grand Lodge and one hundred and seventy subordinate lodges were in line, the brethren numbering over eleven thousand men.

September 28. Cornerstone laid of German Reformed Salem Church, Fairmount Avenue below Fourth Street.

The Roman Catholic Church of Our Mother of Sorrows, Lancaster Avenue near Cathedral Cemetery, dedicated.

Renaissance Hall, in the Masonic Temple, dedicated to the uses of Royal Arch Masons.

September 30. Parade of twenty-six commanderies of Knight Templars.

October 6. Cornerstone laid of Grace Chapel M. E. Church, corner Master and Carlisle Streets.

October 7-8. National amateur regatta on the Schuylkill.

October 9. The returns of the election canvassers showed that the number of citizens entitled to vote is 164,510.

Cornerstone laid of Bethany M. E. Church, southwest corner of Eleventh and Mifflin Streets.

October 23. A locomotive and eleven oil cars were thrown off the track of the Greenwich branch of the Pennsylvania Railroad, Point Breeze, by running over a horse. The engineer, John Frew, killed.

October 26. Chapel of Tasker Street M. E. Church, corner of Snyder Avenue and Fifth Street, dedicated.

November 5. City ice boat No. 3 launched at Kaighn's Point.

November 6. Baptist Home for Old Women, Seventeenth and Norris Streets, opened and dedicated.

November 10. The State Centennial Supervisors adopted the plan of Collins & Autenreeth for the memorial building of the Centennial Exposition.

November 17. First flag on the grand flag staff at League Island hoisted by the Secretary of the Navy, Hon. Geo. M. Robeson.

November 27. Thanksgiving Day, grand review of the First Division National Guards of Pennsylvania, by Governor Hartranft.

1874

January 1. Fire at sugar refinery of McKean, Newhall & Borie, La Grange Place between Second and Third Streets; loss, $200,000.

January 29. New Olympic Theatre, Market Street, south side, below Thirteenth, destroyed by fire; loss, $200,000. Two firemen were killed.

February 8. Miss Hage and Miss Lee, two ballet dancers at Mortimer's Varieties (corner Tenth and Callowhill Streets) burned by their dresses taking fire from a stove. Both subsequently died.

February 6. The Franklin Saving Fund Society adjudged bankrupt. Indignation meeting of depositors held same day at Assembly Building (S.W. corner Tenth and Chestnut Streets).

50th anniversary of the Franklin Institute celebrated at Musical Fund Hall.

February 13. The lager beer brewery of Henry Muller, Thirty-second and Jefferson Streets, fell in from the weight of a great quantity of ice which was being stored in an apartment. There were twenty-eight persons in the brewery at the time; of these nine were killed, and eleven badly injured. Everything in the building was destroyed, the pecuniary loss estimated at $100,000.

February 18. Autopsy upon the bodies of the Siamese twins (Chang and Eng Bunker) finished at the College of Physicians and Surgeons.

February 27. First demonstration made against taverns and lager beer saloons in imitation of proceedings in Ohio and other Western States. About twenty women visited three or four saloons in the neighborhood of Susquehanna Avenue and Fifth Street, sang hymns in front of these places and delivered prayers. None of the saloons closed.

March 5. Ropewalk of John P. Bailey & Co., Otsego and Morris Streets, burned; loss, $20,000.

March 19. Fire at Insall & Dorey's spring factory, 1437 Hutchinson Street; loss, $35,000.

March 24. Machine shops and other buildings at the shipyard of Wm. Cramp & Son, Beach and Norris Streets, burned; loss, $175,000.

April 29. Steamship Mediator burned at Pier 19, Delaware Avenue below Callowhill Street; loss, $250,000.

May 8. Boiler explosion at the Keystone Mills, Callowhill Street near Twenty-fifth; two persons killed.

May 23. Sash-factory and planing-mills of Hazel & Co., northeast corner of Eighth Street and Girard Avenue, burned; loss, $25,000.

May 29. Fire at 11 North Sixth Street, occupied by Edward Stern, printer; loss, $20,000.

May 31. Eighteenth Street Chapel of M. E. Church, corner of Eighteenth and Wharton Streets, dedicated.

June 3. Cornerstone laid of the addition to the German Hospital, corner of Corinthian Street and Girard Avenue.

June 4. University Hospital, Thirty-fourth and Spruce Streets, dedicated by Governor Hartranft.

June 17. Edward Payson Weston, at the Chestnut Street Rink (Twenty-third and Chestnut Streets) commenced an effort to walk two hundred miles at the rate of fifty miles per day in ten hours per day. He accomplished it on the fourth day. Time, first day, 9h. 59m. 15s.; second day, 9h. 56m. 50s; third day, 9 h. 56m. 40s.; fourth day, 9h. 54m. 20s.

June 18-19. Regatta of the Schuylkill Navy. Course, from the Falls Bridge to Rockland, one and a half miles. Prize for four-oared shells won by Argonauta Rowing Association of Bergen Point, N.J.

Prize for pair-oared shells won by Nassau Boat Club, N. Y. Prize for single sculls won by J. R. Keaton of the Harlem Rowing Association of New York.

June 24. Fete champetre at Belmont, West Park, under auspices of Women's Centennial Committee.

June 27. Regatta of the Amateur Rowing Association on the Schuylkill. Course, from Rockland and return, two miles. First prize won by the Nereid; second prize, Lucilla.

July 1. Charles Brewster Ross, a boy four years old, son of Christian K. Ross, of Germantown, together with an elder brother, was carried off and kidnapped by two men. The elder boy was released at Richmond and Palmer Streets, and returned to his home, but the younger one was not heard from. Very large rewards were offered for his recovery, and the case was one which attracted attention all over the United States.

Zoological Gardens at Fairmount Park formally opened to the public.

Public announcement made that the Centennial Board of Finance had accepted the bid of Richard J. Dobbins for the erection of the Centennial buildings. The contract price for Memorial Hall was $972,595, according to specified dimensions, or a maximum cost of $1,249,273, if the cubic capacity of the building shall be increased thirty per cent. The contract cost of the main Exposition Building, covering eighteen acres, was $1,236,000, exclusive of about $80,000 for grading.

July 3. Henry Loth's sewing machine factory, southeast corner of Broad and Wallace Streets, burned; loss, $35,000.

July 4. Cornerstone of the Public Buildings laid at Broad and Market Streets. The buildings had been commenced long before that time.

Girard Avenue Bridge formally opened. Total length, 1000 feet; total width, 100 feet. The widest bridge in the world. Cost, $1,404,445.

July 16. The Athletic and Boston Baseball Clubs sailed for Europe upon a professional tour on the steamship Ohio.

August 4. Fire at mill, northwest corner of Germantown and Columbia Avenues; loss, $22,000.

August 5. Cornerstone laid of Memorial Baptist Church, northeast corner Broad and Master Streets.

August 25. Signor Pedanto made a balloon ascension from Windmill Island. At the office of the Pennsylvania Railroad, Fourth Street and Willings Alley, the aerostat struck a flagpole on the top of the building, which tore a hole in the balloon, causing the gas to escape. The balloon descended rapidly, whereby the persons in the car were injured.

September 1. Fire at James Wright's carpet factory, Twenty-third and Simes Streets; loss, $25,000.

September 5. Centennial celebration of the meeting of the First Continental Congress at Carpenters' Hall.

September 9. Steamship Abbottsford arrived with the members of the Athletic and Bosbon Baseball Clubs on board.

September 26. Annual regatta of the Schuylkill Navy. Course from Rockland, one mile up the river and return. Single scull prize won by J. B. McBeath, of Quaker City Club, time, 16m. 10s; gigs, Pennsylvania Club, time 14m. 18s. Double sculls, Steele and Whitmar of Pennsylvania Club. Barges, Ione of Crescent Club, time, 14m. 38 1/2 s. Four-oared shells, Pennsylvania Club, time, 9m. 15 3/4 s.

October 1. Cornerstone laid of new building for the Women's Medical College, corner of Twenty-first Street and North College Avenue.

October 11. Church of the German Reformed Salem Congregation, Fairmount Avenue below Fourth, dedicated.

October 18. Cornerstone laid of Roman Catholic Church of St. Agatha, northwest corner of Thirty-eighth and Bridge (Spring Garden) Streets.

October 27. F. H. G. Brotherton concluded, at 806 Green Street, the pedestrian feat of walking 1000 half-miles in 1000 half-hours, being 1000 half-hours of consecutive hours, which effort was commenced on October 6.

October 29. Falls of Schuylkill Brewery, belonging to Jacob Hohenadel, burned. Loss, $45,000.

November 2. Fire at glassworks of F. J. Cook, York and Thompson Streets; loss, $35,000.

November 12. Fast traveling on Pennsylvania Railroad from Jersey City to West Philadelphia depot, 1 hour 47 minutes, including two stoppages. From Philadelphia to Baltimore, 2 hours, 15 minutes. From Baltimore to Philadelphia, return, 2 hours, 13 minutes.

November 21. Manayunk and Roxborough inclined railway opened.

December 14. William Mosher and Joseph Clark, abductors of Charles Brewster Ross, shot and killed while attempting burglary at the residence of Judge Van Brunt, at Bay Ridge, Long Island.

1875

February 8. Steam tug Hudson, cut through the ice and sunk in the Delaware.

March 13. First number of Col. Alexander K. McClure's paper, The Times, published.

May 9. Fiftieth anniversary of the pastorate of Rev. Dr. John Chambers celebrated at his church, services lasting for one week.

July 21. Preliminary surveys for the improvement of Independence Square begun.

July 30. People's Passenger Railway (Callowhill Street) opened for travel.

February 9. Fire at Keen & Coates Foundry, 943 North Front Street; loss, $46,600.

February 15. Fire at 113-115 North Third Street; loss, $50,000.

February 27. Fire at Washington Butchers' Sons, meat packing establishment, 146-148 North Front Street; loss, $100,000.

June 7. Fire at John Brown & Sons' cotton and woolen mills, Eighth and

Tasker Streets; loss, $43,000.

August 15. Fire at Perot's malt house, 310 Vine Street; loss, $31,393.

August 24. J. B. Johnson, a professional swimmer of England, swam from the Lazaretto to Gloucester, about ten miles, in a contest with Thomas Coyle of Chester, Pa., who gave up before he had swam more than half the distance.

September 13-22. Cricket Tournament at Germantown. The picked twelve of Philadelphia defeated the Canada twelve by a score of 231 to 144. The British Officers defeated Canada twelve by 353 to 290. The Philadelphia twelve beat the British officers by eight wickets; score, 282 to 281.

September 26. A dummy on the Frankford (Fifth and Sixth Street) railway, smashed by an excursion train from New York at the Harrowgate crossing of the connecting railway; five persons killed, and twenty injured.

October 4. Fire at Burgin & Sons' glass factory, Girard Avenue and Palmer Streets; loss, $20,000.

October 14. Mattress and furniture factory on Randolph Street above Oxford Street, burned; loss, $20,000.

German Hospital formally dedicated.

October 31. Fire at Carlton Woolen Mills, Twenty-third and Hamilton Streets; loss, $500,000.

November 10. J. F. Betz's malt house, St. John (American) Street below Callowhill, burned; loss, $20,000.

November 20. Market Street bridge over the Schuylkill destroyed by fire. Permanent bridge first opened for travel January 1, 1805; rebuilt and widened, 1850-51.

November 21. Moody and Sankey, famous religious revivalists, began a series of meetings in the old Pennsylvania freight depot, southwest corner of Thirteenth and Market Streets.

November 30. South Street bridge opened to pedestrians.

December 2. U. S. Navy Yard at foot of Federal Street sold to Pennsylvania Railroad Company for $1,000,000.

December 8. Fire at Wm. B. Thomas' barrel factory, Willow Street above Twelfth; loss, $20,000.

December 22. Ridge Avenue Farmers' Market, Ridge Avenue below Girard Avenue, opened for business.

1876

The Franklin Institute and Academy of Fine Arts in 1869 memorialized Congress in favor of holding an International Exhibition to commemorate the one hundredth anniversary of the Declaration of Independence. By act of Congress this was authorized March 3, 1871. Congress, on June 1, 1872, incorporated the Centennial Board of Finance with authority to receive subscriptions at ten dollars per share. The State of Pennsylvania gave $1,000,000 to the commission for the purpose of erecting a permanent building, since known as Memorial Hall, and the city of Philadelphia gave $1,500,000 with which were constructed Machinery Hall and Horticultural Hall. On July 4, 1873, the commissioners of Fairmount Park formally transferred to the Centennial Commission and the Centennial Board of Finance, for the use of the exhibition, two hundred and thirty-six acres of ground.

There were one hundred and ninety-four buildings erected. The main buildings were: Main Exhibition building, 1,876 feet long, 464 feet wide; cost,

$1,600,000. Machinery Hall, 1,402 feet long, 360 feet wide; cost, $792,000. Horticultural Hall, 383 feet long, 193 feet wide; cost, $251,937.

Memorial Hall, intended to be an art gallery, permanent building, 365 feet long, 210 feet wide, the dome rising 150 feet above ground; cost, $1,500,000.

Agricultural Hall, a long nave, crossed by three transepts; nave, 820 feet long, and 100 feet wide; central transept 465 feet long and 100 feet wide; cost, $197,000.

The United States government building, built in the shape of a cross. Long nave, 400 feet long, 100 feet wide; cross transepts, 300 feet in depth, 100 feet wide; cost, $62,000.

Women's Pavilion formed by two intersecting naves, each 64x192 feet; cost, $40,000.

Foreign Government and State buildings, etc.

The Centennial Exhibition opened on May 10, 1876, and closed on November 10, 1876. The total admissions were 9,910,966 persons. The exhibition was remarkably successful.

January 1. Grand celebration of the opening of the Centennial year, at the State House, by hoisting the grand Union flag, together with illuminations, ringing of bells, blowing of steam whistles and firing of cannon and firearms, at midnight, between December 31 and January 1. Immense concourse of people present.

January 28. Moody and Snake's meetings at the old Pennsylvania freight depot, southwest corner of Thirteenth and Market Streets, closed. During the time they were in the city they held 210 meetings, and it was estimated that they were attended by more than one million and fifty thousand persons.

February 27. Main auditorium of Siloam M. E. Church, Otis Street above Thompson, dedicated.

March 6. First train of cars from Philadelphia to New York, over the Delaware and Bound Brook Railroad (depot, American and Berks Street) passed through from city to city.

March 18. West End Mills, Sixty-seventh and Lombard Streets, burned; loss, $195,000.

March 26. East Montgomery Avenue M. E. Church dedicated.

March 28. New depot building of Twelfth and Sixteenth Streets

Passenger Railway Co., Twelfth Street and Susquehanna Avenue, fell in, in consequence of heavy rains.

April 1. Municipal census taken by the police. Dwelling houses, 143,936; inhabitants, 817,448; males over twenty-one years, 226,070.

April 22. New building of Pennsylvania Academy of Fine Arts, Broad and Cherry Streets, dedicated.

April 27. New York and Philadelphia Railroad between both cities opened by excursions.

May 1. Continental (horse) Railway opened.

May 3. New branch of the Reading Railroad to the Centennial grounds opened.

May 7. Roman Catholic Church of St. Charles Borromeo, Twentieth and Christian Streets, dedicated, the Empress of Brazil being present.

May 10. Opening of the Centennial International Exhibition of Industry, at the Centennial grounds, Fairmount Park, by the President of the United States, in presence of members of Congress, Supreme Court, Cabinet, and many other National, State and municipal officers, and over one hundred and fifty thousand people. The Emperor and Empress of Brazil were present, participating in the ceremonies which were grand and impressive.

May 26. John Hays' waste paper warehouse, northeast corner of Germantown Avenue and Master Street, collapsed from being over-weighted with materials during alterations. Three persons were killed and four injured.

June 14. First passenger train run over Philadelphia and Newtown Railroad to Fox Chase.

July 3. Centennial service at Christ Church.

July 4. Centennial anniversary of Declaration of Independence. Parade of volunteer troops from all parts of the Union; exercises in Independence Square, oration by William B. Evarts; poem by Bayard Taylor; Senator Ferry, President of U. S. Senate, presided. Emperor of Brazil and large number of distinguished visitors present; grand music by large chorus and orchestra. In the evening a grand display of fireworks was given in Fairmount Park.

Dedication of the Catholic T. A. B. Fountain in Fairmount Park.

Monument to Alexander von Humboldt, in Fairmount Park, unveiled.

Explosion of chemicals at drug store of Henry F. Bucher, Passyunk Road and Moore Street. Four men killed.

Fire at Detwiler & Hartranft's Quaker City Flour Mill, Delaware Avenue above Laurel Street, Landell's soap works, lumber yard of Collins & Co., and B. F. Taylor & Co., and Taxis' screwdock; loss, $90,000.

July 7. Fire, yarn mill of James Meadowcraft & Son, Emerald and Sergeant Streets; loss, $25,000.

Long centre span of the Penrose Ferry Bridge fell into the Schuylkill River.

August 24. "New Jersey State Day" at the Centennial Exposition. Paid admissions, 56,325. Exhibitors, complimentary, etc., 8,709; total, 65,034.

August 31. Prize fight at Pennsville, New Jersey, between Jimmy Weeden and Young Walker for $250.00 a side, won by Weeden. Walker died from the effects of his beating shortly after the fight was concluded. The captains of various boats and the Creedmoor Cutter, a barge, and others, the principal and accessories arrested and held by the Coroner of Philadelphia.

September 3. Fire at Mund & Albrecht's Farm (picnic grounds frequented principally by the Germans) Indian Queen Lane, Falls of Schuylkill. Property entirely destroyed; loss, $50,000.

September 6. Parade of Volunteer Firemen, embodying many of the old volunteer companies of Philadelphia, with companies from other parts of the Union.

September 14. "Massachusetts Day" at Centennial Exposition. Admission to main exhibition, 78,977; live stock show, 6,818; free admissions, etc., 12,075; total, 97,968.

September 22. A number of wooden buildings in Shantytown (in close proximity to the Centennial grounds) were torn down by the police under the direction of Mayor Stokley.

September 25. "New York Day" at Centennial Exposition. Paying visitors at main exhibition, 118,719; at live stock show, 3,284; free admissions, 12,585; total, 134,588.

September 28. "Pennsylvania Day" at the Centennial Exposition. There were 274,919 persons in attendance.

October 1. Audience room of the First Reformed Presbyterian Church (General Synod) York Street near Coral, dedicated.

October 2. Edwin Forrest Home, near Holmesburg, opened. "Instituted for the support and maintenance of actors and actresses decayed by age or disabled by infirmity."

October 3. Philadelphia, Newtown and New York Railroad sold at auction at the Merchants' Exchange for $10,000.

October 5. "Rhode Island Day" at Centennial Exposition. Total attendance, 100,946.

October 12. "New Hampshire Day" at Centennial Exposition. Total attendance, 115,422. Monument and statue to the memory of Christopher Columbus, procured by the Italians of Philadelphia, dedicated in Centennial grounds.

October 18. "Reading Day" at the Centennial Exposition. Total attendance, 138,874.

October 19. "Delaware and Maryland Day" at the Centennial Exposition. Total attendance, 176,407.

October 20. Monument statue in memory of John Witherspoon, signer of Declaration of Independence, dedicated in West Park.

October 21. Fire at George Griffith's shovel factory, Locust above Fifth Street; loss, $50,000.

October 22. Cornerstone laid of Roman Catholic Church of Our Lady of Visitation, Lehigh Avenue and B Street.

October 26. "Ohio Day" and "Merchants' Day" at the Centennial Exposition. Attendance, 135,661.

October 27. "Vermont Day" at Centennial Exposition. Attendance, 108,080.

October 30. Girls' Normal School at Seventeenth and Spring Garden Streets, dedicated.

November 2. "German Day" at the Centennial Exposition. Attendance, 128,022.

November 7. "Women's Day" at the Centennial Exposition. Attendance, 87,859.

November 9. "Philadelphia Day" at the Centennial Exposition. Attendance 193,078. In the evening, display of fireworks.

November 10. The Centennial Exposition was formally closed with appropriate ceremonies. During the 159 days that it was open the paying visitors were 8,004,274; free, 1,906,692. Total, 9,910,966. The free admissions were mainly those of exhibitors, attendants and employes.

1877

January 1. The Supreme Court took possession of their new apartments, City Hall, Broad and Market Streets.

January 19. Fire at the flour mills of Detwiler & Co., 3042-44 Market Street; loss, $75,000.

January 20. Fire at Baeder & Adamson's glue factory, Allegheny Avenue and Richmond Street; loss, $20,000.

Fire at sash and blind factory of Keller & Krouse, St. John (American) Street; loss, $30,000.

February 5. New fire station of Truck D, Union Street below Fourth, formally occupied by the company.

February 6. New police station at Girard Avenue and Vienna (E. Berks) Street, 11th District, formally occupied.

February 22. Citizens of Philadelphia presented to John Welsh, president of the Centennial Board of Finance, $50,000 in commemoration of his zealous and unselfish labors in promoting the success of the Centennial Exhibition. The money was transferred to the University of Pennsylvania for the perpetual support of "the John Welsh Professorship of History and English Literature."

February 23. Synagogue of the Hebrew Congregation Beth-el-Emeth, Franklin Street above Green, re-dedicated.

February 25. Fox's American Theatre, Chestnut Street above Tenth, with Rodger's carriage factory, and other buildings burned; loss, $300,000. One man killed.

February 26. Meeting of butchers at Institute Hall, Broad and Spring Garden Streets. Strong resolutions against the proposition that all the butchers shall have their slaughtering done at the abattoirs.

March 10. Planing mill of Turner, Larrish & Co., Noble Street between Eleventh and Twelfth Streets, destroyed by fire; loss, $30,000.

March 21. Trial of steam passenger cars on the West Philadelphia (Market Street) P. R. W. Co. Seven dummy engines in use.

April 2. An exhibition of the powers of Elisha Gray's telephone at office of Western Union Telegraph Co., Tenth and Chestnut Streets. Music played at Philadelphia was heard in New York by an audience assembled at Steinway Hall.

April 4. Menagerie storage building and stables of Adam Forepaugh, Wister Street near Godfrey Avenue, burned; loss, $20,000.

May 1. Union Banking Co., Chestnut Street above Third, failed. Same day United States Banking Co., corner of Tenth and Chestnut Streets, failed.

May 10. Permanent Exhibition formally opened in Philadelphia by President Hayes and ex-President Grant. Admissions estimated at 100,000.

June 25. Cornerstone laid of new building of Central Presbyterian Church, on west side of Broad Street, north of Fairmount Avenue.

July 8. The new Philadelphia and Atlantic City Railway (narrow gauge) opened by an excursion of officers of the road and others.

July 16. Trial of the transmission of sound through Edison's vocal telephone at the Permanent Exhibition Building. Vocal music at the Central-Station telegraph office, at Fifth and Chestnut Streets, was transmitted over the wires, and heard with great clearness at the Exhibition Building.

July 19. Fire at Swift & Courtney's match factory, 219 North Fourth Street; loss, $45,000.

August 13. Swimming match on Delaware River between Thomas Coyle, of Chester and George H. Wade, of Brooklyn. Course from Red Bank to Gloucester, 4 miles. Race won by Wade. Time, 1 hour and 40 minutes.

September 17. Jefferson Medical College Hospital, Sansom Street between Tenth and Eleventh Streets, formally opened.

September 22. Great excitement among brokers and bankers in consequence of the discovery of an over-issue of stock of the Market Street Railway Co., which it was subsequently ascertained amounted to about 11,000 shares. John S. Morton, President of the company, who with the Treasurer and Secretary had made the over-issue, resigned the office of President, and also resigned his position as President of the Permanent Exhibition Company.

September 28. John S. Morton and others implicated, bound over to answer a charge of conspiracy to cheat and defraud.

The 101st Anniversary of the adoption of the old Constitution of Pennsylvania celebrated at the Hotel La Fayette (west side of Broad Street below Chestnut, now site of Land Title Building).

September 29. Fire at morocco factory of W. Schollenberger & Sons, S.W. corner of Mascher and Putnam Streets; loss, $250,000.

September 30. New Roman Catholic Church of Sacred Heart, Third Street below Reed, dedicated.

Siloam Primitive Methodist Church, Otis (E. Susquehanna Avenue) and Moyer Streets, re-dedicated.

October 6. New Farmers' Market, N.W. corner of Broad Street and Columbia Avenue, opened for business.

October 19. First annual regatta of the Fairmount Rowing Association over the national course on the Schuylkill.

November 3. Fox's new American Theatre, Chestnut Street above Tenth (rebuilt after the fire) was opened for performances.

November 7. Fire at Randolph Mills, Randolph Street above Columbia Avenue, occupied by Weil & Sons, Harvey & Good, and others; loss, $50,000.

November 22. Fire at southwest corner of Ninth and Chestnut Streets; loss, $100,000.

November 27. Farewell banquet to Hon. John Welsh, minister to England, at the Aldine Hotel. Public reception at the Academy of Fine Arts on next day.

December 9. German Lutheran Church of Holy Trinity, Sixteenth and Tioga Streets, formally opened.

December 15. Fire at the building in which Thomas Jefferson wrote the Declaration of Independence, at the southwest corner of Seventh and Market Streets; loss, $15,000, suffered by Simon & Co., trunk manufacturers, and Longacre & Co., wood engravers.

December 25. The Alhambra Theatre on Broad Street re-opened by John S. Clarke, under the title of the Broad Street Theatre.

1878

January 1. William S. Stokley inaugurated for his third term as mayor of the city of Philadelphia.

January 11. Chatham Mills, Howard and Berks Streets, burned; loss, $50,000.

January 20. New iron bridge at Penrose Ferry, on the Schuylkill, opened for foot-passengers.

January 22. Excitement among dealers in morocco leather, caused by the failure of ten firms engaged in that trade.

January 23. John M. Armstrong, a music typographer, while on a visit to Camden, N. J., murdered. Coroner's jury at Camden found that Benjamin Hunter was guilty of the crime. Hunter, after a trial at Camden, lasting twenty days, was convicted of murder in the first degree on July 3, 1878.

January 31. Fire at wholesale dry goods store of H. P. & W. P. Smith, 224-226 Chestnut Street; loss, $400,000.

February 2. Philadelphia, Newtown and New York Railroad formally opened for business.

February 10. Nine of the western arches of the South Street bridge fell. Loss estimated at S85,000.

February 14. Fire at the carriage factory of Jacob Rech, southeast corner of Eighth Street and Girard Avenue; loss, $12,000.

February 20. New building of the Kensington National Bank, Frankford and Girard Avenues, opened for public inspection. Business commenced Saturday the 23d.

March 11. The office of Prothonotary of the Supreme Court was removed from State House Row to the new Public Buildings.

March 16. Fire at the bedstead factory of Meyer, Tufts & Co., Richmond Street above Montgomery Avenue; loss, $15,000.

March 25. Fire at southeast corner of Fourth and Cherry Streets in the store of H. K. Wampole, extended nearly down to Arch Street; total loss, $750,000.

April 13. Steam dummy cars, after a trial of almost a year by the Market Street Railway Co., were withdrawn from service. Too expensive.

April 29. The gallery of Pompeiian views deposited with Fairmount Park Commission by John Welsh opened to the public in the Art Building, East Park.

May 6. Ridgway Library building and grounds, corner of Broad and Carpenter Streets, formally transferred to the Library Company of Philadelphia by Henry J. Williams, executor of the late Dr. James Rush.

May 10. Fire at phosphate manufactory on Venango Street, near the Delaware River; loss, $75,000.

May 16. Iron steamship State of California launched from the shipyard of William Cramp & Sons.

Hall of Moyamensing Lodge, No. 330, I.O.O.F. at Eighth and Reed Streets, dedicated.

Fire at Southwark Cotton and Woolen Mills, Moyamensing Avenue and Moore Streets; loss, $42,000.

June 8. Spring regatta of the Schuylkill Navy. Course, Falls Bridge to Rockland Landing. Pair-oared prize won by University crew, time, 11.20; double sculls by Crescent Club, 10.12 1/4; four-oars by Crescent Club, 9.31.

First regatta of the Schuylkill Yacht Club. Course from Ellsworth street wharf, Schuylkill to Chester buoy and return. First-class prize won by the T. B. Doyle; second-class, the Bently; third-class, the Vindex.

June 15. Annual regatta of the Schuylkill Navy. Prizes for four-oared boats won by Crescent, time, 9.33 1/2; for four pair oars by University; double sculls and single sculls by Crescent; four-oared gigs by University; and six-oared barges by Crescent.

June 29. Western section of Brown Street River Market on Delaware Avenue, opened for business.

July 10. Explosion at the blast furnace of S. Robbins & Son, at Beach and Vienna Streets, by which seven persons were injured. John McChesney died. Two others died subsequently.

Rifle contest at Saenger Park (21st and Diamond Streets) between the Norristown Rifle Club and the Keystone Rifle Club of Philadelphia. Eight men on each side, ten shots each. Keystone, 342; Norristown, 339. Average, 42%. Time, 1 hour.

August 1. Destructive rain and wind storm. The Coliseum market house (iron building) Broad and Locust Streets, was struck by lightning.

August 5. River pirates attempting to rob the schooner L. Stillman of Great Egg Harbor, N. J., anchored in the Delaware, shot at by the master of the vessel. One thief killed and two wounded.

New American Theatre, Chestnut Street above Tenth, sold by the Sheriff for $75,000 to H. H. Morrell of New York.

August 15. Swimming match between T. Butler, of Philadelphia, and Robert Ward, of New York, from Bridesburg to Point Airy (southern end of

Windmill Island, opposite Spruce Street in the Delaware river) distance, 5 miles. Won by Butler in 40 minutes.

September 2. Ground broken for the building of Eden M. E. Church, Lehigh Avenue below Fifth Street.

September 5. Stalls in new (Zimmerman) market house, southwest corner of Frankford Avenue and Adams Street, sold, and the market opened. (Now site of Weisbrod & Hess brewery).

September 13. New Delaware River Market, at the foot of Brown Street, formally opened.

October 3. International cricket match at the grounds of the Germantown Cricket Club between the Australian cricketers and a select team of Philadelphia players. The game was closed on Saturday, while unfinished, by the stumps being drawn. Score, Philadelphia, first innings, 196; second innings, 53; total, 249. Australians, first innings, 150; second innings, 56; total, 206.

October 4. The Continental Telegraph Company opened its line between Philadelphia and New York.

October 5. Second annual regatta of the Fairmount Rowing Association on the Schuylkill River, over the national course. Prize for single shells won by C. Hamilton in 11 minutes, $11^{1/2}$ seconds; single shells, J. Schnall, 14 minutes, $46^{1/4}$ seconds; double sculls, W. Tapper and C. Reitze, 12 minutes, $37^{3/4}$ seconds; four-oared barges, Fairmount, 14 minutes, 10 seconds; six-oared barges, Washington, 10 minutes, $43^{3/4}$ seconds.

Fall regatta of the American Rowing Club on the Schuylkill River below the dam, from Callowhill Street bridge to Chestnut Street bridge and return, estimated two miles. Prize for single sculls won by W. Wood; four-oared barges, Atlantic, 18 minutes, 52 seconds; six-oared barges, Belmont, 15 minutes, 26 seconds; double-outriggers, won by the Eddie; single shell match, three miles, J. Meek, 12 minutes, 42 seconds.

October 7. Free drawing schools of the Spring Garden Institute formally opened at Broad and Spring Garden Streets.

October 12. Hero Glassworks of W. A. Leavitt, at Aramingo, Cedar, Gaul and Adams Streets, destroyed by fire; loss, $60,000.

October 20. Roman Catholic Church of St. Agatha, Spring Garden and Thirty-eighth Streets, dedicated.

October 21. New freight station of Pennsylvania Railroad Company opened at Thirty-first and Market Streets.

October 23. Great cyclone and wind storm. There was a great flood in the "Neck" which submerged the whole territory below Mifflin Street from the Delaware to the Schuylkill. Loss of life, about ten persons, thirty injured. Properties destroyed, 4 church steeples blown down. Immense loss.

November 5. Edward Shippen school house, Cherry Street above Nineteenth, destroyed by fire; loss, $15,000.

November 9. Fire at ice house of Bergner & Engel Brewery, Thirty-second and Thompson Streets; loss, $150,000.

November 12. Fire at chair factory and lumber yard of Hutchinson, Nichols & Co., American Street above Susquehanna Avenue; loss, $10,000,

November 14. Rifle shooting contest at Saenger Park, Twenty-first and Diamond Streets, between Keystone Rifle Club of Philadelphia and Norristown Rifle Club, 100 yards, offhand. Score: Norristown, 354; Keystone, 345.

December 1. Norris Square M. E. Church, Mascher Street above

Susquehanna Avenue, dedicated.

December 11. Offices of Department of Highways removed from Sixth and Chestnut Streets, and opened in the new Public Building, Broad and Market Streets.

December 17. John S. Morton, formerly president and Samuel B. Hahn, formerly treasurer of the Market Street Passenger Railway Company, sentenced to pay a nominal fine, the costs of trial, and to undergo ten years imprisonment, for fraudulently issuing stock of the company.

December 30. Meeting of citizens of Twenty-third Ward, formerly of the township of Byberry and Moreland, at which it was resolved to petition the Legislature to separate that territory from the city of Philadelphia and annex it to Bucks County.

1879

January 6. Octavius V. Catto school for colored children, Lombard Street above Twentieth, formally opened.

January 6 and 7. Largest sheriff's sale of real estate ever known in Philadelphia. Nearly 700 properties were levied upon and advertised to be sold.

January 10. Benjamin Hunter, convicted of the murder of John M. Armstrong, music typographer of Philadelphia, hanged at Camden, N.J.

January 15. United States Centennial Commission met for the last time at the Continental Hotel, and received and adopted the final report of the committee on finance and accounts.

January 20. Cotton and woolen mills of John Brown & Son, corner of Eighth and Tasker Streets, burned; loss, $200,000.

February 8. Machinery Hall, Fairmount Park, originally built for the use of the Centennial Exhibition, and which cost the city of Philadelphia $634,867.48, was sold at auction to W. P. Allison & Son for $24,600. The building consisted of a main hall 360 feet wide and 1,402 feet long, and an annex 208x210 feet.

March 1. Cracker bakery of Walter G. Wilson & Co., 212-214 North Front Street, destroyed by fire; loss, $40,000.

March 10. The building formerly the Arch Street Opera House, opened as "The Park Theatre," under the management of George K. Goodwin.

March 24. Fire at packing establishment of Washington Butchers' Sons, 146-148 North Front Street; loss, $30,000.

March 25. British bark Tulchen, while being towed from Kaighn's Point, N. J., to Girard Point, capsized and sunk in twenty-two feet of water at the mouth of the Schuylkill.

March 31. Fire and explosion at Belmont Oil Works, Twenty-fourth and Mifflin Streets. Two men burned to death; loss, $80,000.

April 6. Fire broke out in factory building, northeast corner of Race and Crown (Lawrence) Streets, extended to the building northwest corner of Fourth and Race Streets and to properties on south side of Race Street; loss, $800,000. One person killed.

May 11. Brewery of Sebastian Nagel, Paoli Avenue, Roxborough, destroyed by fire; loss, $21,000.

May 15. The directors of the Philadelphia and Reading Railway Company announced that they had leased for a period of 990 years the North Pennsylvania Railroad to Bethlehem, with its connection, and the Bound Brook Railroad to New York, lease to date from May 1, 1879.

HAPPENINGS IN YE OLDE PHILADELPHIA

June 11. Lightning struck the oil canning shed of LaComte & Perkins, at Point Breeze, setting it on fire. The flames were communicated to several vessels moored at the wharves; loss, over $150,000.

June 14. Annual regatta of the Schuylkill Navy. Course from below the Falls Bridge to Rockland, one and a half miles straight away. Prizes as follows: Four-oared shells, won by Crescent Club, 9.30; two-oared shells, Philadelphia Club, 10.46; double shells, Quaker City, 10.48; four-oared gigs, College Club, 10.35; single shells, Pennsylvania Club, 10.47.

Steamer Wanderer, for New Orleans and Havana Line, launched from shipyard of Birely, Hillman and Streaker, foot of Montgomery Avenue.

June 20. Fire at factory building, Ridge Avenue below Master, G. W. Smith, furniture finishers; loss, $20,000

June 24. Inter-collegiate regatta between the crews of Columbia and Princeton Colleges and University of Pennsylvania, on the Schuylkill River. National Course, Falls Bridge to Rockland, one and a half miles. Won by the University crew in 9.23.

June 27. Fire at southeast corner of Seventh and Cherry Streets, doing great damage to Hasting's gold leaf establishment, Stern's printing office, etc.; loss, $20,000.

Steam boiler exploded in the planing mill of Alpheus Wilt & Sons, Front Street, below Brown. Four persons killed and several injured.

July 17. Fires at the stores 7-9 South Water Street; loss, $30,000.

July 31. Seventeenth and Nineteenth Streets Passenger Railway formally opened as a portion of the Continental Passenger Railway.

August 14. An excursion train on the Philadelphia and Atlantic (narrow gauge) Railroad, came into collision with a freight train near Clementon; five persons killed and several injured.

August 28 and 29. International Cricket match at the Young America grounds at Stenton, between the Hamilton Club, of Hamilton, Canada, and the Young America Club, of Philadelphia. Score: Young America, first innings, 28; second innings, 50; total, 78. Hamilton, first innings, 74; second innings, 5; total, 79, with ten wickets to spare.

October 23. Match game of cricket between the Nottinghamshire and Yorkshire players of Daft's English professional team, reinforced by English players. Score: Nottinghamshire, first innings, 148.

September 25, 26 and 27. International cricket match at the grounds of the Germantown Cricket Club, near Wayne Station, between the Gentlemen of Ireland and a picked team of Philadelphia. Score: Irish Gentlemen, first inning, 58; second inning, 82; total, 140. Philadelphia, first and only inning, 149.

September 28. Return game between the Irish and Philadelphia Cricketers. One inning, Ireland, 122; Philadelphia, 108.

September 30. Cricket match between the Irish twelve and fifteen of the Merion Club on the grounds at Ardmore. Score: Ireland, first inning, 138; second, 170; total, 308. Merion, first inning, 81; second, 130; total, 211.

Keystone wool and yarn Mill, Callowhill Street above Twenty-fifth, destroyed by fire; loss, $28,000.

October 2. Boat race on the Schuylkill between six-oared barges of Fairmount and Neptune Clubs. Course from Chestnut street bridge to the red buoy at Gibson's Point, three miles. Won by Fairmount in 19 minutes, 20 seconds.

October 4. Annual fall regatta of the Schuylkill Navy. National course, Schuylkill River. Prize for single sculls won by W. B. Cobb, Pennsylvania Club, 11.2; double sculls, Vesper Club (no opponents); four-oared gigs, Malta, 9.53 1/4; senior singles, C. V. Grant, Philadelphia Club, 10.53; eight-oared shells, Undine, 8.55.

October 5. Cornerstone laid of new Roman Catholic Church of the Gesu, to replace Church of the Holy Family, Eighteenth and Stiles Streets.

First through train from Philadelphia to New York run from the Reading Railroad depot, Ninth and Green Streets, via the Bound Brook Railroad.

October 10, 11 and 13. International cricket match at Germantown Cricket grounds, Nicetown, between Daft's English professional eleven and fifteen selected amateurs. Score: English, first inning, 149; second, 133; total, 282. Philadelphia, first inning, 70; second, 67; total, 137.

October 12. Cornerstone laid of new building of the German Evangelical Reformed Bethlehem Church, Blair and Norris Streets.

October 17. Cricket match between Daft's All-English professional eleven and Young America eleven at Stenton. Young America, first inning, 64; second, 47; total, 111. Daft, first and only inning, 171; second, 22 (when the game was stopped with the first wicket down); total, 170. Yorkshire, first inning, 51; second, 118; total, 169.

November 1. Fire at the grain storage house of Brooke & Harper, 1729-33 Market Street; loss, $150,000.

December 3. Oxford Presbyterian Church, corner Broad and Oxford Streets, burned; loss, $50,000.

December 4. The controlling interest in the Union Passenger Railway Company, 12,600 shares, purchased by a combination, principally composed of officers and stockholders of the Continental Passenger Railway Company, at $100.00 a share. (This was the nucleus to the formation of combinations, eventually forming the Philadelphia Rapid Transit Company).

Ridge Avenue Passenger Railway Company commenced to sell five tickets for the conveyance of passengers for 25 cents. Single fares remained at 6 cents.

December 8. Work commenced on dismantling and taking down the Coliseum Building, corner Broad and Locust Streets (site of Hotel Walton) in order to remove the same to Boston.

December 16. Grand public reception of General U. S. Grant upon his return to Philadelphia and the conclusion of his journey around the world. Military and civic procession which required four hours and 40 minutes to pass a given point. It was 6 1/2 miles in length, and was estimated to have been participated in by 40,000 persons and seen by 350,000 spectators.

December 25. George Sheppard badly injured in Shackamaxon Street above Richmond, by oil of vitriol being thrown on him, as was alleged, by George Wood.

1880

January 12. Brickmakers' Union formed at a meeting held at Federal Hall, Seventeenth and Federal Streets.

January 14. Fire at spring factory of John Scott, Newmarket and Pollard Streets, which also destroyed Jacob J. Plucker & Co.'s furniture factory and damaged the furniture factory of S. Oetzel, J. Worthington's machine shop, and J. Buckley & Co.'s hub and spoke works. Loss, $55,000.

January 15. The Darby Plank Road from Forty-ninth Street to the county line passed into the possession of the city by purchase.

January 25. Fire at the establishment of Stephen S. Whitman & Sons, S.W. cor. of Twelfth and Market Streets. Loss, $70,000.

January 26. Twenty-two locomotive engines belonging to the Reading Railroad Company were seized at the Port Richmond depot by U. S. Internal Revenue Collector, by instruction from Washington, upon a claim of the U. S. Government for taxes on scrip issued by the company in 1878-79.

February 2. Fire at furniture factory of John A. Ebert, on Edward and Lydia Streets, above Hancock. Loss, $60,000.

Fire at Keystone Flour Mill, cor. of Leopard Street and Girard Avenue, occupied by Stetler & Co., millers. Loss, $25,000.

February 9. Fire at Clifton Mills, Berks Street between Hope and Howard Streets. Loss, $190,000.

Meeting of subscribers to a proposed bank, at which it was resolved that the institution should be organized with a capital of $600,000, under the title of "The Merchants' National Bank of Philadelphia."

February 19. Philadelphia Library building, N.E. cor. Fifth and Library Streets, closed.

March 8. Birth of a female elephant, said to be the first born in captivity, at Cooper & Bailey's London Circus and Menagerie stables, Ridge Avenue and Twenty-fourth Street.

March 25. The new Merchants' National Bank commenced business at the former building of the Provident Insurance Company, Fourth below Chestnut Street.

Stable of the Richmond branch of the Union Passenger Railway Company, Thompson and Norris Streets, burned. Loss, $20,000.

April 1. Fire at N.W. cor. Twelfth and Noble Streets, factory occupied by J. Conaway & Co., manufacturers of umbrella frames. Loss, $100,000.

April 7. Fire at the tea and coffee store of John Lamont (an eccentric character) 51 South Second Street. Loss, $20,000.

April 11. Mrs. Elizabeth E. Goersen died at the house of her husband, 255 East Cumberland Street. Coroner's jury found that her death was occasioned by poisoning with arsenic, administered by her husband, Dr. Alfred G. F. Goersen. On the 19th of April Coroner's jury also found that Mrs. Elizabeth F. Souder, mother-in-law of Dr. Goersen, who died on the 25th of March, was poisoned by him. Dr. Goersen was convicted of murder.

April 29. Under the name of Ridgway Park, Smith's Island, in the Delaware opposite the city, improved with new buildings and other arrangements, was opened to the public as a place of resort.

May 17. Fire at Gardener's Continental Brewery, Twenty-first Street and Washington Avenue. Loss, $75,000.

May 21. Reading Railroad Company and Reading Coal and Iron Company suspended payment, causing great excitement.

June 4. Fire at Patton, Allison & Jones cotton-mill, Washington Avenue above Twelfth Street. Loss, $30,000.

June 16. New railroad to Atlantic City, via the West Jersey Railroad to Newfield, formally opened.

June 24. Fire at Nice's Sash Mill, Third and Marriat Streets. Loss, $100,000.

June 28. Inter-collegiate boat-race for the Childs' challenge cup, on the Schuylkill River, between the crews of Columbia College, N. Y.; University of Pennsylvania, and Princeton, N. J., won by Columbia, beating the University 7 inches. Time, 9.04³/₄.

Fire at hosiery mills, Crease Street above Girard Avenue. Loss, $30,000.

July 4. Steamboat Argonauta, of the Ridgway Park line, ran down a small boat near the foot of Otis Street. Kate Mahey and three children were drowned.

July 7, 8, 9. Eighth annual regatta of the National Association of Amateur Oarsmen, national course, Schuylkill River. Prizes, single sculls, J. A. Whitaker, Pawtucket Club, R. I., 10.43; senior single sculls, F. J. Mumford, Perseverance Club, New Orleans, La.; double sculls, Pawtucket Club, R. I., 9.41; pair-oars, Gorman Bros., Albany Club, N. Y., 10.17; four-oared shells, Hillsdale Club, Mich., 8.53; six-oared shells, Mutual, Albany, N. Y., 8.51; eight-oared shells, Douglas, New York City, 8.53.

August 11. Excursion by congregation of St. Anne's Roman Catholic Church to Atlantic City by the West Jersey Railroad route, carrying about 1,300 persons. Collision between two sections of the train on the return trip at May's Landing, N. J., at 6.30 P. M. One person was killed outright. Thirty-two persons were scalded by escaping steam, of whom twenty-five subsequently died.

August 18. Arrival of the steam yacht Anthracite, claimed to be the smallest steam vessel that ever crossed the Atlantic. Length, 85 feet; breadth of beam, 16 feet; depth of hold, 10 feet; tonnage, 28 tons.

August 25. Fire at the W. B. Thomas flour-mill, N.W. cor. Thirteenth and Noble Streets. Loss estimated at $200,000. William Miller, foreman of the mills, overwhelmed in the falling ruins and killed.

September 3. Fire at Marshall Bros.' Rolling Mill, Beach and Marlborough Streets. Loss, $50,000.

September 6. Tenth anniversary of the Declaration of the French Republic celebrated at Rising Sun Park, Allegheny Ave. and Germantown Ave.

September 12. Monument and bronze statue of the Benevolent and Protective Order of Elks dedicated at Mount Moriah Cemetery.

September 13-14. International cricket-match at the Nicetown field between twelve Canada and twelve United States players. Score, United States, first inning, 70; second inning, 168; total, 238. Canada, first inning, 83; second, 7; total, 90. There were six wickets down in the second Canada inning when at night the stumps were drawn, and the game declared a draw, according to the rules.

September 15-16. Cricket at Ardmore between the Canadian players and the Merion Club. Score, Canada, first inning, 57; second inning, 85; total, 142. Merion, first inning, 138; second, 6; total, 144, with eight wickets to go down.

September 17. Ninety-third anniversary of the adoption of the Constitution of the United States celebrated by the Keystone Club by a commemorative dinner at the Girard House (northeast corner of Ninth and Chestnut Streets).

September 20. The new Chestnut Street Opera House, formerly Fox's American Theatre, rebuilt and refurnished, opened for the first time, under the management of George K. Goodwin, with the drama of the Danicheffs.

October 4. The epizooty, or horse disease epidemic in the city. Large numbers of animals affected, but the disease much milder than was the case in 1872.

October 12. Stone flour mill, Mill Street, Holmesburg, totally destroyed by fire. Loss, $12,000. This mill was the oldest in Pennsylvania, having been erected in 1697.

October 17. New Roman Catholic Church of St. Joachim, Frankford, dedicated.

October 22. Fire at the yarn factory of Dixon & Roberts, Canal Street above Lawrence Street and Girard Ave., also occupied by Alexander & John McConnell, morocco manufacturers. Loss, $86,000.

October 27. Cornerstone laid of East Baptist Church, Hanover Street above Girard Avenue.

November 3. New House of the Good Shepherd, Thirty-fifth and Silverton Ave., Roman Catholic, first occupied by the sisterhood.

November 7. St. Peter's P.E. Church, Germantown, was consecrated, being out of debt.

Fourth Moravian Church, Hancock Street above Dauphin, dedicated.

December 23. Fire at B. Crawford's tannery, Sixth Street (east side) above Thompson. Loss, $25,000.

1881

January 2. Delaware River frozen over from shore to shore. Persons passed over the ice to Camden; skating lasted for some days.

January 5. New building of Beneficial Savings Fund Society, S.W. corner Twelfth and Chestnut Streets, opened for business.

January 14. Fire at Columbia Shoddy Mill, Columbia Avenue and Fifth Street. Loss, $15,000.

January 18. Fire in the carpet-yarn mill of James Whitaker, Trenton Avenue and Sargent Street. Loss, $16,000.

Explosion and fire at the works of the Atlantic Petroleum Refining Co., Point Breeze. Loss, $60,000.

January 19. Malt-mill of G. F. Rothacker, Thirty-first and Master Streets, burned. Loss, $30,000.

January 31. Beth-Eden Baptist Church, N.W. corner Broad and Spruce Streets, totally destroyed by fire. Loss, $60,000.

February 1. Fire in the six- and eight-story factories, 212-224 Carter Street. Loss, $200,000.

February 2. Waltzing against time by Julian and Constantine Carpenter, at Carpenter's Dancing Hall, Thirteenth and Chestnut Streets, who waltzed for sixteen and a half hours without stopping "The best time on record."

February 6. Tioga M. E. Church, corner Nineteenth and Tioga Streets, dedicated.

February 7. By formal vote the congregation of Sixteenth Street M. E. Church decided to unite and consolidate with Trinity M. E. Church, Eighth Street above Race.

February 10. The ice above Columbia Bridge, Schuylkill River, started, but formed a gorge at the bridge, backing up the water as far as Manayunk. The river rose from 15 to 18 feet, flooding the mills and other buildings on the banks of the Schuylkill and overflowing Ridge Avenue, stopping horse-car traveling.

February 16. First train run over the new elevated railroad of the Pennsylvania Railroad Company, on Filbert Street to Broad, with an excursion-party composed of members of the American Institute of Mining Engineers.

February 20. New Oxford Presbyterian Church, cor. Broad and Oxford Streets, built on the site of one destroyed by fire December 3, 1879, dedicated.

February 22. Pythian Temple, Pine Street below Third, built for the order of the Knights of Pythias, opened for inspection.

March 6-7. Farewell services at Trinity M. E. Church, Eighth Street above Race, the congregation having abandoned the building and united with the Sixteenth Street M.E. Church.

March 9. Fire at Belmont Oil Works of W. L. Elkins & Co., Long Lane near Twenty-fourth and Mifflin Streets. Loss, $80,000.

March 21. Retail Grocers' Association formed at a meeting held at Association Hall.

March 24. The trustees of the University of Pennsylvania accepted an endowment of $100,000 from Joseph Wharton for the foundation of the Wharton School of Finance and Economy in the University.

March 26. Iron steamship Perseus, built for Iron Steamship Company of New York, launched from Cramp's Shipyard.

April 5. Farmers' bone and fertilizer works and ninety boat houses of the Southwark Yacht Club destroyed by fire. Loss, $110,000.

April 7. Iron steamboat Pegasus, built for Iron Steamboat Company of New York, launched at Cramp's Shipyard.

April 9. Iron Steamship Caraccas, built for New York and Venezuela line, launched from Cramp's Shipyard.

June 1. Steam-boiler in dye-house of Thomas Gaffney & Co., 2430 Collins Street, exploded, causing the death of three, and injuring five others. Loss, $31,000.

Children's Sanitarium at Point Airy (Windmill Island) opened for the season.

All Saints Roman Catholic Church, Brown and Bockius Streets, Bridesburg, struck by lightning and damaged by fire.

June 11. First annual meet of Bicycle Club at West Park and road race to Ardmore, in which 67 wheelmen participated.

June 18. Annual regatta of the Schuylkill Navy; 25 contesting crews. National course, $1^1/2$ miles, straight away. Prizes as follows: Juniors singles, Vesper Club, $11.33^1/2$; senior singles, Quaker City Club, $10.25^1/4$; pair oars, Undine, $10.40^1/2$; junior four-oared gigs, Vesper, 10.03; four-oared shell, College, $8.58^3/4$; double sculls, Vesper, 10.13; senior gig, Vesper, 9.48; six-oared barge, College, $9.39^1/4$; eight-oared shells, College, 8.33.

June 24. A syndicate represented by the People's (Callowhill Street) Railway Company and others bought 15,309 shares of stock in the Germantown City Passenger Railway Company, being a controlling interest.

July 6. Inter-collegiate boat race for the Childs' challenge cup on the Schuylkill between the crews of Princeton College and University of Pennsylvania. The University came in ahead, the Princeton being a quarter of a mile behind. The cup was awarded to the Princeton crew upon the ground that one of the crew of the University Club was ineligible.

July 16. Annual regatta of the American Rowing Association on lower Schuylkill. Course from Callowhill Street bridge to Market Street and return. Prizes for six-oared barges won by the Riverside; four-oared, Pythias; double sculls, the W. J. Temple crew; single scull, John Hobbs.

July 20. Cornerstone laid of the new building of Heidelberg Reformed Church, cor. Nineteenth and Oxford Streets.

Fire at Pequea Cotton and Woolen Mills, Pennsylvania Avenue and Twenty-second Street. Loss, $160,000.

July 27. The Lombard and South Street Passenger Railway leased to the

West End and Angora Passenger Railway Company.

July 28. The trotting mare Maud S. undertook, at Belmont Park, to exceed her previous performance of one mile in 2.10^1/$_2$. She trotted three heats as follows: First, 2.12; second, 2.13^1/$_4$; third, 2.12^1/$_2$. This was stated to be the quickest time on record for three consecutive one-mile heats.

August 1. Eighth Street Theatre, Eighth Street below Vine, opened for the first time. Address, music and the play "Little Emily."

August 5. Four colored men appointed substitutes on the city police by Mayor King, they being the first in Philadelphia.

August 6. Iron screw steamship Allegheny, built for the Merchants and Miners Transportation Company, launched from the shipyard of Wm. Cramp & Sons.

August 10. A fast train on the Camden and Atlantic Railroad made the trip from Camden to Atlantic City in 76 minutes.

August 22. Meeting of colored citizens at Liberty Hall, Lombard Street above Seventh, to return thanks to Mayor Samuel G. King for his course "in recognizing the just and equal claims of colored men in his appointments to the police force."

August 26. Lager-beer brewery of Henry Mueller, Thirty-first and Jefferson Streets, burned. Loss, $75,000.

August 29. Fire at Globe Mills, Germantown Avenue below Girard Avenue, occupied by Schatchard & Hoffman, silk-yarn spinners, and the Midnight Yarn Co. Loss, $15,000.

September 3. Steamship Berkshire for Merchants and Miners Transportation Company, launched at shipyard of Wm. Cramp & Sons.

September 14. Fire at the Union Hub, Spoke and Wheel Works of Fitler & Dubois, cor. Otter and Leopard Streets. Loss, $30,000.

September 15. Swimming-match for the championship of the Delaware from Blockhouse to Ridgway Park, a distance of 7^1/$_2$ miles; 8 contestants. First prize won by Dennis F. Butler; second, Duke Marr, of Schuylkill; third, George Bird, of Atlantic City; fourth, Thomas Coyle, of Chester.

September 19. Intelligence of the death of President James A. Garfield, who died at Elberon, N. J., at 10.35 P. M., received before midnight.

September 20. Public buildings, churches, stores, factories, etc., draped in mourning colors. In the evening all the theatres and places of amusement were closed.

September 26. Day of humiliation and prayer in consequence of the death of President Garfield. General suspension of business.

David Kalakaua I, King of the Sandwich Islands, arrived in the city and took lodgings at Continental Hotel.

September 27. Cornerstone of Cookman M. E. Church, corner Twelfth and Lehigh Avenue, laid.

September 29. Fire at stables of Adams Express Company, Twenty-second Street below Market. Loss, $10,000.

Swimming-match on the Delaware River, for the championship and a purse of $400 between Joseph Marrow and Dennis F. Butler. Course, from the red buoy at Chester to Ridgway Park, 15 miles. Upon reaching the old Greenwich Point docks, a distance of about 12^1/$_2$ miles, Butler succumbed, and the prize was awarded to Marrow. Time, 3.50m. This was said to be the longest swim yet accomplished in the United States.

October 1. Linseed-oil works of Grove & Brothers, at Greenwich Point, First

Ward, burned. Loss, $50,000.

International cricket match commenced at the grounds of the Germantown Club, near Nicetown, between Alfred Shaw's English professional team and twelve amateurs of Philadelphia, selected from the Young America, Merion, Germantown and Girard Clubs. Score: Englishmen, first inning, 277; Philadelphians, first inning, 126; seconds 47.

October 7. International cricket match at the grounds of the Germantown Club, near Nicetown, between Shaw's professional team and eighteen Americans chosen from Philadelphia, New York and Boston clubs. Score: Englishmen, first inning, 114; second, 166. Americans, first inning, 71; second, 77.

October 12. Fire at the Randolph cotton and woolen mill, occupied by Charles H. Landenberger, Randolph Street above Columbia Avenue. There were thirty-eight workmen and girls in the building, all of whom were cut off from escape by the rapid progress of the flames. Nine were killed by jumping from the windows or burned to death while in the building, or died afterward from their injuries; thirteen were seriously maimed or injured; sixteen escaped. Loss by the fire on the building, $10,000; on stock and machinery, heavy.

October 18. By vote of 18,463 shares in favor to 3,501 against the proposition, the stockholders of Germantown Passenger Railway (Fourth and Eighth Streets) resolved to lease their road and franchises to the People's Passenger Railway (Callowhill Street) for 999 years at a maximum rental of $4.50 per share, or nine per cent. on the capital stock.

Steamship City of Puebla, 2,900 tons burden, for New York and Havana line, launched from shipyard of Cramp & Son.

October 24. Fire at the stationery store of William F. Murphy's Sons, Chestnut Street above Fifth. Loss, $25,000.

November 7. The disease called "pink-eye," or epizooty, affecting horses, made its appearance in this city, and continued about three weeks. Probably ten thousand horses belonging to passenger railway companies, etc., were affected, but few fatally.

November 27. Thomas E. Conaty and Owen Burns instantly killed while riding on a car on Fourth Street above Master by the pole of a steam fire-engine drawn by runaway horses.

December 3. Chestnut Street first illuminated with the electric light (forty-nine lamps) from the Delaware to the Schuylkill.

December 5. New Broad Street Station of Pennsylvania Railroad Company, connected with the elevated railroad at Market and Broad Streets, opened for business with the regular running of passenger trains.

1882

January 16. Telegraph line of Bankers' and Merchants' Telegraph Company, from Philadelphia to New York, first opened for business.

January 26. Keystone hub, spoke and wheel works, Charles Scott's railway car spring factory, and N. H. Harned's silk fringe factory, New Market Street above Laurel, destroyed by fire. Loss estimated at $125,000.

March 18. Iron steamship Valencia launched from shipyard of William Cramp & Son, for New York and Venezuela Line. Dimensions, 260 feet long, 34.6 feet beam, 22 feet deep. Engines, 900 horsepower, 1,800 tons.

Directors of Union Passenger Railway Company resolve to adopt the cable-motor system for propulsion of their cars on Columbia Avenue branch from

Twenty-third Street to East Park entrance.

March 19. Cornerstone laid of German Roman Catholic Church of Our Lady of the Nativity, at Allegheny Avenue and Belgrade Street.

March 23. The boiler of the tug-boat Henry C. Pratt, at Pier No. 8, South Wharves, exploded, killing five persons and totally destroying the boat. The tug-boat Ella, lying near by, caught fire and was destroyed. Station of Philadelphia and Atlantic City Railroad burned and adjoining property damaged. Loss, $20,000.

Last rail of the River Front Railroad laid on Delaware Avenue and thereby complete railroad connection made between the Pennsylvania Railroad tracks at Greenwich Point and the tracks of the same road and the Reading Railroad at Kensington and Port Richmond.

March 25. Fire at cork manufactory of C. N. Rossel, Third Street above Callowhill; adjoining buildings damaged. Loss, about $45,000.

March 29. Store-building of Jacob Rorer & Son, Old York Road, Branchtown, totally destroyed by fire. Loss, $30,000.

Ground broken for new armory for First Regiment Infantry, National Guards Pennsylvania, southeast cor. Broad and Callowhill Streets.

April 1. Fire at Philadelphia Sewing Machine Company's works, N.W. cor. Thirteenth and Buttonwood; property of R. Moorehouse damaged. Loss, $25,000.

April 8. Philadelphia Recreation Park, Ridge Avenue and Twenty-fourth Street, opened for sports with a game of baseball.

April 9. Armory of Third Regiment National Guards of Pennsylvania, N.E. cor. Twelfth and Reed Streets, opened with religious services, Bishop Stevens, of P. E. Church, officiating.

April 19. Cornerstone of the armory building for First Regiment National Guards of Pennsylvania laid at Broad and Callowhill Sts. by the Grand Lodge of Pennsylvania with Masonic ceremonies, a military parade, review, and an oration. Reception in the evening at the Academy of Music.

April 22. Mill buildings, Sophia St. between Edward and Van Horn, occupied by Isaac Casson & Co., machinists, Joseph Weiss, and Roher & Noell, furniture manufacturers, destroyed by fire. Loss, $30,000.

April 29. Four-oared gig race between the classes of the University of Pennsylvania, National Course, Schuylkill River. Distance, $1^1/2$ miles. Sophomores, 9 min. 22 sec.; Seniors, 9 min. 24 sec.; Juniors, 9 min. 39 sec.; Freshman time not taken. The Sophomores' time was faster by 9 seconds than any previous 4 oared gig-time on the course.

May 16. Composing-rooms and foundry of the *Public Ledger* lighted for the first time by means of the Edison incandescent electric light.

June 6. Spruce and Pine Streets Passenger Railway cars commenced to run for five-cent fares to Fairmount and Gray's Ferry from Delaware Ave.

June 13. Fire at round-house of Philadelphia and Atlantic City (narrow gauge) Railroad, Bulson St., Camden. Seven locomotives destroyed. Loss, $100,000.

June 17. Spring regatta of Schuylkill Navy; twenty-nine entries. National Course, $1^1/2$ miles straight away. Prizes as follows: Junior singles, to West Philadelphia Club, 12.14$^1/2$; Senior singles, to Quaker City, 11.15$^3/4$; four-oared shells, College, 10.16$^1/4$; pair-oars, West Philadelphia, 11.44$^3/4$; Junior four-oared gigs, College, 10.40$^3/4$; Senior four-oared shells, College, 9.45$^1/4$; double sculls, Crescent, 11.5$^1/4$; Senior four-oared gigs, College, 10.31$^1/4$; six-oared barges, Vesper, 10.40$^{3}/_{4}$.

June 20. Lombard and South Street, and Spruce and Pine Street Passenger Railway Companies (five-cent fare roads) began a system of exchanges for six cents over both roads, between West Philadelphia, Zoological Garden, Delaware Ave. and Dock St. and Exchange, Fairmount Park and Gray's Ferry.

June 23. Inter-collegiate boat-race for the Childs' challenge cup, on the Schuylkill River, between the crews of Princeton College and University of Pennsylvania. National Course, 1$^{1}/_{2}$ miles straight away. Won by the University of Pennsylvania by two or three lengths. Time, 9 min. 32 sec.

June 24. At a special meeting of the stockholders of the Camden and Atlantic Railroad Company, resolution adopted in favor of the purchase of the interest of William Massey in the Philadelphia and Atlantic City (narrow gauge) Railroad Company for $500,000, which included stock, first-mortgage bonds, claims for interest, floating debt, track, motive-power and rolling stock, worth at par and full value $824,807.57, payment to be made in bonds of Camden and Atlantic Railroad. Stock vote in favor of purchase, 13,057 shares; against purchase, 312. Subsequently (July 26) the Chancellor of New Jersey granted an injunction prohibiting the sale and transfer as contrary to law.

July 1. Auction-house of M. Thomas & Son, 139 and 141 South Fourth St. totally destroyed by fire. Loss, $250,000.

Iron Steamship Tacoma launched from the shipyard of Cramp & Son. Length, 350 feet; beam, 42 feet; depth of hold, 30 feet; burden, 3,500 tons; owners, Central Pacific Railroad Company; engines, 2,000 horse-power. Vessel intended for collier service.

July 8. Fire at malt-house of Bergner & Engel's Brewery. Thirty-second and Thompson Sts. Loss, $20,000.

July 14. Fire at factory of M. L. Shoemaker & Co., fertilizers, Delaware Ave. and Venango St. Loss, $20,000.

July 26. Stockholders West End Passenger Railway Company, by a vote of over 6,000 shares to 3,300, agree to consolidate their company with Lombard and South Streets Passenger Railway Company. Same day Court of Common Pleas granted a preliminary injunction to restrain the consolidation.

August 3. Excitement in business circles in consequence of the discovery of extensive forgeries and frauds by Charles M. Hilgert, sugar-refiner, refinery, Lawrence St. below Girard Ave., estimated to amount to $1,000,000. Hilgert absconds.

August 20. Roman Catholic Church of the Nativity of the Blessed Virgin Mary, at Allegheny Ave. and Belgrade St., dedicated.

August 22. Eighth General Convention of the American St. Cecilia Society for the culture of Catholic church music assembled at St. Peter's Roman Catholic Church, Fifth and Girard Ave.

August 24. Iron steamship San Pedro, built for Central Pacific Railroad Company, launched at shipyard of William Cramp & Son. Length, 350 feet; breadth, 42 feet; depth, 30 feet, carrying capacity 3,500 tons.

September 1. Warrant issued for the arrest of Major Ellis P. Phipps, superintendent of the Almshouse, on a charge of defrauding the city out of $5,000 by a fraudulent warrant. Phipps entered bail to appear before a magistrate, and then absconded. Subsequently large quantities of goods and supplies belonging to the Almshouse were found on premises in which Phipps resided.

September 2. Boat-race for a champion flag for barges between the Falls of

Schuylkill and George W. Mallison barge clubs; four oars and coxswain. National course 1 1/2 miles straight away. Won by Falls of Schuylkill Club. Time, 10 min. 30 sec.

September 15. Public reception of Chief-Engineer Melville and Seamen Noros and Nindermann, survivors of the Jeanette Arctic expedition, at Continental Hotel.

September 18. Ellis P. Phipps arrested at Hamilton, Ontario.

September 19. First railroad car lighted by electricity arrived at station of Pennsylvania Railroad Company, being also the first using this light in America.

September 20. Sanitarium (Point Airy) closed. During the season there were received and made comfortable there 36,860 children.

September 28. Fire at candy manufactory of Philip Wunderle, New Market St. above Pegg. Loss, $40,000.

October 4. President and directors of the People's Passenger Railway Company (Callowhill Street), which also controlled the Germantown, Fourth and Eighth, Girard Avenue and Green and Coates Street lines, resigned, and Charles J. Harrah, who had obtained the controlling interest of the stock, was elected president, with a new board of managers.

Buildings in Rising Sun Park, Germantown Road at. Rising Sun Lane, destroyed by fire. Loss, $11,000.

October 8. New edifice of St. Peter's Lutheran Church, Reed St. below Ninth, consecrated.

Cornerstone laid of new Roman Catholic hospital of St. Agnes, corner Broad and Mifflin Streets.

October 12 and 13. International cricket-match between the Australian eleven and the Philadelphia eighteen at Nicetown grounds. Score: Philadelphia, first inning, 82; second inning, 76. Total, 158. Australia, first inning, 106; second inning, 53. Total, 159, with nine wickets to spare.

October 16. At Hamilton, Ontario, Judge Sinclair decided that Ellis P. Phipps, formerly steward of the Philadelphia Almshouse, was subject to extradition on charge of forgery. Phipps' counsel appealed.

Freight and passenger station of Philadelphia and Atlantic City (narrow-gauge) Railroad at Pier 8, South Wharves, destroyed by fire, also steam-tug, Major, belonging to the company. Steam-tug Argus, with some adjoining shipping, considerably damaged. Loss estimated at $40,000.

October 24. Landing Day. Bi-centennial celebration. A vessel representing the ship Welcome, bearing as passengers persons representing William Penn and other Friends, came up the river, followed by a grand procession of steamboats and tugs.

October 25. Trades' Day. Procession including persons engaged in different industries.

October 26. Festival Day.

October 27. Military Day.

December 5. Arrott's mill, N.W. corner Coral and Taylor Sts., destroyed by fire January 31, 1881, having been rebuilt, reopened.

Arrott's mill, N.W. cor. Coral and Taylor Sts., occupied by Joseph Greer, cotton and woolen manufacturer, Jaggard & Jones, Henry Grant, Stead Bros. and Robert Beatty, yarn spinners, burned. Loss, $115,000.

Fire at Rebman & Ruhland's iron foundry, Twenty-second and Master Sts. Loss, $25,000.

December 6. Great excitement in the southern part of the city in consequence of the discovery that a number of graves had been robbed of the dead in Lebanon Cemetery for Negroes, and that the bodies had been carried to a medical college.

December 20. Goldsmith's Hall, Library St. east of Fifth, totally destroyed by fire. Occupants, E. G. Haehnlen & Co., dealers in chamois skins; E. C. Markley & Sons, printers; A. C. Farley & Co. manufacturing stationers; Lehman & Bolton, lithographers; Custom-House and note-brokers, lawyers, etc. Loss, $350,000.

December 25. Joseph Jarvis, police-officer, stabbed severely, while in the discharge of his duty, at Leopard St. and Girard Ave., by William Rusk, with whom at the time was Jacob Rusk (twin brothers). The two escaped to Trenton, New Jersey, where, having learned that officers of the law were in pursuit of them, they committed suicide by drowning.

1883

January 3. Bucks and Montgomery County Farmers' Market opened in building some years abandoned, formerly erected for market-house purposes, at S.E. cor. of Sixth St. and Columbia Ave.

January 26. Underground electric light apparatus on the Thomson & Houston plan went into operation for business purposes on Market St. between Seventh and Eleventh Sts.

January 29. New freight-station of Pennsylvania Railroad Company, Shackamaxon St. and River-front Railroad, open for business.

January 30. James F. Brown, ex-storekeeper in the Almshouse, charged with forgery and conspiracy with Ellis P. Phipps, ex-steward, to cheat and defraud the public, was found guilty.

Fire at 250-256 N. Broad St., occupied by Levi, Knowles & Co., J. Allen & Co., E. H. Graham & Co., flour and grain merchants, Edmund Hill & Co., machinists, and E. W. Siegeman & Co., dealers in agricultural implements. Loss, $100,000.

February 5. Furniture manufactory of Julian Kraan, 942 N. Ninth St., totally destroyed by fire. Loss, $20,000.

March 14. New building of the Homeopathic Hospital for children, No. 914 Broad Street, formally opened.

March 24. United States steel-plated monitor Terror launched from the shipyard of Cramp & Sons. Length between perpendiculars, 250 feet; extreme breadth over armor, 55 feet, 10 inches; extreme depth over armor, 17 feet, 3 inches; depth of hold, 14 feet, 8 inches. Keel laid October 2, 1874.

April 7. Cable-motor branch of Union Passenger Railway, Columbia Ave., from Twenty-third St. to the Park, commenced regular operations.

The iron steam pleasure yacht Atlanta, built for Jay Gould, of New York, launched from the shipyard of Cramp & Sons. Length from knighthead to taffrail, 230 feet, 3 inches; beam, 26 feet, 4 inches; depth, 16 feet; rigged with three masts. No. 246.

April 10. Warrant for the extradition of Maj. Ellis P. Phipps to Philadelphia, signed by the governor-general of Canada.

April 13. Maj. Ellis P. Phipps, extradited from Canada, brought back to the city and lodged in the county prison.

April 14. Fire at the plumbers' metal-works of C. A. Blessing, Montgomery Ave. bel. Sixth St. Loss, $70,000.

April 26. Fire at the Arch Street Opera House, by which the interior was burned out. Loss, $18,000.

April 28. Four-oared gig-race between the classes of the University of Pennsylvania, national course, Schuylkill River. Distance, $1^1/_2$ miles. Juniors, class of '84, 9 min., 15$^5/_8$ sec; Seniors, '83, 9 min., 33 sec.; Freshmen, '86, 9 min., 30 sec. Medical class time not taken. The Junior time was 6$^1/_8$ sec. faster than any before made on the river by four-oared gigs.

May 3. Iron steamship Alameda, built for the Oceanic Steamship Company, San Francisco, launched at the shipyard of Cramp & Sons.

Fire at S.E. cor. Germantown Ave. and Master St., occupied by D. F. Rawle, flour dealer; John Richardson, furniture manufacturer; Montague & White, hosiery; John Patterson, hosiery; Walton Ritter, cotton goods. Loss, $23,000.

May 4. Maj. Ellis P. Phipps, tried for forgery, committed as an officer of the Almshouse, found guilty in the court of Quarter Sessions and sentenced, June 30, to five years' imprisonment, at hard labor.

May 6. Cornerstone laid of new Roman Catholic Church and School of St. Edward the Confessor, N.E. cor. Seventh and York Sts.

New chapel of Trinity M. E. Church, Fifteenth and Mount Vernon Sts., dedicated.

May 13. Fire at 1512-16 Spring Garden St., occupied by North American Smelting Works; Pennsylvania Brass Works; D. W. Bing, foundry and machine shops; D. B. Birch, miller; Fayer, cigar-moulder, and James Kerr, manufacturer. Loss, $35,000.

May 22. Fire at saw and planing mill and steam packing-box factory, Marshall St. above Girard Ave., occupied by W. H. Howard, Williwar & Yiest and William Stone. Loss, $11,500.

. May 27. Cornerstone laid of Mount Airy Presbyterian chapel, Germantown Ave. and Mount Pleasant St.

June 5. Fire at furniture manufacturing establishment of John Ebert, Edward St. west of Hancock, also occupied by D. R. Dover, bobbin-turner, and William W. Altemus & Son, manufacturers of knitting machines; adjoining properties damaged. Loss, $85,000.

June 12. Cornerstone laid of infirmary attached to Presbyterian Home for Widows and Single Women, Fifty-eighth St. and Woodland Ave.

Ground broken for Cohocksink M. E. church, S.W. cor. Seventh and Norris Sts.

June 15. Inter-collegiate boat-race for the Childs challenge cup on the Schuylkill River between the crews of Princeton College and the University of Pennsylvania. National course, $1^1/_2$ miles straight away. Won by the University of Pennsylvania by two clear lengths. Time 9.31$^1/_5$ minutes.

June 23. Spring regatta of Schuylkill Navy, National course, Schuylkill River, $1^1/_2$ miles straight away. Prizes, Junior single scull to Vesper Club, time, 10.19; Senior singles, Malta, 10.27$^1/_2$. Pair-oared shells, West Philadelphia, 11.12$^1/_2$. Junior four-oared gigs, Malta, 9.18. Senior four-oared shells College, 8.39. Double sculls, Crescent, 9.10$^1/_2$. Six-oared barges, Malta, 9.42$^3/_4$.

July 1. Henry Disston Memorial M. E. Church, Tacony, dedicated.

July 19. At 12 o'clock M. the telegraph operators of the Western Union Telegraph Company, to the number of two hundred and forty, struck and left their work—a movement which was general with the operators of that company all over the United States at the same hour. The strike lasted until August 17th, when the members of the Brotherhood were officially informed by their officers, "The strike is a failure. All the members who can may return to work immediately."

July 23. The direction taken by the cars on the Thirteenth and Fifteenth Streets Passenger Railway reversed, running up Thirteenth St. and down Fifteenth.

August 7. Fire at stable and ice-house of Knickerbocker Ice Company, Willow Street Wharf; thirty-three horses and four mules burned to death. Loss, $35,000. Reading freight depot, adjoining, damaged.

Fire at chemical works of Hance Bros. & White, N.W. cor. Marshall and Callowhill Streets. Loss, $28,000.

August 8. Exhibition of "walking on the water" on the Delaware River by C. D. Fort. He wore shoes of light cedar. Course, from Walnut St. Wharf to Ridgway Park. In consequence of a strong tide, which carried the walker far out of his course, the time required to reach the goal was two hours.

August 14. The Subsidiary High Court of the Ancient Order of Foresters began its annual session in Lincoln Hall.

August 22. Collision in the Delaware River, off Point Airy, between the ferry-boat Dauntless, of the Gloucester line, and the steam yacht Emma A. Kline. The latter was sunk, and William Young, drowned.

August 29. Fire at woolen-mill, N.W. cor. Cumberland and Third Sts., occupied by Gilmour & Morris, finishers; Lee & Bowers, woolens; Robert Laycock, woolens; Garner & Co., worsted; Joseph P. Murphy, shawls, etc. Loss, $50,000.

August 30. Accident on Philadelphia and Atlantic City Narrow-Gauge Railroad, near Pleasantville, New Jersey, caused by defect in a switch. Cars overturned, twenty-eight persons seriously injured.

September 3. William J. Menow shot and killed on Front St. above Poplar by Mrs. Emily Bickel, who claimed to be the wife of Menow.

September 12. Steamboat Moses Taylor, of the Bridesburg and Tacony line, sunk at Bridesburg Wharf.

September 17. The new Arch Street Opera House, Arch St. west of Tenth, rebuilt after being burned, opened by Rice's Comic Opera Company.

September 19. Saw and planing mill, Norris and Richmond Sts., occupied by Jesse W. Taylor & Sons, and Henry Bradshaw, hardwood goods, burned, and adjoining property damaged. Loss, $30,000.

Fire broke out in the lumber yard of James Gill, 1168 N. Third St., which spread and destroyed nearly the whole block of buildings bounded by Third St., Canal St., Charlotte St. and Girard Ave., occupied by Gill's lumber yard, Eagle Iron Works of Hoff & Fontaine, and from fifteen to twenty dwelling houses, shops and other buildings. Loss estimated at $75,000.

September 19. Workmen commenced laying the cable road of the Union Passenger Railway Company on Columbia Avenue east of Twenty-third Street.

September 20. Philadelphia and Atlantic Railroad (narrow-gauge) sold at public sale at Camden, N. J., and bought by G. W. R. Kercher for the Reading Railroad Company.

September 24. New Central Theatre, on site of old Grand Central Theatre, Walnut St. above Eighth, opened. Front, 80 feet; depth, 135 feet, height to the cornice, 58 feet; auditorium, 76 feet deep; stage, 74 feet wide, 40 feet deep; height of rigging-loft, 76 feet; proscenium opening, 28 feet square. Seating capacity (orchestra, orchestra circle, balcony and gallery), 2,600.

New hall of the Philadelphia Turn Verein, 433 and 435 N. Sixth St., dedicated.

September 29. Saw and planing mill, Willow between Eleventh and Twelfth Sts., property of the assignees of William B. Thomas and occupied by J. J. Crout & Son, sash, blind and door manufacturers, and Henry A. Hunsicker, planing mill, burned. Loss, $20,000.

First annual meeting of the Pennsylvania division of the League of American Wheelmen at Fairmount Park, followed by bicycle races at the Gentlemen's Driving Park. About four hundred wheelmen in line.

October 1. Filemyer's brewery, 2527 N. Broad St., partly destroyed by fire. Loss, $15,000.

Reception of the Athletic Base Ball Club after its return from the West, where it had won the champion pennant of the American Base Ball Association. Parade, participated in by base ball clubs, yacht clubs, social clubs and other organizations.

October 8. Improvements in Franklin Square having been finished it was opened to the public and illuminated for the first time with electric lights.

October 24. The Letitia house, the cottage of William Penn, built in 1682, which was the first State House of the province and was the oldest mansion in the city, having been removed from Letitia court to Fairmount Park, was formally presented to the Park Commissioners on behalf of the Bi-Centennial Association of Pennsylvania.

November 10. Iron steamship San Pablo, built for the Pacific Improvement Company, launched from shipyards of Wm. Cramp & Sons. Length, 350 feet; width, 42 feet; depth, 29 feet; engines, 2,000 horse-power; carrying capacity, 4,000 tons.

November 17. Fire at the sheds of the American Line Steamship Company at Christian St. Wharf. Cotton and other merchandise intended for shipment burned, also the tugboat Pallas, some hoisting-floats, lighters and other vessels. Loss estimated at $112,000.

November 18. The new eastern standard of time adopted by the railroad companies of the eastern division of the country went into operation at noon. By resolution of City Councils, the public clocks were set thirty-six seconds faster than the current time, that being the time of the seventy-fifth meridian and the difference at Philadelphia.

November 28. The fences on Carpenter St. and on Washington Ave., on the line of Fifteenth St., which blocked up travel by reason of the occupancy of the ground by the Philadelphia, Wilmington and Baltimore Railroad Company, taken down.

1884

January 1. New hall of the Improved Order of Red Men, 928 Race St., formally opened.

January 15. Fire at hosiery mill of J. R. Bridges & Co., 1347 N. Front St. Loss, $11,000.

January 21. New post-office building at Ninth and Chestnut Sts., opened for the first time to the public, a session of the United States Circuit Court being held there.

January 26. Perseverance Wood Works of Mahlon Fulton, Ninth St. above Oxford, totally destroyed by fire. Loss, $75,000.

January 27. Farewell services in Cohocksink M.E. Church, Germantown Av. above Columbia Av., building then abandoned by the congregation.

HAPPENINGS IN YE OLDE PHILADELPHIA

January 28. New post-office, Ninth and Market Sts., put in use by the opening of the Money Order Department.

February 6. Workshop of the Phillips Underground Electric Cable Manufacturing Company, Willow St. above Twelfth, destroyed by fire; four firemen injured. Loss, $27,500.

February 16. Fire at the flour warehouse and depot of E. Lathbury & Co., Vine St. above Broad. Loss, estimated, $60,000. The western wall fell on February 17th, crushing in adjacent buildings on Vine St. and Leeds Ave., and killing two men, one of them being a fireman.

February 22. New armory of the First Regiment Infantry, Cor. Broad and Callowhill Sts., formally opened.

Hall of St. Michael's T. A. B. Society, Germantown Ave. above Columbia Ave. dedicated (formerly Cohocksink M. E. Church).

February 29. Fire in the laboratory of the chemical works of Powers and Weightman, extending from Brown to Parrish St., and from Ninth to Knox St. Loss, estimated, $200,000.

March 6. Fire at the oil-cloth works of George W. Blabon & Co., Nicetown, destroying the coating, grinding and printing buildings. Loss, $150,000.

March 15. Fire at spice manufactory of A. Colburn & Co., Broad St. above Arch. Loss, $75,000.

March 31. The first trains run on the Schuylkill Valley branch of the Pennsylvania R. R., from Broad Street station to Bala, Philadelphia city.

April 7. New city government organized. William B. Smith inaugurated as Mayor; James R. Gates elected president of Select Council and Charles Lawrence president of Common Council.

Fire at malt-house of Frederick Fischer, Thompson St. west of Thirty-second. Loss, $55,000.

May 7. Fire at the Philadelphia home-made bread and biscuit bakery of George W. Jones, 1429-1431 N. Twelfth St. Loss, $16,000.

May 11. Cornerstone laid of monastery of the Redemptorist Fathers of St. Bonifacius' Church, Hancock and Diamond Sts.

May 12. Stockholders of the West Philadelphia Passenger Railway Company ratified a lease of their road to the Philadelphia Traction Company for nine hundred and ninety-nine years, on a contract to pay each stockholder ten dollars per share annually, in half-yearly Payments.

New Schuylkill Valley branch of the Pennsylvania P. R. Company formally opened as far as Manayunk.

May 14. Iron side-wheel steamer Hero, built for service on the Orinoco River, South America, launched from the yard of the America Shipbuilding Company, Port Richmond. Length, 110 feet; beam, 22 feet; depth of hold, 8 feet.

May 18. West Tasker Street Presbyterian mission chapel, Eighteenth and Tasker Sts., dedicated.

June 4. Iron steamship Eureka, built for the Morgan Line, between New York and New Orleans, launched from the shipyard of Wm. Cramp & Son. Length, 350 feet; breadth of beam, $42^{1/2}$ feet; depth of hold, $32^{1/2}$ feet; engine, 1800 horse-power.

June 14. Collision on the Camden and Amboy R. R. near Ashland; two trains going in opposite directions on the same track ran into each other. Eight persons killed and nine badly wounded.

June 15. Spring regatta of Schuylkill Navy National Course; $1^{1/2}$ miles straight away. Prizes: Junior sculls West Philadelphia Club, time 10 m. 39$^{1/2}$ s.; Senior sculls, Pennsylvania, 10 m. 17$^{1/2}$ s.; pair-oar shells, West Philadelphia, 10 m. 38$^{1/4}$ s.; light four-oared shells, Crescent, 9 m. 46$^{1/2}$ s.; Junior four-oared gigs, Pennsylvania, 9 m. 30 s. Senior four-oared shells, Pennsylvania, 8 m. 52 s.; double sculls, Pennsylvania, 10 m. 17$^{1/2}$ s.; Senior four-oared gigs, Pennsylvania, 9 m. 1 s.; six-oared barges, Malta, 9 m. 23 s.; eight-oared shells, University, 8 m. 12$^{1/2}$ s.

June 17-19. Tournament of the Quaker City Bicycle Club for all wheelmen in the United States and Canada commenced at Jumbo Park, Broad and Dickinson Sts.

June 18. Fire at Carr & Crawley's hardware and malleable iron works, Ninth and Jefferson Sts. Loss, $45,000.

June 19. Sixth inter-collegiate boat race for the Childs challenge cup, between the crews of Princeton College, New Jersey, of Cornell University, New York, and of the University of Pennsylvania. Flat-Rock course, on the Schuylkill; 1$^{1/2}$ miles straight away. Won by the University of Pennsylvania by half a length. Time, 7 m. 6$^{1/4}$ seconds.

June 20. Second race between the trotting-horse Scotland and John S. Prince on a bicycle at Jumbo Park; 10 miles. Won by Prince in 33 minutes and 35$^{1/4}$ seconds.

June 29. Closing exercises at Tabernacle Presbyterian Church, cor. of Broad St. and Penn Square, the building having been sold by the congregation.

June 30. Stockholders of the Union Passenger Railway Company at a special meeting agreed to lease their road to the Philadelphia Traction Company for nine hundred and ninety-nine years.

July 10. Eight-oared boat-race for the Sharpless challenge cup over the National Course, Schuylkill River, 1$^{1/2}$ miles. Won by the Columbia Boat Club, of Washington, D. C., in 8.06$^{3/4}$, being 5$^{1/4}$ seconds faster than any previous record.

July 17. Ground broken at N.E. cor. Susquehanna Av. and Twentieth St. for the hospital of the Woman's Homœpathic Association.

August 1. The old Chestnut Street skating rink, N.W. cor. Twenty-third and Chestnut Sts., occupied by John Wanamaker for the manufacture of furniture and for storage purposes, and Phelan's lumber-yard, Twenty-third St., burned, together with considerable property on the south side of Chestnut between Twenty-third and Twenty-fourth Sts. Loss, $160,000.

August 4. Machine-shop, store-room and pattern-loft of Baldwin Locomotive Works, Broad and Buttonwood Sts., partially burned. Loss, $150,000.

August 10. At 2.09 P. M. an earthquake shock, followed by another was felt in the city, accompanied by a rumbling sound. Buildings were shaken, bells rung, sashes rattled, doors sprung, various articles in some places thrown off of shelves and tables, and people prostrated. Several chimneys in various parts of the city were overthrown. The time of continuance of the shock was estimated at from 4 to 8 seconds.

August 13. Fire at drying-room of Theodore Morgenstern's dye-house, Third and Huntingdon Sts. Loss, $35,000.

August 15. At Belmont Park the trotting-horse Jay-Eye-See, on a trial with the intention of excelling the former record of a mile in 2.10, trotted one heat in 2.10$^{1/4}$. Phallas, with the intention of beating his former record of 213$^{3/4}$, trotted one heat in 2.14$^{1/4}$.

HAPPENINGS IN YE OLDE PHILADELPHIA

August 20. Most Rev. P. J. Ryan, D. D., LL. D., archbishop of the archdiocese of Philadelphia, installed at the Cathedral by bishops and clergy of the Roman Catholic Church.

September 2. International Electrical Exhibition, under the auspices of the Franklin Institute, formally opened by Mayor William B. Smith and Governor Robert E. Pattison. Main Exhibition Building bounded by Lancaster Ave., Thirty-second and Thirty-third Sts. Front on the avenue, 283 feet; towers at the corners, 60 feet high; main roof central Gothic arch, 100 feet span, with two smaller arches 30 feet span. There were annexes, principal among which was the old Pennsylvania Railroad station, on the east side of Thirty-second St. with railroad sheds and other buildings. Exhibition closed October 11th. Visitors, 285,000.

September 4. Councils passed resolutions directing the superintendent of electrical department to notify all telegraph, telephone, and electric-light companies operating in city to remove their overhead wires, in compliance with ordinance of June 13, 1882, and place the same under ground before January 1, 1885.

September 12. Saw-mill of Bonta & Fenderich, Nos. 1063-1067 Germantown Ave., burned. Loss, $15,000.

September 13. Annual regatta of the Fairmount Rowing Association on the National Course, Schuylkill River. Huhn challenge cup won by N. Hayes; time, 10.03^1/$_5$. Four-oared shells won by the Hayes crew, 9.38^1/$_2$; six-oared barges, Walsh crew, 10.34.

September 14. Cornerstone laid of new parochial building of St. Vincent de Paul's Roman Catholic Church, Germantown.

Cornerstone laid of new building for Monumental Baptist Church, Forty-first above Chestnut St.

September 15. Fire at wood carpet factory of J. W. Boughton & Co., Willow St. below Thirteenth. Loss, $50,000.

Forepaugh's Dime Museum, Eighth St. below Vine, opened for the first time.

September 18. Bronze equestrian statue of Major General John Fulton Reynolds, by John Robers, sculptor, unveiled on the northern front of the new City Hall.

September 20. Fire at repairing-shop of W. D. Rodgers & Co.'s carriage-works, Tenth and Chestnut Sts. Loss, $50,000.

September 21. Chestnut Street Dime Museum opened in the old Masonic Hall building, Chestnut St. above Seventh. Closed October 29th.

September 23. Annual convention of the National Council of the Order of United American Mechanics, at Elks' Hall, Eleventh and Chestnut Sts.

September 25. Penn National Bank commenced business in its new building, S.W. cor. Seventh and Market Sts.

September 26. New building of P. E. Church of the Crucifixion, Bainbridge St. above Eighth, dedicated.

September 29. Centennial celebration of the foundation of Freemasonry in the United States among colored persons by the establishment of African Lodge at Boston, Mass. Parade of Grand and Master Masons' Lodges of fourteen States and a reception.

October 1. New grounds of the Philadelphia Cricket Club, Wissahickon station, Schuylkill Valley Railroad, formally opened.

October 5. Cornerstone laid of Roman Catholic Church of St. Leo, cor. Keystone and Unruh Sts., Tacony.

74

Track of the Philadelphia and Atlantic City Railroad between Camden and Atlantic City changed from narrow gauge to standard gauge.

October 13. Collision of trains on West Jersey Railroad, Camden. One man killed and six injured.

October 21. Fire at oil-refinery of Crew, Levick & Co., 111 and 113 Union St. Loss, with damage to adjoining buildings, $30,000.

November 23. St. Mark's German Reformed Church, Fifth St. above Huntingdon, rebuilt, rededicated.

Fire at furniture manufactory of W. T. Richardson, 1204-1210 Frankford Ave. Loss, $15,000.

November 24. New line of People's Passenger Railway Company, via Susquehanna Ave., from Eighth to Twenty-second St., and by way of Islington Lane and Twenty-third to Norris St. and east on Norris to Germantown Ave., on Fourth St., to Walnut, and Eighth St., to Susquehanna Ave., opened for travel.

December 9. Fire at 526 and 528 North St., occupied by Scott Paper Company (Limited), Edwards & Docker and Henry P. Heppe, paper-bag manufacturers, and George Miller & Son, confectioners. Loss, $60,000.

December 10. Fire in furniture-factory of Clark Bros. & Co., 239, 241, 243 Levant St. Communicated to adjoining properties on Levant St. and west side of Second St. Loss, estimated, $145,000.

1885

January 8. New monastery of Redemptorist Fathers attached to Roman Catholic Church of St. Boniface, Diamond St., Norris Square, dedicated.

January 26. Cable passenger railway of the Philadelphia Traction Company went into operation on Columbia Ave. and Master St.

January 29. Fire in livery stable of Charles S. Smith and John D. Cooper, 716, 718 and 720 Marshall St., with injury to adjoining buildings. Thirty-four horses burned to death, a large number of carriages and sleighs destroyed, with other property. Estimated loss, $35,000.

February 12. Insane department of Philadelphia Almshouse, Blockley, totally destroyed by fire; twenty-four lives lost.

February 16. High-tide in the Delaware River. Delaware Ave. was flooded from Callowhill to Chestnut St. the water in some places entering first floor of stores. Kaighn's Point ferry-house flooded and a portion of Eighth Ward submerged. Freshet on the Schuylkill, water 6 feet above ordinary stages.

February 19. Fire on Chestnut St. east of Second, north side, which destroyed or greatly damaged store-buildings 117, 119, 121, 123, 125 and 45 and 47 S. Second St. and damaged adjoining properties.

February 21. Fire at 504 and 506 Market St., occupied by Ruth, Bennett & Co., china and glassware; S. A. Rudolph, paper; Joseph I. Meaney, boots & shoes, with some damage to adjoining buildings. Loss, estimated, $100,000.

March 29. Parish building of Trinity P. E. Church, Forty-second St. and Baltimore Ave., dedicated.

April 2. John L. Sullivan and Dominick McCaffrey, professional pugilists, who had arranged for a contest at Industrial Hall, arrested for violating the laws in reference to prize-fights, and bound over each in $5,000 to answer for conspiracy, and in $5,000 to keep the peace.

April 28. Repair-shops of Pullman Palace Car Company, Forty-first St. and Pennsylvania R.R., burned. Loss, $150,000.

April 26. Malt-house of Continental Brewing Company, Twenty-first St. and Washington Ave., burned. Loss, $50,000.

May 9. Fire at station and stables of Knickerbocker Ice Company, Noble St. and Delaware Ave., nine horses and mules burned Loss, $25,000.

May 10. Cornerstone laid of new St. Luke's Evangelical Lutheran Church, at Seventh St. and Montgomery Ave.

May 12. Fire at planing-mill of A. H. Higham & Sons., Nos. 1043-1053 East Cumberland St. Loss, $12,000.

May 24. Services in new P. E. Church of the Annunciation, Twelfth and Diamond Sts.

Cornerstone laid of Roman Catholic convent of Immaculate Heart of Mary, adjoining St. Teresa's Church, Broad and Catharine Sts.

Closing services at P. E. Church of Evangelists, Catharine St. above Eighth, before tearing down the building.

May 28. Explosion of benzene and fire at the furniture-store and manufactory of Henry Vehmeyer, S.W. cor. Second and Market Sts., with damage to hat-stores of Henry Kayser and Evans & Betts, adjoining. One lady passing by in the street killed by the falling walls, and two persons injured. Loss, $60,000.

May 29. Shackamaxon Bank, cor. Frankford Road and Norris St., failed in consequence of the allowance and payment of heavy over-drafts upon the funds.

May 31. First appearance of the cicadas, usually called "Seventeen-year locusts," in Washington Square.

June 11. Formal opening of the new grounds of the Belmont Cricket Club, at Elmwood, Fifty-eighth St. and Darby Road.

June 13. New cable of the Traction Company, on Columbia Ave. between Twenty-third St. and East Park, put into operation.

June 17. Lard-oil works of Washington Butcher's Sons, Moore St. above Sixth, totally destroyed by fire. Loss, $120,000.

June 19. Fire at Farmers' Western market-house, Twenty-first and Market Sts., used as a depot for the sale of Bradley's Chicago beef. Loss, $10,000.

Seventh intercollegiate boat-race for the Childs cup, between Cornell University, New York, and the University of Pennsylvania. Course, Shawmont, above Flat Rock, on the Schuylkill, 1 1/2 miles straightaway. Won by Cornell by a length and a third. Time, 8 m. 51s.; Pennsylvania, 8 m. 54 s.

June 27. Annual regatta of Schuylkill Navy National course, 1 1/2 miles straightaway; 21 entries. Prizes: Junior single, Bachelor Club, 11 m. 50 3/4 s.; senior single, Pennsylvania; junior four-oared gigs, Pennsylvania, 10 m. 24 1/4 s.; pair-oared shells, West Philadelphia, 11 m. 32 1/4 s.; senior four-oared gigs, Pennsylvania, 10 m. 23 1/4 s.; senior four-oared shells, College, 9 m. 37 3/4 s.; double sculls, Pennsylvania, 10 m. 28 1/2 s.; eight-oared shells, Malta, 8 m. 54 s.

July 3. Mayor Smith signed the ordinance, which had previously passed Councils, authorizing the construction of the Baltimore and Philadelphia and the Schuylkill River East Side railroads within the city.

July 7. William H. Bumm, George W. Bumm and Samuel P. Milligan, late teller of Shackamaxon Bank, bound over on the charge of conspiracy to defraud the bank.

July 9. Eight-oared boat-race for the Sharpless challenge cup. National course, Schuylkill River, 1½ miles; 5 entries. Won by Fairmount Rowing Association of Philadelphia, beating Columbia, of Washington, D. C., by two-thirds of a length. Time, 8 m. 32 s.

July 12. East Montgomery Avenue M. E. Church, rebuilt, reopened.

July 14. Walls of boiler-house of Star Mill, Mascher and Jefferson Sts., fell in. One person killed; nine injured.

Ninety-sixth anniversary of destruction of the Bastille, celebrated by French societies and citizens at Renz Park.

July 18. Fire in operating-room of Western Union Telegraph Company, N.W. cor. Tenth and Chestnut Sts., destroying all the wires there. Loss, $20,000.

July 23. News of the death of Gen. U. S. Grant, at Mount McGregor, N.Y., received at Philadelphia at 8.12 A. M. The State House bell was tolled sixty-three times, one stroke for each year of his age. Immediately flags were hoisted at half mast in all parts of the city. The Mayor's office was draped with mourning, and emblems of woe were displayed at public and private offices, stores, factories, dwellings and other buildings.

Cornerstone laid of the new building of Young Mænnerchor Vocal Society, N.W. cor. Sixth and Vine Sts.

August 3. Heavy rains at intervals, with sharp lightning and thunder from 11.35 A. M. to 9.50 P. M. About 3.30 P. M. a tornado of great force crossed the river Delaware from Gloucester Point Three large buildings in the Neck at the Pennsylvania salt-works were entirely prostrated, and other property in the neighborhood was damaged. The course of the wind was nearly north by east. The tornado crossed the Delaware to New Jersey. The steamboat Major Reybold, of the Salem Line, and the Peerless ferry-boat, of Gloucester line, were struck by it in the river, had all their upper works, pilothouses and cabins carried away, and the pilot of the Reybold was drowned. At Kaighn's Point the storm took the shore and pursued a northwardly course, by way of Front, Second and Third Sts., to Federal and Linden Sts., extending eastward to Fourth and Fifth Sts., and then upward to Cooper's Point where again crossing the Delaware, it struck the Port Richmond coal-wharves, at the foot of William St., passed to the north to the neighborhood of Harrowgate Lane and Kensington Ave., where its force was spent. In Camden large factory-buildings were thrown down or greatly damaged. The round-house of the Pennsylvania Railroad Company was totally demolished and locomotives damaged. Dwelling-houses, stores, etc., were unroofed, or the walls blown in; trees in great numbers were thrown down; 400 buildings were damaged. In Kensington similar destruction took place. Houses were partially blown down, walls blown in and roofs taken off, with other damage; 150 buildings in this part of the city were damaged. The value of property destroyed was immense. In the city there were 3 lives lost and 38 persons injured; in Camden 4 were killed and 48 injured. In Camden the damage to real estate was estimated at $500,000, in Kensington, at $250,000. The value of personal property destroyed was impossible to compute. The course of the tornado was from 200 to 300 yards in width. In the afternoon there was a heavy flood in the Schuylkill. At the Falls the water, rushing down from the streets and descending to Ridge Ave. rose on the road 7 feet, carrying away small houses and fences, flooding cellars and the first stories of mills and buildings.

August 8. Day of funeral solemnities of Gen. Ulysses S. Grant in New York observed with due solemnity throughout the country. The State House bell was tolled from 10 to 12 o'clock A. M. and bells of churches and public buildings.

There was a general suspension of business throughout the city.

August 9. Fire at the Richmond paper-mill of Alexander Balfour, corner of Brabant and Tioga Sts. Loss, $22,000.

August 17. Explosion, supposed to be by dynamite, on the steamboat Samuel L. Felton, of the Wilmington Line, shortly after leaving Chestnut St. Wharf. About 175 passengers were on board. Eleven or twelve persons were injured, one of whom afterward died. Damage to the boat estimated at $4,000.

September 14. Temple Theatre and Egyptian Musee, Old Masonic Hall building, Chestnut St. between Seventh and Eighth Sts., opened for the first time, with the comedy of "Sealed Instructions."

September 19. International cricket-match, between the "Gentlemen of England" and "Gentlemen of Philadelphia." Result: Philadelphia first inning, 200, second inning, 178, total 378; Gentlemen of England, first inning, 147, second inning, 122, total 269.

September 25 and 26. Second international cricket game at Nicetown. Gentlemen of England first inning, 293, second inning, 317, total 510; Gentlemen of Philadelphia, first inning, 147; second inning, 120, total 267.

September 29. Industrial Art School under control of the Board of Education, opened in Hollingsworth schoolhouse, Locust St. above Broad; 150 pupils.

October 8. Robert White attacked and killed, by the elephant Empress at winter-quarters of Forepaugh's circus and menagerie, Lehigh Ave. and Edgemont St.

December 3. New hall of Young Mænnerchor Musical Society, N.W. corner Sixth and Vine Sts., dedicated.

New gymnasium of the University of Pennsylvania formally opened.

December 6. Consecration of new building of St. Luke's Lutheran Congregation, at Seventh St. and Montgomery Ave.

December 7. At the winter quarters of Forepaugh's menagerie, Lehigh Av. and Edgemont St., the Nubian lion Prince escaped from his cage and attacked the elephant Bolivar. He was disabled by a blow from the trunk of the latter, who finished by tramping upon the lion's body.

December 16. Fire in five-story building, 224 Carters Alley, below Exchange Place, occupied by Morrell & Bros., printers and bookbinders, Electric Motor Supply Company, Newman & Ergen, shirt manufacturers. Loss, $60,000.

December 24. Cornerstone laid of Girard Avenue Farmers' Market cor. Ninth St. and Girard Ave., 198 ft. on Girard Ave. by 194 ft. on Hutchinson St.

1886

January 10. Tugboat James Kelly caught fire off mouth of Pennypack Creek. Loss, $5,000.

Fire consumed the whole block of buildings between Emerald and Letterly, Taylor and Coral Sts., Thirty-first Ward.

January 13. Tug William G. Boulton, Capt. Peterson, sunk by ice on Fourteen-Feet Bank lightship, Delaware River.

January 16. A majority of the stock in the People's Passenger Railway (Callowhill Street) Company, which was the lessee of the Fourth and Eighth, Green and Coates, Girard Avenue and Norris and Susquehanna roads, sold to a syndicate composed principally of stockholders of the Lombard and South Streets, P. B. W. Company, and reorganized by the latter.

January 20. Fire and explosion at the oil and lamp-fixture establishment of

R. J. Allen, Son & Co., 115 Arch St. The flames spread to premises of King, Son & Co. and the Riverside Oil Company, Nos. 113, 117 and 119. One person was killed by the explosion. Loss $50,000.

January 25. Tenth National Bank (new) cor. Columbia Ave. and Camac St. (below Broad), opened for business.

January 26. Great fire on Arch St. west of Seventh, which commenced in the five-story Morris Building, Nos. 715, 717 and 719, occupied by Monroe Brothers & Co., shoe-dealers, Lehman & Bolton, lithographers, William H. Butler, lithographer. The Crosscup & West Engraving Company extending on the west to the building formerly occupied by the Fourth National Bank and tax-receiver's office, used by S. May, millinery straw-goods, Julius Gerstler, artificial flowers and feathers, Schœdler & Hilery, kid glove importers, and Weaver Electric Mail-Box Company on the east to the St. Cloud Hotel, kept by G. K. & G. H. Mullen, the upper stories of which were burned and all the furniture and contents damaged by fire and water; on the north dwelling-houses on Winfield Place were overwhelmed by falling walls and partially burned. The flames crossed to the south side of Arch St. and burned the upper stories of No. 712, Fred. Gutekunst, photographer, No. 714, Fahy & Co., furs, No. 716, P. C. Fulweiler, tobacco and cigars, No. 718, George S. Harris, printing, 720, Gillender Son, glassware, No. 722, Hunter & Brother, laces, Nos. 724-726, Custer & Son, millinery, with injury to adjoining properties on the west. Total loss, estimated, $500,000.

February 9. New building of First Unitarian Church, Chestnut St. east of Twenty-second, dedicated.

February 14. Brick dwelling-house No. 1225 Lawrence St. fell to the ground and totally destroyed; eleven persons in it at the time injured and bruised by the falling walls, joists and floors.

February 16. Fire at Nos. 613 and 615 Cherry St. which also damaged Nos. 611 and 617. Loss, $28,000.

March 3. Fire at the stable of People's Passenger R. W. Company, at Eighth and Dauphin Sts. Loss, $5,000. It contained 128 horses, which were rescued.

March 20. Steam ferry-boat Cooper's Point, owned by the Camden and Atlantic R. R. Company, burned at her dock, Camden, and passenger-cars near by damaged. Loss, $24,000.

Daniel Coyle, electrical engineer in employ of the Northern Electric Light Company, instantly killed at No. 1116 N. Second St. while readjusting a light, by the full current of electricity being turned on.

March 27. Hand type-setting contest at Dime Museum, Ninth and Arch Sts., which continued for 11 days and 3 hours. First prize won by Alexander Duguid, of the *Cincinnati Enquirer*, total, 69,200$^{1/4}$ ems. Other contestants were Joseph McCann, *New York Herald*, 68,907$^{1/2}$; W. C. Barnes, *New York World*, 65,714$^{1/4}$; Thomas Levy, *Chicago Herald*, 61,299$^{1/4}$; Peter Thienes, *Philadelphia Times*, 59,498; J. A. Washington, *Philadelphia Inquirer*, 53,289$^{1/2}$; James J. Nolan, *Philadelphia North American*, 52,575$^{1/2}$; W. A. Crane, *Philadelphia Evening News*, 47,434$^{1/4}$.

April 2. The traction company withdrew the night cars running on the Richmond, Columbia Ave., Seventeenth and Nineteenth Sts., and Chestnut and Walnut Sts. branches.

April 8. Fire at the Academy of Fine Arts, Broad and Cherry Sts. Forty paintings burned, among them St. Sebastian, by Murillo. Loss to the academy and artists, estimated, $70,000.

April 14. New line of night-cars commenced, on the Hestonville, Mantua and Fairmount (Arch St.) Railway from Second and Arch Sts. to Forty-third St. and Lancaster Ave.

Night-cars resumed running on the railways formerly furnished with that service by the traction company.

April 18. St. Luke's Lutheran Church, Seventh St. and Montgomery Ave., consecrated.

New building of Second Reformed Presbyterian Church, Seventeenth St. below Race, formally opened.

April 21. Iron steamboat Newburgh, intended for passenger service on the North River, launched from the shipyard of Neafie & Levy, Kensington. Length, 245 feet; beam, 43 feet; depth of hold, 15 feet; engines, 1100 horse-power; burden, 1000 tons.

April 23. Spinning-mill of J. Meadowcraft & Sons, Emerald and Sergeant Sts., burned. Loss, $29,000.

May 3. East Baptist Church, Hanover St. below Thompson, dedicated.

May 6. New Northwestern National Bank opened for business at No. 1812 Girard Ave.

May 8. Steamboat John S. Ide, of Bridgeton and Philadelphia Line, sank at the mouth of Cohansey Creek.

May 9. St. Joseph's Roman Catholic Church, Fourth St. and Willing's Alley, remodeled, rebuilt and improved, formally re-opened

May 11. The first train, carrying the president and other officers of the Baltimore and Ohio Railroad, passed over the railroad from Baltimore to the western abutment of the new bridge, below Gray's Ferry.

May 12. The Hayes Mechanics' Home, established under the will of George Hayes, who died in 1857, was formally opened on Belmont Ave. near Christ Church Hospital.

May 24. Fire at paint and chemical works of Harrison Bros. Co., Gray's Ferry Road. Loss, $60,000.

June 6. Basement of St. Stephen's Roman Catholic Church, Broad and Butler Sts., dedicated.

June 10. Formal opening of the new grounds of Belmont Cricket Club, at Forty-ninth St. station, Pennsylvania R. R.

Fire at the J. & P. Baltz brewery, Thompson St. above Thirty-first. Loss, $5,000.

June 11. Cornerstone laid of the parish building of St. Barnabas Protestant Episcopal Church, Third and Dauphin Sts.

June 21. Fire at George Smith's scroll and carpenter mill, Philadelphia St. between York and Dauphin. Loss, $10,000.

June 22. The four-oared shell of the College Club of the University of Pennsylvania rowed over the course on the Schuylkill River, and won the Childs cup, there being no competitors.

June 24. Cornerstone laid of the new house of the Bicycle Club, at Twenty-sixth and Perot Sts.

June 25. Iron steamship El Monte, built for the Morgan Line, between New York and New Orleans, launched from the yard of Cramps' Shipbuilding Company. Length, 338 feet; beam, 42 feet 8 inches; depth of hold, 31 feet 8 inches; carrying capacity, 9,000 bales of cotton; engines, 2500 horse-power.

June 26. Annual regatta of the Schuylkill navy, National course, $1\frac{1}{2}$ miles straightaway. Twenty entries. Prizes: Junior singles, Pennsylvania Club, 11m.

28½ s.; senior singles, Malta, 11m. 57½ s.; junior four-oared gigs, Iona, 10m. 1½ s.; double sculls, 10m. 32½ s.; four-oared shells, Undine, 9m. 11½ s.; senior gigs, Iona, 9m. 21s.; pair-oared shells, Undine, 10m. 13s.; eight-oared shells, Malta, 8m. 11½ s.; being 43½ s. faster than the best record heretofore made, that by the Dauntless in 1880. Commodore's prize, single paper shell, to the Malta Club, for the most entries, crews coming in not more than 40s. behind the winning boat.

June 28. Fire at warehouse and factory, Northwest cor. Oxford and Randolph Sts., occupied by C. W. Hall, chair manufacturer, and B. F. Richardson, furniture manufacturer. Loss, $11,500.

June 30. Defalcation discovered in the accounts of the Chesapeake and Delaware Canal Company, amounting to $652,200.60; of this sum, $615,260 was an over issue of bonds of the company. J. L. Wilson, treasurer and secretary, and Henry V. Lesley, charged with being the guilty parties, absconded.

July 1. New Produce National Bank opened for business at No. 104 Chestnut St.

The Casino, formerly Lauber's Garden, Broad St. above Columbia Ave., opened for the production of light operas with the "Crimson Scarf," by Legroix, and the "Cantrabandista," by Sir Arthur Sullivan.

July 5. Fairmount Park lighted with electric light for the first time, ten double-arc lights being placed on the Lemon Hill Observatory, 225 feet above the ground.

July 7. Ground broken for the new Park Avenue M. E. Church, at Park Ave. and Norris St.

New bridge of the East Side Schuylkill (B. and O.) R. R. Company across the Schuylkill at Gray's Ferry finished and put in use.

July 10. Cornerstone laid of new building of East Montgomery Ave. M. E. Church, Montgomery Ave. and Frankford Road.

July 13. Fire at packing-box factory and saw-mill of Tunis Manufacturing Company, Otsego and Moore Sts. Loss, $10,000.

Eight-oared boat-race for the Childs challenge cup, on the National course, Schuylkill River, 1½ miles. Two entries. Won by the Malta Boat Club by two lengths; time 8m. 6½s.

July 19. Southwestern National Bank (new) opened for business, on Broad St. above South.

July 23. Southern section of Long Beach R. R. to Beach Haven, N.J., formally opened by Pennsylvania R.R. Company.

July 31. Samuel R. Shaw was struck by a stone while on a boat near Pine St. Wharf, Delaware River, knocked overboard and drowned. John, Timothy and Richard McLaughlin, George Flynn and Thomas, all boys, were held to answer and John Hillard as accessory.

August 2. Swimming match for the championship of America, on the Delaware River, between Dennis F. Butler, American champion, and W. B. Johnson, champion of England. Course, from off Cooper's Point to Ridgway Park, 1 mile. Won by Butler in 15m. 45s.

August 5. Second champion swimming-race on Delaware River between Butler and Johnson; 3 miles. Won by Butler in 45m.

August 7. Fire at shoe factory of John Mundell & Son, cor. Thirteenth and Cherry Sts. Loss, $10,000.

August 14. Third and last swimming match on Delaware for championship of America between Butler and Johnson. Won by Butler. Course 5 miles; time 1h. 12m. 55s.

New Columbia Theatre opened in rink building, formerly Ridge Avenue P.R.W. depot, N.E. cor. Twenty-third St. and Columbia Ave.

August 16. Baltimore and Ohio R. R. Company open depots for reception of freight for transmission to all points at Pier 35 1/2 N. at Brown St.; Pier 24 S., foot of Lombard St., and Piers 62 and 63 S., at Dickinson St., on the Delaware River.

August 28. Steamship Cherokee launched from the shipyard of William Cramp & Sons, built for William P. Clyde & Co. Length, 290 feet; beam, 43 feet; depth, 29 feet; measurement, 2500 tons.

August 29. Cornerstone laid of Cayuga Presbyterian Chapel, Sixteenth St. below Cayuga.

September 8. The assessors of the different wards made returns of the number of voters in the election divisions of the city as 229,092 an increase of 8,510 over last year.

September 16. First regular passenger-train over the Schuylkill River East Side (B. and O.) R. R. left station Twenty-third and Chestnut Sts., for Baltimore.

September 17. Wholesale grocery store and warehouse of Thompson Fry & Co., No. 131 Market St., destroyed by fire. Confectionery manufactory and store of Knight & Horebach, adjoining, wool-house of Coates Brothers and hardware stock of Robers, Duor & Miller, damaged by fire. Loss, $100,000.

Fire at the bonded warehouse of Fitzpatrick & Pemberton, at Front and Lombard Sts.; Section A, at the corner of Lombard St., entirely destroyed. Loss, estimated, $50,000.

September 18. Ground broken for the new Third Regiment Armory, east side Broad St. above Wharton.

September 21. Fire at No. 25 N. Seventh St., occupied by Buchanan Smedley & Bromley, dealers in photographic materials, Davis Brothers, printers, D. W. Odiorne, umbrella materials, and Enterprise dining-rooms. Loss, $25,000.

September 23. First international cricket match, at Nicetown Park, between Gentlemen of England, and Gentlemen of Philadelphia. Score, Philadelphia, first inning, 168; second inning, 70; total, 238. England, first and only inning, 323.

September 24. New temple of the Jewish congregation, Adath Jeshurun, Seventh St. above Columbia Ave., consecrated.

September 25. Cornerstone laid of the new building of Park Avenue Methodist Episcopal Church, cor. Park Ave. and Norris St.

Iron steamship Seminole launched from the yard of William Cramp & Sons, ship and engine builders; vessel built for William P. Clyde & Co. Length, 290 feet; beam, 43 feet; depth, 29 feet; measurement, 2500 tons.

September 28. Planing and sash-mill of Gotlieb Hoersch, American St. above York, burned. Loss, $16,000.

September 30. Windsor Theatre, Vine St. below Eighth, opened for the first time by Mahn's Opera Company, with "Olivette."

October 3. Fire at the terra-cotta works of Harvey, Moland & Co., Seventh and York Sts. Loss, $27,500.

October 4. New Fourth Street National Bank, capital $1,500,000, commenced business on the east side of Fourth St. below Chestnut.

Second international cricket match at Nicetown Park, between Gentlemen of England and Gentlemen of Philadelphia. Score: Philadelphia, first inning, 128; second inning, 146, total, 274. England, first inning, 235; second inning, 40 for four wickets, total, 275.

October 6. Fire in the finishing department of the shovel-works of T. Rowland's Sons, on Tacony Creek. Loss, $20,000.

October 9. Cornerstone laid of Presbyterian Church of the Evangel, Eighteenth and Tasker Sts.

October 10. New building of Temple Baptist Church, Twenty-second and Tioga Sts., dedicated.

Cable-cars commenced running on the Columbia Ave. branch of the Union Passenger Railway.

October 24. Fifth Reformed Church (Dutch Reformed), Otis St. near Cedar, dedicated.

October 25. Bronze statue of Schiller by Henry Manger, sculptor, formally unveiled in West Fairmount Park, near Horticultural Hall.

October 30. New Girard Avenue farmers' market-house, Girard Ave. and Ninth St., opened for business.

November 1. New buildings of the Second National Bank of Frankford, Main St. below Unity, opened for business.

November 10. Fire at John Bromley & Sons' carpet-mills, Front and Jasper Sts. Loss, $10,000.

Fire at Nos. 22, 24, 26 and 28 N. Front St. occupied by J. M. Sharpless & Co. and others. Loss, $65.000.

November 11. Explosion and fire at cigar-box factory of Henry H. Sheip & Co., Randolph St. above Columbia Ave. One woman killed; fourteen persons burned and injured.

Cornerstone laid on grounds of German Hospital of the Mary J. Drexel Home, for old men and old women, Mother-House for Deaconesses and Nurse-training School, the gift of John D. Lankenau.

November 25. Fire at furniture factory of John D. Raggio, Fourth and Reed Sts. Loss, $75,000.

November 28. New building of Beacon Presbyterian Church, Cumberland and Cedar Sts., dedicated.

December 3. Fire at factory-building, Callowhill St. above Twelfth, occupied by Philadelphia Drop Forge Company and F. A. Wheeler & Co., straw-board linings. Loss, $10,500.

December 4. Old Post-office building, Chestnut above Fourth, sold at auction to A. J. Drexel for $413,000.

December 11. Steamship Herman Winters, for the Metropolitan Steamship Company of New York, launched from the shipyard of William Cramp & Sons. Length, 286 feet, breadth of beam, 41 feet; depth of hold, 29 feet; burden, 2500 tons.

December 15. New tunnel of the Baltimore and Ohio B. R. on Twenty-fifth St. from Callowhill St. to the Reading Railroad, opened for the passage of freight trains.

December 16. Fire in mill-building at Coral and Dreer Sts., occupied by H. Davenport & Co. and Davenport & Hepworth, manufacturers of curtains and upholstery goods. Loss, $19,000.

December 17. Dye-house of J. G. Haley, Gorgas Lane, Roxboro, burned. Loss, $20,000.

December 20. A portion of Pier No. 54 S. Wharves, occupied by the Pennsylvania R. R. Company and the American and Red Star Steamship Lines, gave way, and sank into the Delaware, carrying down merchandise, etc. Loss, $50,000.

December 21. No. 711 Market St., occupied by Kneedler, Patterson & Co., drygoods, and John M. Maris & Co., druggists' supplies, destroyed by fire. Loss, $150,000.

December 25. Seventy-two hours' walking-match, go-as-you please at the Elite Rink, Twenty-third and Chestnut Sts., closed. Won by Strokel, 386 miles 3 laps, being 14 miles 2 laps beyond any competitor.

December 27. Temple Theatre and Egyptian Musee, old Masonic Hall building, under management of George C. Brotherton, totally destroyed by fire, together with the stores and salesrooms, in the first story, of Fairbanks & Co., scale-manufacturers, Remington Typewriter Co. and the Niles Tool Company. Losses also by Hubbard Bros., publishers and paper-manufacturers, 723 Chestnut St., and at the Washington Hotel, with partial damage to adjoining property. Loss estimated at $450,000. Two firemen killed and one injured by the falling walls.

December 31. Fire in spinning-room of Roxborough cotton and woolen-mill of J. Leech & Brother, Shur's Lane below Pechin St. Loss, $12,000.

Market-sheds and stalls on Girard Ave. between Sixth and Twelfth Sts. sold at auction preparatory to the abandonment of the public markets there.

1887

January 3. Fire at J. R. Applegate's photograph gallery, Eighth and Vine Sts. Loss, $5,000.

January 7. Fire at the office of the Evening Telegraph newspaper, at Nos. 106 and 108 S. Third St., C. E. Warburton, proprietor, which also damaged the office of Howard Bell & Co., brokers, No. 110, and of MacDonald & Conrad, grain-merchants, No. 106. Loss, $30,000.

January 9. Explosion—supposed of dynamite—in a shanty at Thirtieth and Stiles Sts. Building totally destroyed and a watchman killed. The report was heard as far north as Chestnut Hill and the shock felt at Burlington and Princeton, N. J. Houses on Girard Ave. and from Twenty-eighth to Thirty-first St., and in intersecting streets, suffered by breakage of sashes and window-panes.

January 10. New Lyceum Theatre, Vine St. below Eighth, formerly Miller's Varieties, rebuilt and improved, reopened with the play of Jack Cade by Collier's company.

January 11. Ninth National Bank opened for business at its new building, Front and Norris Sts.

January 12. The examiner and master to whom had been referred the equity suit arising in consequence of the failure of the Shackamaxon Bank filed his report, deciding that the amount lost by the bank was $430,210.29, and that the defendants, Thomas L. Huggard, cashier of the bank, and Samuel P. Milligan, teller, were chargeable with the whole amount; also that Joseph Concklin was liable for $149,538.23, the estate of William Bumm, deceased, $285,823.42; G. W. and W. H. Bumm, surviving partners, $136,285.13, and G. W. and W. H. Bumm, new partners, $4,720.39.

Fire at curled-hair and glue factory of Delany & Co., Hancock and Jefferson Streets. Loss, $12,000.

Fire at No. 511 Market Street, occupied by Louis Echner & Bros., manufacturers of neckwear. Loss, $22,000.

January 13. Fire at North Star Hotel, Main Street, Frankford, which destroyed the barn, haysheds and hay. Thirty horses perished in the flames. Loss, $20,000.

January 14. Fire at No. 236 Market Street, occupied by M. Garlic, boots and shoes; W. Allshin, leather, and Gibbs & Wesley, shoe manufacturers, with damages to Wolf & Marks, clothiers, No. 238. Loss, $26,000.

January 23. New chapel of East Montgomery Avenue M. E. Church, corner Frankford Road and Montgomery Avenue, formally dedicated.

January 27. Fire at Armstrong, Craig & Co.'s wholesale paper warehouse, Nos. 12 and 14 So. Sixth Street, and Garrett & Buchanan, paper dealers. Loss, $50,000.

February 1. New building of the Northwestern National Bank, Ridge and Girard Avenues, opened for business.

February 2. The toboggan slide erected for the use of the public in Fairmount Park at the expense of William M. Singerly, used for the first time. Width of the slide, 34 feet; length of the slide and the ground to be covered, 2200 feet.

February 18. Lawrence Donovan of New York, who jumped from the New York and Brooklyn Bridge into the East River, and from the suspension bridge at Niagara, jumped from Chestnut Street bridge, Schuylkill, a distance of 82 feet. When rescued, he was arrested and bound over to keep the peace.

February 21. Six days go-as-you-please race for the championship of the world commenced at the Chestnut Street Rink. Forty-one entries; forty starters. During the week thirty-two men dropped out. Final score: Robert Vint, 530 miles, securing diamond belt and large proportion of entrance money. The remainder of money was distributed to F. Hart, 518 miles 8 laps; Peter J. Panchot, 511 miles; A. Bennett, 506 miles 3 laps; George D. Noremac, 500 miles. The other men who were in the race at the close were Elson, 362 miles; Tilly, 352 miles 2 laps, and Newhart, 291 miles 8 laps.

February 25. The Philadelphia Traction Company gave notice that on and after the 1st of April the fare on all lines controlled by the company would be five cents for a single ride, with privileges of transfer at certain points and additional charge of two cents for transfer at other points formerly freely given.

March 1. The Traction Company announced a reduction of fare to five cents, and transfers without extra charge.

March 4. People's Passenger Railway Company reduced fare for all passengers except infants in arms to five cents, including all existing transfer privileges.

March 7. The Traction Company and all the other passenger railway companies commenced carrying passengers at five cent fares. Exchange tickets between other roads than the Traction, Ridge Avenue and People's Passenger Railway systems, seven cents.

March 21. Stable and hayloft of the Thirteenth and Fifteenth Streets Passenger Railway Company, at Cumberland and Carlisle Streets, burned. Loss, $8,000.

March 22. Ground broken at N.E. corner Ninth Street and Lehigh Avenue, for new German Lutheran Church of the Cross. Church dedicated November 6.

The firm of James and John Hunter, manufacturers of cotton goods, at Hestonville and Norristown, failed, and made a general assignment in favor of creditors. The failure was caused by the discovery that of $400,000 worth of promissory notes issued by the firm, less than $55,000 had genuine endorsements; the rest were forged. The assets appraised at $154,344.28.

April 4. The amended charter of the city of Philadelphia—usually called the Bullitt Law—went into operation, the principal change being investing in the Mayor full authority to act as the chief executive officer of the city, to cause the ordinances of the city and the laws of the State to be enforced, and to be responsible for the good order and efficient government of the city; the Mayor also to be responsible for the appointment and removal of heads of the departments of Public Safety, Public Works and Charities and Corrections. Edwin H. Fitler was inaugurated as Mayor, and announced his appointments to be as follows: Director of Public Works, Genl. Louis E. Wagner; Director of Public Safety, William S. Stokley; Director of Charities and Correction, Dr. James W. White, president; Richard C. McMurtrie, Dr. Richard A. Cleeman, Robert Laughlin, James Stewart, directors.

April 8. John Wanamaker announced that he would introduce the plan of profit-sharing with his employes.

April 13. Steam ferry boat Atlantic, of the Cooper's Point ferry line, burned in the upper portion at Vine Street Wharf, Camden. Loss, $30,000.

April 25. Manufacturers' Club of Philadelphia, formed at a meeting held at the Continental Hotel.

May 1. At midnight, at the Elite Skating Rink, corner Twenty-third and Chestnut Streets, six days go-as-you-please walking match commenced. There were forty-eight entries and forty-one starters. The match ended May 7 with the following records for the winning contestants: Strokel, 515 miles; Albert, 505 miles; Noremac, 492 miles; Hart, 485 miles.

May 4. Annual class races of the University of Pennsylvania for the Powel cup, eight-oared shells, won by juniors. Time, 8.32 4/5. The prize was awarded to the sophomores upon claim of irregularity in the makeup of the junior crew.

May 6. Special jury to inquire into the mental condition of W. Ellwood Rowan, Sheriff, reported to the Court of Common Pleas that by reason of lunacy he was incapable of managing his estate, and that he had been incapable for eight months last past and upward, without lucid intervals.

May 7. Last block of marble required for the construction of the new City Hall placed on the tower, at a height of 337 feet 4 inches from the ground.

May 12. Hay sheds and other buildings at Burgin & Sons', glass factory, Montgomery Avenue above Girard Avenue, destroyed by fire, with damage to dwelling houses on Palmer Street. Loss, $42,000.

May 19. Girard College grounds lighted for the first time with thirty-five electric lights placed upon seven towers, each 125 feet high.

Iron steamship Josefita, intended for the Cuban trade, launched from the shipyard of Neafie & Levy. Length, 230 feet; beam, 34 feet; depth of hold, 21 feet; 1500 tons register.

May 22. Margaret Harvey, Theodore Murphy, Catharine Murphy, Jeremiah Murphy and Dennis Crimmins drowned in the Delaware River by the upsetting of a boat, which Coroner's jury found was caused by the carelessness of Thomas O'Connor. The latter pleaded guilty June 29 to indictments for involuntary manslaughter, and was sentenced to three years' imprisonment.

May 23. Market Street National Bank, capitol $600,000, commenced business at No. 1017 Market Street.

Six days walking match, go-as-you-please, commenced at Chestnut Street

Rink; fifteen entries. First prize won by Burns, 485 miles.

June 18. Henry V. Lesley, late secretary of the Chesapeake and Delaware Canal Company, arrested in Philadelphia, and James H. L. Wilson charged as confederate, arrested in Toronto, for the defalcation of $661,490 which occurred in June, 1886.

June 25. Fire at kindling wood factory of Longton & Crawford, No. 1112 S. Thirteenth Street with damage to John Stockdale public school-house, John A. Smith's coal yard and other adjoining property. Loss, $15,000.

Annual regatta of the Schuylkill navy. National course, 1 1/2 miles straight away. Prizes: junior singles, Iona, 10m. 44 1/2 s.; pair-oared shells, Philadelphia, 9m. 47s.; junior four-oared gigs, Pennsylvania, 8m. 56s.; senior four-oared shells, Iona, 8m. 33s.; double sculls, Pennsylvania, 10m. 23s.; senior four-oared gigs, Iona, 8m. 56s.; senior singles, Pennsylvania, 10m. 23s.; eight-oared shells, Vesper, 8m.

June 26. Norris Square M. E. Church, Mascher Street above Susquehanna Avenue, dedicated.

July 3. Cornerstone laid of German Lutheran Church of the Cross, Ninth Street and Lehigh Avenue.

July 5. New Chestnut Street National Bank opened at the N.W. corner Tenth and Chestnut Streets.

July 11. George M. Palmer, a baker residing at No. 504 Lehigh Avenue, held to bail by Coroner Ashbridge to answer the charge of having poisoned four persons by adulteration of buns and cakes which he baked with chromate of lead (chrome yellow), used to give the articles a rich yellow color.

July 12. George M. Palmer and F. Schmidt, bakers, and George W. Millett, salesman, charged with poisonous adulteration of food with chromate of lead (chrome yellow), bound over to answer.

July 13. Explosion of two stills filled with petroleum at the oil-works of the American Refining Company, Point Breeze, setting fire to three or four other stills and adjoining property. Several persons scalded by the hot oil. Loss, $10,000.

July 15. Fire in the Bergdoll Company brewery, Twenty-ninth and Poplar Streets. Loss estimated at $100,000.

July 16. Fire at mill building corner Mascher and Putnam Streets, occupied by William Shellenberger, hides and fats, Bakeman & Smith, card-cloth and carpets, and Gilpin & Martin, hosiery. Loss, $8,000.

July 21. Frederick Schmidt, a baker at Vienna Street and Frankford Avenue, was by the verdict of a Coroner's jury found guilty of having caused the death of Anna E. Helm by the use of poisonous matter (chromate of lead) in the preparation of buns and other breadstuffs which were eaten by the deceased.

July 23. A compressor of ammoniacal gas for an ice machine at the Bergner & Engel Brewery, Thirty-second and Thompson Streets, burned. The vapor was ignited and seriously burned nine men (two of whom afterward died) besides setting fire to the building.

July 27. Alfred Krumm, manufacturer of noodles, held to answer on a charge of adulterating them with chrome yellow (chromate of lead).

July 30. The yacht Minerva capsized opposite Kaighn's Point during a squall. Two persons drowned.

The Columbian Bank, a State institution doing business on Chestnut Street below Fifth, failed and made an assignment. Capital, $200,000; liabilities stated to be $278,901.32; estimated assets, $278,901.32; which were appraised at $95,159.25.

August 4. An electric car built by William Wharton, Jr., & Co., and run with the electric power and energy of storage batteries on the car was run from Gray's Ferry over the Spruce and Pine Street Passenger Railway to Dock and Walnut Streets with passengers, making two trips.

August 26. The bulkhead and about 70 feet of the wharf at the foot of Sansom Street fell into the Schuylkill River. It was used for storing cars of the Baltimore and Ohio R. R., but no cars were on it at the time of the accident. Loss, about $10,000.

September 5. Thirty-third annual fair of the Pennsylvania State Agricultural Society opened at the grounds, Lehigh Avenue and Broad Street.

September 15. First day of the centennial celebration of the adoption of the Constitution of the United States. Grand civic procession, showing the progress of a century in trades, manufactures and industries, also in education, with participation in the parade of societies, firemen, etc. There were floats and wagons with allegorical figures, machinery, persons at work, models, etc., and the procession required about seven hours to pass any point on the route. It was estimated that half a million people were spectators of the display.

September 16. Second day of the constitutional celebration. Grand military parade, under command of Lieut.-General Philip H. Sheridan, U.S.A. It was participated in by about twenty-five thousand men, including detachments of cavalry, artillery and infantry of the regular army and marines and seamen from the navy, organizations of the national guard from seventeen States and the District of Columbia and by posts of the Grand Army of the Republic.

October 16. Cornerstone laid of Roman Catholic Church of Our Lady of the Rosary, Haddington.

October 18. Bronze equestrian statue of General George Gordon Meade, by Alexander Milne Calder, unveiled in Fairmount Park with appropriate ceremonies, which included a parade of the First Brigade, N. G. P., Grand Army Posts, and others.

November 2. Lease of the Lombard and South Street Passenger Railway lines by the People's Passenger Railway Company rescinded.

Fire at stone factory building, and engine house, Wister Station, Germantown, belonging to estate of John Bromley and occupied by Henry F. Scatchard, William R. Taylor and Stirling & Son, manufacturers of yarns. Loss, $115,000.

November 4. Fire at saw and planing mill Broad and North Streets, occupied by the Fite, Arbelo Company and D. W. Nudd, sash, door and blind manufacturer. Loss, $21,000.

November 6. New German Lutheran Church of the Cross, Ninth Street and Lehigh Avenue, dedicated.

November 12. Fire at saw and planing mill, Nos. 928 and 932 N. Third Street, occupied by John Dick, tool-grinder; Casper Miller, turner; J. H. McCloskey, carpet-cleaner; H. B. & J. C. Petty, picture frames and others. Loss, $25,000.

November 11. Explosion of gasoline at No. 908 Sansom Street. Fourteen men burned and injured. Six died.

November 21. The southern section East Park Reservoir, being completed, was formally placed in use.

Henry V. Lesley and James A. L. Wilson, formerly secretary and treasurer of the Delaware and Chesapeake Canal Company, pleaded guilty in the Court of Quarter Sessions to an indictment to defraud the company, and were sentenced respectively to eight and six years imprisonment.

November 26. Six days go-as-you-please pedestrian contest, at Chestnut Street Rink, finished. Score: Littlewood, 569 miles; Albert 530; Panchot, 511; Noremac, 501; Elson, 500.

November 29. The Harbor Commission and the Advisory Board of United States Engineers held a meeting at the office of the Wardens of the Port to consult with merchants and citizens, and to hear their views in reference to the improvement of the harbor of Philadelphia by the removal of Smith's and Windmill Islands, in the Delaware, and the extension of wharves into the stream.

December 27. Thomas L. Huggard, late cashier of the Shackamaxon Bank; Samuel P. Milligan, late teller; George W. Bumm and William H. Bumm, directors, put on trial to answer the charge of conspiracy to defraud the bank previous to the failure which took place May 29, 1885. Huggard pleaded guilty, and sentenced to one year and three months' imprisonment; Milligan and George W. Bumm convicted and sentenced to one year's imprisonment each; William H. Bumm acquitted. George W. Bumm pardoned July 17.

1888

January 10. Cable cars of the Traction Company began running on Seventh and Ninth Streets between Columbia Avenue and McKean Street.

February 10. John Wanamaker bought the business and stock of Hood, Bonbright & Co., wholesale drygoods merchants.

February 15. Roman Catholic Cemetery of the Most Holy Redeemer, Richmond Street below Orthodox, Twenty-fifth Ward, opened for use.

February 27. George M. Palmer, a baker residing at No. 504 Lehigh Avenue, convicted of causing the death of Louisa Drebel by adulterating cakes and buns with chromate of lead, sentenced to six months' imprisonment. For like adulterations, Frederick Schmidt, a baker residing at Vienna Street and Frankford Avenue, sentenced to six months. Albert Krumm, a manufacturer of noodles, charged with a similar offense, sentenced to six months' imprisonment and a fine of $100.

March 11. Commencement of stormy season known as the blizzard. The morning was cloudy. Light rain commenced at 3 P. M. and very heavy rain at 10 P. M. At 11 P. M. the rain changed to snow, and the wind, steadily increasing in violence, soon blew a full gale. The 12th of March came in with heavy snowfall and a violent gale, the wind reaching 46 miles an hour and with frequent terrific squalls. Direction of the wind due North; temperature at 15°. During the morning the temperature continued to fall and the wind to rise, but the fall of snow was checked. Owing to the high wind, which attained a velocity at times of 60 miles an hour, the loose snow was blown into enormous drifts. Streets and roads became impassable, all railroad trains were blocked, telegraphic communication was cut off, and a great amount of damage was done by the blowing down of trees and telegraph poles. Chimneys, roofs and other portions of buildings were also damaged in many parts of the city. At noon on the 12th the snow ceased, but the high winds continued all that day and the next. The greatest difficulty was experienced outside the city in getting communication in any way. The roads and railway-cuttings were drifted full of snow, through which neither carriages nor trains were able to proceed.

Many trains were snowed in and either abandoned or lost in the drifts. The first train to reach the city from New York left the latter place on Monday at 6 A. M., and reached Philadelphia on Thursday at 5 P. M.; the first train from Philadelphia to Pittsburgh reached there on the 15th. There was no telegraphic communication in any direction except to Harrisburg through Norristown and Reading. The long-distance telephone to New York, however, acted admirably throughout the crisis. Business on the 12th was almost entirely suspended; the schools, courts and many places of amusement were closed. On the Delaware River and on the coast, especially at the Breakwater, the injury to shipping was very great, over thirty vessels being sunk or stranded, and several of the seamen being drowned. On the 13th the blizzard continued, although traveling was to some extent renewed. High winds continued and the temperature was very low, ranging from 8° minimum to 15° maximum. The force of the wind showed a velocity of 47 miles an hour. The wind gradually subsided, and on the 14th the snow began to melt; but several days elapsed before the interrupted travel could be resumed, and the snow lay in sheltered places for several weeks.

April 3. Claus Spreckels, of California, bought 10 acres of ground on the river Delaware, at Reed Street, for the purpose of erecting a new sugar refinery with buildings and machinery to cost $5,000,000. Ground broken May 27.

April 4. Broad Street Theatre, owned by John S. Clarke, sold at auction to J. M. Fox, for $141,000.

April 6. Dinner to Dr. D. Hayes Agnew in honor of the fiftieth year of his graduation as a doctor of medicine from the University of Pennsylvania, given by the medical profession at the Academy of Music.

April 11. The pneumatic dynamite gun built by William Cramp & Sons for the Italian Government sent to Fort Lafayette, where it was tested under the direction of Lieutenant Zalinski.

April 17. Meeting of citizens at the Board of Trade rooms to protest against the erection of the proposed elevated railroad by the Reading Railway Company between Twelfth and Market and Ninth and Green Streets.

April 19. Reading Railroad elevated terminal ordinance introduced into Select Councils and referred to the Railroad Committee.

April 28. Launch of the gunboat Yorktown and the dynamite cruiser Vesuvius from Cramps' shipyard, Kensington. Secretary Whitney and a number of members of Congress and other distinguished guests attended the launching.

May 1. The "State in Schuylkill"—the Schuylkill Fishing Company—established in 1732, removed its "Castle" from the banks of the Schuylkill below Gray's Ferry to the banks of the Delaware, near Andalusia.

The new crematory, at E. Washington Lane and Stenton Avenue, Germantown, used for the first time for the cremation of the body of Damon Y. Kilgore.

May 7. The first year of the system of profit-sharing adopted by John Wanamaker resulted in the distribution of $109,439.68 to the employes, in addition to their usual salaries.

May 15. St. Agnes' Hospital, at Broad and Mifflin Streets, dedicated and formally opened.

May 21. New Market Street National Bank opened for inspection; ready for business May 24.

May 30. New passenger depot of the Baltimore and Ohio Railroad at Twenty-fourth and Chestnut Streets, formally opened.

June 1. New liquor licenses went into effect. Number of saloons licensed, 1347; number licensed in 1887, 5773.

June 14. New system of attaching the cars of the Fairmount branch of the Philadelphia Traction Company to the cable motor cars at Franklin and Wallace went into effect.

June 16. A new steamer, the Elizabeth Monroe Smith, the gift of Mr. John F. Smith to the Sanitarium Association, made its trial trip.

June 19. The Sanitarium Association opened its twelfth season at Red Bank, N.J.

July 19. Industrial school and home of St. Frances de Sales, founded at Eddington and maintained by the Misses Drexel, opened with religious ceremonies by Archbishop Ryan.

July 24. The "Penny Savings Bank" organized by members of the Bethany Presbyterian Church. Opened for business August 1.

July 31. The boiler of a locomotive of the Reading Railway Co., exploded while standing at Columbia Avenue station, killing Andrew Pond, the engineer, and Peter Graklow, the fireman.

August 4. Steamship Corona, built for the Oregon Steamship Company, launched from the yards of Neafie & Levy. Sailed for San Francisco, October 27.

August 10. Eight-cent exchanges inaugurated on the Traction Company's system.

August 21. A tornado struck the Delaware River below Fort Delaware doing considerable damage to shipping. The same afternoon a heavy rainstorm passed over this city, the total precipitation being nearly two inches. Considerable damage done to sewers, etc.

September 13. A row boat containing two men and two women swept over Flat Rock dam, on the Schuylkill. Frank Carver and Mrs. Minnie Tuful drowned.

September 18. Managers of the House of Refuge completed the purchase of 385 acres of ground at Glen Mills, Delaware Co., for a new building and farm for the boys' department.

September 26. Tug W. W. Graham capsized and sunk in the Delaware off Edgemoor; the engineer, Seth M. Long, drowned. The Graham was successfully raised and towed into port.

October 6. United States cruiser Baltimore launched at Cramps' Shipyard in the presence of the Secretary of the Navy, and a distinguished party from Washington.

October 18. Northeastern Elevated Railroad bill passed by Select Councils.

October 20. John D. Cruice fatally burned by an explosion of "flash powder" at Wiley & Wallace's drug establishment.

December 3. Keystone Bank Building opened for business.

December 6. Mary J. Drexel Home and Philadelphia Mother-House of Deaconesses, attached to the German Hospital, handed over to the trustees and consecrated according to the services of the Lutheran Church.

December 17. New building of the Western Saving Fund occupied.

1889

January 11. Dynamite cruiser Vesuvius on her official trial trip made a speed of 21.64 knots per hour.

January 14. Third Regiment Armory formally opened.

January 18. Portion of the Reading Railway wharf at the foot of Willow Street sank into the river. No lives lost.

January 26. New building of the Medico-Chirurgical College and the Philadelphia Dental College formally opened.

March 25. Gunboat Yorktown formally accepted by the government.

April 19. The family of the late George L. Harrison presented $200,000 to the Episcopal Hospital to found and endow a building for incurables.

April 23. U.S. warship Yorktown put in commission, and sailed for New York two days later.

May 10. Philadelphia Belt-Line Railroad Company organized, and received a charter.

May 13. A salmon weighing 12½ pounds caught in the Delaware—the first salmon caught in the Delaware for many years.

May 31. Walt Whitman's seventieth birthday anniversary celebrated in Camden by a banquet, at which distinguished guests from all parts of the country were present.

June 23. A rowboat containing John H. DeBarry, Jr., William S. Castnett, Mary A. Young and Rosaline Eattock carried over Fairmount dam and the occupants drowned.

August 2. Claus Spreckels announced that he would double the size of his great sugar-refinery at Reed Street Wharf, making a total investment of $4,000,000 to $5,000,000.

September 2. Labor Day. Celebrated as a legal holiday for the first time in Pennsylvania.

September 3. Contract for the metal work of the clock tower of the new Public Buildings awarded to the Tacony Iron and Metal Company, the price to be paid estimated at $325,000 and four years being required to complete the work.

September 6. Mass meeting of property owners and residents along the line of the Cohocksink sewer urged the finance committee of Councils to take immediate measures to prevent further breaks in the sewer.

September 9. Annie E. Leconey brutally murdered at her home, near Merchantville, New Jersey. Francis Lingo was suspected of the crime and was arrested, and subsequently the murdered girl's uncle, Chalkley Leconey, was also arrested and held to answer.

September 12. New Park Theatre opened for inspection.

October 1. A storm caused the extension of the break in the Cohocksink sewer. William F. Keppler was carried down in the break and drowned.

October 4. Mr. Joseph Wharton presented $25,000 to the University of Pennsylvania to found a library for the Wharton School of Finance.

October 17. Cornerstone laid of the administration building of the new House of Refuge at Glen Mills, Delaware county.

November 6. The schoolship Saratoga arrived at the League Island navy yard.

November 13. U. S. cruiser Baltimore started on her second trial trip being successfully accomplished.

December 11. Joseph G. Ditman, a well-known wholesale paper dealer, left his home to take a drive to the park. His horse and carriage were found the same evening on the towpath, but no trace of the missing man's body was found until January 26. The coroner's jury found a verdict of accidental drowning.

1890

January 16. Steamer Edwin Forrest driven on the sand-bar off Burlington Island. No one was injured, and the steamer was afterward floated without injury.

January 20. George W. Wright pleaded guilty to the embezzlement of $38,660.20 from the order of Tonti, and was sentenced to pay a fine of $1000 and to undergo an imprisonment of four years and nine months in the penitentiary.

January 26. David Alexander, a monomaniac, fired a shot from a revolver at Bishop Whitaker of the Protestant Episcopal Church while the latter was conducting services in St. John's Church. The bullet missed its mark. Alexander was afterward adjudged insane and sent to the Danville Asylum.

February 1. Spring Garden market house opened for business.

February 21. The roof of the Grand Opera House fell while efforts were being made to raise it, injuring seven workmen.

March 1. Cars began running on the Catharine and Bainbridge Streets branch of the Philadelphia Traction Company. Coaches of the Omnibus Company General began running on Broad Street.

March 10. A special train on the Bound Brook division of the Reading Railway made the trip between Philadelphia and Jersey City in 85 minutes, claimed to be the fastest time ever made between these points.

April 30. The Bank of America and its numerous branches suspended payments. On the following day the Gloucester City National Bank suspended. This was followed by the suspension of the Fidelity Surety Trust and Safe Deposit Company of Camden and its branches through their officers, as was the American Life Insurance Company, which suspended business on May 10, in compliance with a writ of *quo warranto* issued by the Attorney-General of the State. Numerous suits were brought against the officers of the various institutions involved.

May 1. Parish house of St. Simeon's Protestant Episcopal Church dedicated.

The new building of the First Penny Savings Bank of Philadelphia opened for business.

Lehigh Avenue electric cars began regular service with six cars.

May 14. Steamer City of Seattle launched at Neafie & Levy's shipyard.

May 28. Steamer Essex launched at Cramps' shipyard.

May 29. Smith's and Windmill Islands formally transferred to the United States in the mayor's office.

May 30. John C. File, late treasurer of the Lutheran Orphans' Home, confessed that he had made away with almost the whole endowment fund of the institution.

June 3. The dynamite cruiser Vesuvius formally transferred to the Government by Cramp & Sons. She sailed for the Brooklyn navy yard on June 18.

June 6. Announcement made that Cramp & Sons had increased their capital stock to $3,500,000 for the purpose of establishing new and extensive shipbuilding yards near Greenwich Point.

Severe electrical storm. Alice Farrel, six years old, killed by lightning. Lightning also struck G. & H. Barnett's oil storehouse, setting it on fire and burning 38,500 gallons of oil. Many minor casualties occurred.

City Avenue Bridge over the Schuylkill formally opened.

June 12. A freight train wreck at Beach and Otis Streets threw two freight cars into the Aramingo Canal and killed John Fallack, a rolling mill employe.

June 16. A street car struck by a railroad train at Ninth and Green Streets. Several passengers injured, one seriously.

June 19. Two men fatally scalded by the bursting of a mash tub at Betz's brewery.

June 24. Joseph Buecher shot and killed Dennis Crowley at Fourth Street and Girard Avenue.

July 2. The Fairmount Park Motor Company to build and operate a gravity railroad in the Park, formed.

July 14. New police station at Manayunk opened.

July 17. Severe storm. One man drowned in the Delaware River. Part of the roof of the Second and Third Streets car stables fell on a car, killing a horse. Numerous minor accidents caused by high wind and lightning.

July 24. Gambling establishments at Gloucester raided by Camden county constables.

July 29. Wooden steamer Pawnee launched at Charles Hillman & Co.'s shipyard.

July 30. Conference of citizens with the Board of United States Engineers on the matter of improving the harbor and removing the islands of the Delaware.

August 19. Lighthouse-tender "Armenia" launched at Dialogue's shipyard.

August 21. A severe windstorm partially demolished the car stables of the Twelfth and Sixteenth Streets and the Tenth and Eleventh Streets railway companies. Six persons were killed and seven injured. Considerable other damage was done by the storm.

August 25. A forty-six-inch supply pipe of the Corinthian Avenue Reservoir burst, doing considerable damage.

September 4. A Pennsylvania Railroad locomotive overturned while rounding a curve at Beach and York Streets, killing the engineer and firemen and seriously injuring the conductor.

September 5. Roman Catholic High School dedicated.

September 18. New public manual training school on Howard Street below Girard Avenue, began in regular sessions.

September 25. Mrs. Annie Miller brutally murdered near Merchantville, N. J. Francis Lingo arrested for the crime.

October 14. The Master Brewers' National Convention opened at Mannerchor Hall. Delegates from all parts of the United States attending. Entertainment of delegates, Kommers, banquet, drive through Fairmount Park, etc.

November 19. Contract for building a new reservoir at Roxborough awarded to John B. Reilly.

November 20. Barker Brothers & Co., bankers, suspended and made an assignment. The senior member of the firm had been in active business for fifty-three years.

December 1. First day of the run on the Keystone National Bank, which, though temporarily allayed, finally led to the suspension of the bank, the exposure of its fraudulent methods and those of other bank officers and of City Treasurer Bardsley.

December 20. The cruiser Newark left Cramps' shipyard for her trial trip, which took place on December 22. The trip was very successful.

1891

January 16. The main building of John and James Dobson's carpet-mills at the Falls of Schuylkill destroyed by fire. Loss, about $1,000,000.

January 20. The contract between the city and the Philadelphia and Reading Terminal Company signed. The company entered a bond of $1,000,000.

January 23. Three floors of a building on Willow Street, occupied by the John Y. Huber Publishing Company, the Bunting Iron Car-Seat Company and A. Falkenau, machinist, fell through to the basement, owing to a heavy weight of paper stored on the upper floor.

February 5. Market Street Elevated Railroad ordinance passed finally by both branches of Councils. The mayor signed the bill on February 16.

February 25. Lewis E. Pfeiffer pleaded guilty to a charge of re-hypothecating stocks and securities in connection with the failure of the Bank of America, and took the witness-stand against his co-conspirators, George F. Work and James S. Dungan. The latter were convicted of the crime on February 27. Pfeiffer was sentenced to two years' imprisment. Work to four years' imprisment and Dungan to three years' imprisment in the Eastern Penitentiary.

March 5. The J. O. Schimmel Preserving Company's building, Eighth and Berks Streets, burned. Loss, $125,000.

March 20. The Keystone Bank closed by order of the Controller of the Currency. Later investigation showed gross frauds by the president, cashier and other officers.

March 24. Dr. Edward Brooks elected Superintendent of Public Schools by the Board of Education.

March 28. Reading Railway offices and station at Kaighn's Point destroyed by fire. Loss, about $80,000.

Cresswell's Eagle Iron Foundry, 812-820 Race Street, burned. Loss, $75,000.

April 9. Bids for the removal of the islands in the Delaware River opened. The lowest bid was $2,229,200, made by James A. Mundy & Co.

April 23. Mr. J. Pierpont Morgan's steel yacht Corsair launched at Neafie & Levy's yard.

April 26. The National Publishing Company's five-story building at Eighth and Cherry Streets, destroyed by fire. Loss, $200,000.

May 3. Joseph Beucher, who shot and killed Dennis Crowley at Fourth Street and Girard Avenue, convicted of murder in the first degree. Sentenced to be hung. Afterward sentenced to life imprisonment. After a lapse of about four years pardoned.

March 4. Gideon Marsh, late president, and Charles Lawrence, ex-cashier, of the Keystone National Bank arrested and held under $20,000 bail on the charge of fraud and conspiracy. Marsh, after securing bail, fled.

The centennial anniversary of the adoption of the Polish constitution celebrated by Polish residents of this and neighboring cities by a parade and other ceremonies.

May 8. The Spring Garden National Bank closed by order of the Controller of the Currency. The Penn Trust and Safe Deposit Company, which was connected with the bank, made an assignment.

May 14. Large fire at the Belmont Refinery of the Standard Oil Company.

Loss, $40,000.

The Philadelphia Bourse organized in the Board of Trade rooms.

May 20. President Francis W. Kennedy and Cashier Henry H. Kennedy of the Spring Garden Bank were arrested. Charges accumulated against them and they finally pleaded guilty of charges of fraud and conspiracy.

June 9. John Bardsley pleaded guilty to charges against him. He was sentenced on July 2 to fifteen years solitary confinement at labor in the Eastern Penitentiary, and to pay fines aggregating $237,530.

June 14. Martin Fuller & Co.'s abattoir at the Philadelphia stock-yards, West Philadelphia, destroyed by fire. Loss, $373,000. Charles Hocke fatally injured by an explosion.

June 24. Mayor Stuart signed the Northeastern Elevated Railway ordinance.

July 24. Campbell & Elliott's textile mills, Twelfth and Washington Avenue, destroyed by fire. Loss, $750,000.

August 1. The permit for the construction of the Reading Terminal Depot at Twelfth and Market Streets, issued by the building inspectors.

August 15. A. G. Elliott & Co.'s paper warehouse, Sixth and Minor Streets, burned. Loss, $60,000.

August 17. Francis W. Kennedy, president; H. H. Kennedy, cashier, of the Spring Garden National Bank, and Charles Lawrence, assistant cashier of the Keystone National, pleaded guilty to the charges against them. The latter was sentenced to seven years' imprisonment and a fine of $100. The Kennedys were each sentenced on September 15 to ten years' imprisonment.

August 28. Guano & Raggio's macaroni factory. Seventh and Marriott Streets, burned. Loss, $35,000. Two firemen were severely injured.

September 25. International cricket match between Gentlemen of England and Gentlemen of Philadelphia begun. The Philadelphians won the first game, the visitors the subsequent game.

September 28. Phillips & Cunningham's oil warehouse, the Jessup & Moore Paper Co.'s warehouse, and other buildings on Water Street near Race, burned. Nine firemen were injured during the fire. Total loss, $220,000.

September 29. The commission appointed by the Secretary of the Treasury to recommend a site for the new Mint reported in favor of the block bounded by Walnut, Sansom, Sixth and Seventh Streets.

October 3. School-ship Saratoga arrived in port, after a journey to Madeira and the Azores.

November 7. Inter-collegiate football match between the University of Pennsylvania and Princeton College. The latter won, 24 to 0.

November 9. Lippincott, Johnson & Co.'s cloth warehouse, Market Street below Seventh, destroyed by fire. Loss, $300,000.

November 23. The Mayor approved the bond presented by the Northeastern Elevated Railroad. The Board of Highway Supervisors granted the company permission to begin work on the public streets on November 25.

December 2. The new armored cruiser New York launched at Cramp's shipyard.

December 6. William F. Shaw's music publication house, Vine Street below Eighth, destroyed by fire. Loss, $200,000.

December 15. Fire caused by an explosion of benzene destroyed a large building on Delaware Avenue near Fairmount Avenue, occupied by several firms. Aggregate loss, about $50,000.

December 16. The Associated Alumni of the Central High School gave a reception to Dr. Edward Brooks, the Superintendent of Public Schools.

December 29. Policeman Elmer E. Findley shot and instantly killed by Robert J. Cascaden, aged eighteen, whom he detected in the act of breaking and entering a store. Another policeman was shot in the arm by the youthful desperado, who was, however, captured.

1892

January 28. Applegate's carrousel, or "Palace of Flying Animals" raided by the police. About 215 persons, of whom 106 were females, were arrested.

February 9. The Quaker City Elevated Railroad bill passed Councils finally. The ordinance was signed by the mayor on February 21.

February 11. Ontario Mills, Second Street and Columbia Avenue, destroyed by fire. Loss, $15,000.

February 15. Dobson's blanket mills at the Falls of Schuylkill, burned. Loss, $150,000.

February 17. The trustees of Jefferson Medical College confirmed the purchase of the ground on South Broad Street, for the new college and hospital buildings.

February 23. The directors of the newly-organized Philadelphia Bourse selected the plot of ground bounded by Fourth, Fifth, Merchant and Ranstead Streets, as the site for their new building.

February 25. Rev. Dr. Ignatius F. Horstmann consecrated a Roman Catholic Bishop of Cleveland by Archbishop Elder of Cincinnati, at the Cathedral of St. Peter and St. Paul, with imposing ceremonies. The attending prelates and clergymen were entertained at a dinner at the Academy of Music in the afternoon.

March 1. The will of Mrs. Anna H. Wilstach made public. It bequeathed about $2,000,000 to the city for an art-gallery, and bequests amounting in all to about $5,000,000 were made to the various charitable institutions.

Permission granted by Councils to the Society of the Cincinnati to erect a monument of Washington in Independence Square. The mayor signed the ordinance on March 10.

March 11. Greaves & Bro.'s cotton and woolen yarn factory in Nicetown destroyed by fire. Loss, $50,000. James Greaves, a member of the firm, was suffocated by smoke, and died a few days later.

March 14. The steamer Hartford launched at Neafie & Levy's shipyard.

March 16. The barrel factory connected with the Spreckels sugar refinery destroyed by fire. Loss, about $200,000.

March 17. A portion of the Philadelphia Market Company's building at Thirtieth and Market Streets, destroyed by fire. Loss about $200,000.

March 22. The Schuetzen Park site approved by Common Councils as the best situation for the new subsiding reservoir.

March 26. John Bromley & Sons' mill, Front and Lehigh Avenue, damaged by fire. Loss estimated at $375,000.

March 27. The jury in the case of Robert Cascaden, charged with the murder of Policeman Findlay, discharged, being unable to agree.

Fire at H. O. Wilbur & Son's cocoa and chocolate manufactory on Third Street near New. Loss, about $175,000.

April 1. The Frankford and Southwark Passenger Railway Company took possession of the Tenth and Eleventh Streets Passenger Railway.

April 3. The Mutual Banking, Surety, Trust and Safe Deposit Company closed by order of the State Commissioner of Banks.

April 5. The work of demolishing the Twelfth Street Market to make room for the Reading Terminal was commenced.

April 21. The Methodist Episcopal Hospital at Broad and Wolf Streets was dedicated by Bishop Foss.

April 27. A fire which originated in the Central Theatre destroyed that building, the Times newspaper office on Sansom Street above Eighth Street, and several stores on Eighth Street. Six performers were buried in the ruins of the theatre, and seven persons in the audience were fatally injured. The loss amounted to nearly $1,000,000.

May 7. Applegate's Palace of Flying Animals was destroyed by fire.

May 8. The Reading Railway in-bound freight depot, at Delaware Avenue and Noble Street, sustained about $50,000 damage by fire.

May 11. Police Captain Joseph M. Schooley committed suicide by shooting in the City Hall.

May 12. The Hammett-Souder ordinance, authorizing the Mayor to grant to the Traction Company the privilege of operating their cars by the trolley system, was passed by both branches of City Councils.

May 14. The coroner's jury which investigated the Central Theatre fire, found that the lessee of the theatre was grossly negligent in not providing sufficient means of escape.

June 26. The fast, protected cruiser, Columbia, claimed to be the most formidable war-vessel in the world, was successfully launched at Cramp's shipyard. The vessel was formally christened by Miss Edith Morton, daughter of the Vice-president of the United States.

August 3. James Hunter, who for five years had been a fugitive from justice in South America, returned to Philadelphia to make answer to the charges of forgery to be made against him.

August 12. The Board of Port Wardens unanimously voted in favor of granting permission to the Belt Line Railroad Company to build its roadway along the Delaware River front at Bridesburg.

August 15. The construction of the Traction Company's electric trolley line on Catharine and Bainbridge Streets was commenced.

August 16. The officers of the Mutual Banking, Surety, Trust and Safe Deposit Company made an assignment for the benefit of creditors to A. E. Stockwell.

August 18. Stockholders of the Ridge Avenue Passenger Railway Company leased the line to the Traction Company, the lease to go into effect September 1.

August 19. The construction of the Quaker City Elevated Railroad begun by the breaking of ground at Belmont and Elm Avenues.

September 3. The steam-yacht Yankee Doodle, which her owners claimed to be the fastest boat afloat, was destroyed by fire off Tinicum Island.

October 17. The first free public library established by the city was opened at the Wagner Institute.

1893

December 1. The old Thornton Worsted Mills, at Tenth Street and Columbia Avenue, owned and operated by James E. Cochran & Brother, were destroyed by fire. Total loss, about $225,000.

December 11. Henry S. Cochran, ex-Chief Weigher of the Mint, who pleaded guilty to stealing gold from that institution, was sentenced in the United States District Court to seven years and six months in the Eastern Penitentiary and to pay a fine of $1,000 and costs.

December 27. Common Council passed an ordinance reducing the price of gas to $1.00 per 1000 feet.

1894

January 10. Theodore F. Baker, Paying Teller of the Consolidation National Bank, admitted to the bank officers that he had embezzled about $47,000 of the bank's funds in small sums during the last twenty years. He was committed in default of $15,000 bail to answer in the United States District Court. On January 13, Matthew J. Van Dusen, individual bookkeeper of the Consolidation National Bank was placed under arrest, charged with aiding Theodore F. Baker in embezzling its funds. Baker pleaded guilty, and was sentenced to seven years and six months in the Eastern Penitentiary on March 3. Van Dusen, on February 24, was acquitted.

February 3. George W. Childs, editor and philanthropist, died, in the sixty-fifth year of his age.

February 13. Robert Ellis Thompson, D.D., LL.D., elected President of the Central High School.

March 14. Fire destroyed the building of Eaney, White & Co., 2730-32-34 North Broad Street, and caused an estimated loss of nearly $100,000. Four horses belonging to the firm were burned to death.

March 19. Mill buildings on Huntingdon Street, extending from Palethorp to Hancock Street, were destroyed by fire; total loss on the buildings estimated at $138,000, total insurance at $250,000.

May 20. The millinery establishment of the Julius Sichel Company was totally destroyed and the wholesale millinery stores of L. Dannenbaum & Co., were partially destroyed by fire. Loss estimated at about $350,000.

June 5. The new cruiser Minneapolis left Cramps' shipyard on her builders' trial trip, in which she showed a speed of 21.75 knots per hour.

June 13. John Kauffman, fifty-five years old, of Cramer Hill, near Camden, driven to desperation through poverty, murdered his wife and three children by cutting their throats, and then ended his own life by hanging.

June 14. The terra-cotta coping of an ornamental balcony on the third-story front of the Tenth National Bank, Broad Street and Columbia Avenue, fell. One person was killed and others injured, one dangerously.

August 1. The Secretary of the Navy accepted as a site for the new Mint the property bounded by Sixteenth, Seventeenth, Spring Garden and Buttonwood Streets.

August 2. A fire in a mill building at Jefferson and Randolph Streets resulted in the suffocation of two firemen and the loss of $70,000.

August 6. Fire destroyed the pavilion and field seats of the Philadelphia Ball Park, and burned the buildings of the Omnibus Company General, a car barn of the Philadelphia Traction Co., and damaged several dwellings. Loss about $100,000.

August 7. The boiler of the American Dredging Company's steam dredging machine, Philadelphia, exploded, killing two men and injuring five others.

Eleven horses were burned to death at a fire which also destroyed the stable of Stead & Murphy, 2107 East Somerset Street.

August 12. Trolley cars of the People's Traction Company began running to

Mt. Airy.

September 18. Charles F. Phillips, ex-President of the Columbian Bank, which failed in 1887, held in $10,000 bail on the charge of embezzlement.

October 4. The new annex to the Penn Asylum for Indigent Widows and Single Women dedicated.

October 12. The will of Richard Smith, type-founder, authorizing the erection of a monumental arch in West Fairmount Park, at a cost not exceeding $500,000 admitted to probate.

October 16. At the first annual meeting of the Electric Traction Company, it was reported that during the year the Company had carried 41,046,346 passengers; the receipts were $1,916,936.77, and the expenditures $1,823,562.82.

October 18. The Home for Wives and Widows of Odd Fellows, at 3519 North Seventeenth Street, was opened and dedicated.

October 20. The cornerstone of the new Central High School for boys, at Broad and Green Streets, was laid by President Sheppard.

October 24. The bronze equestrian statue of General George B. McClellan was unveiled in the presence of a distinguished gathering.

October 28. The shoe factory of John Mundell & Co., Thirteenth and Cherry Streets, was damaged by fire to the extent of $30,000.

October 29. Exercises commemorating the landing of William Penn were held in the public schools.

November 9. The People's Passenger Railway Co. reduced the fare to Germantown from ten to five cents.

December 8. The five-story brick building at the northwest corner of Front and Walnut Streets, damaged by fire to the extent of $35,000. The fire was of incendiary origin, and started in the factory of the Quaker City Paper Box Company, on the second floor.

The Washington Hotel, on Chestnut Street above Seventh, closed its doors, being unable to meet expenses.

December 9. The agreement between the People's and Electric Traction Companies, under which free transfers are made at nearly every point where lines intersect, went into effect.

December 19. The new police and patrol station on Fairmount Avenue above Third Street, opened; the Mayor and other city officials being present.

1895

February 12. Isaac R. Sheppard sent to the Board of Education his resignation as President of that Board. The Board refused to accept it, but granted Mr. Sheppard six months' leave of absence, and elected Simon Gratz, President, pro tem.

February 17. Madge Yorke, 22 years old, an actress in the "Baggage Check" Company, was shot and killed in her room at Zeisse's Hotel, by her lover, James B. Gentry, 30 years old, a member of Willie Collier's Company. Gentry, who was very drunk at the time, escaped, but was afterwards arrested.

February 27. The new fire station on Fourth Street above Girard Avenue, the largest in the city, opened.

March 14. The Hotel Bellevue and the residence adjoining on Walnut Street purchased by George C. Boldt, in order to erect on the site a palatial hotel, at an estimated cost for the structure alone of $1,500,000.

March 25. About 30,000 people assembled in and about Cramps' shipyard to witness the launch of the big American Line steamer St. Paul for the International Navigation Company. The vessel stuck on the ways owing, it is said, to the quality of the tallow furnished the builders and the launch was postponed.

The funeral of ex-Mayor Richard Vaux was held.

April 12. The American Line steamer St. Paul successfully launched at Cramps' shipyard.

April 12. The explosion of a gasoline stove in George Kurzschenkel's bakery, 1174 North Third Street, set fire to the clothing of Mrs. Mary Kurzschenkel, aged 27 years, and her infant son, Charles, aged 7 months, and both were burned to death.

April 15. The magnificent new house of the Mercantile Literary and Social Club, Broad Street below Jefferson, was dedicated in the presence of a large and brilliant assemblage.

April 18. The bakery of the New York Biscuit Company, on Front Street above Race, destroyed by fire. Wm. Dreydoppel's soap factory adjoining, was badly damaged. Loss, $250,000. Five firemen were injured.

April 21. By the capsizing of a small sailboat in the Delaware, on the eastern shore of Petty's Island, Julius Hæfelin, aged 18 years, his brother Ernest, aged 16 years, and John Miller, aged 16 years were drowned.

April 29. Stephen Borden, aged 45 years, and George West, aged 19, entered the Pegg's run sewer at Third and Willow Streets, to clean out a drain from John A. Duncan & Co.'s morocco factory. They were swept off their feet by the current and carried to the Delaware River. Borden was drowned, but West kept afloat, and on reaching the Delaware was saved by a tugboat.

May 28. In the suit brought in 1875 by the Ridge Avenue Passenger Railway Company against the city to recover $100,000 damages occasioned that company by certain changes of grade in the roadbed of Ridge Avenue Turnpike, made in 1873 and 1874, the referee decided in favor of the city.

June 29. The Veteran Fireman's Association dedicated its new hall at 803 North Tenth Street.

July 19. While the hose cart of Engine Company No. 18 was going to a fire it upset at Nineteenth and Vine Street. Hoseman John F. Ryder was killed, and four other firemen who were riding on the cart were injured.

July 22. Leading stockholders of the People's and Electric and the Philadelphia Traction Companies agreed to consolidate and form a company with a capital of $30,000,000, a charter for which was afterwards obtained and consolidation effected, dating from October 1.

August 5. Announcement was made that arrangements had been effected for a partnership between the Baldwin Locomotive Works and the Westinghouse Electric Manufacturing Company, of Pittsburgh, for the purpose of constructing electric locomotives and elective motive power equipment, and the development of a new electric railway system.

August 13. Archbishop Ryan signed the agreement for the purchase of the Davis Farm at Fatlands, Montgomery Co., containing 184 acres for the site of the Catholic Protectory for Boys.

September 24. Fire destroyed the building No. 116 Chestnut Street, occupied by Charles J. Webb & Co., wool and yarn merchants, and all its contents. Loss estimated at $250,000.

September 29. The American Line's new steamship St. Paul sailed for the Massachusetts coast for her official trial trip. About 20,000 people inspected the vessel at Cramps' shipyard, and between $4,000 and $5,000 was received from the sale of admittance tickets.

October 1. The plant of the Horn & Brannen Company, manufacturers of gas and electric fixtures, at Broad and Willow Streets, was destroyed by fire. Loss on buildings, stock and machinery, $175,000.

Fire destroyed Dingee's brick works, at Twenty-sixth and York Streets and a number of dwelling houses and stables at Twenty-seventh and Huntingdon Streets, two squares away. Loss, $80,000.

October 2. The armored cruiser, Brooklyn, was successfully launched at Cramps' shipyard. Miss Ida May Schieren, daughter of the Mayor of Brooklyn, christened the vessel. Postmaster General Wilson and Mayor Schieren were prominent among the spectators.

October 6. The lease of the Philadelphia Traction Company to the Union Traction Company was signed, and the consolidation of the Philadelphia, People's and Electric Traction systems was consummated, the Union Traction Company taking control. John R. Beetem, General Manager of the People's Traction Company, was appointed General Manager of the Union Traction Company.

October 16. Directors of the Union Traction Company decided to fix the rate of fares on all lines at five cents for a straight ride, except to certain suburban points, with eight cents for exchange tickets, abolishing free transfers.

November 16. The Orphans' Court took formal possession of its new quarters in the City Hall. Addresses were delivered by Samuel C. Perkins, ex-Judge F. Carroll Brewster and Judge Hanna.

December 10. The oil-storage plant of the Crew-Levick Company at Swanson and Jackson Streets, were destroyed by fire, and thousands of gallons of oil were burned. The loss was estimated at from $50,000 to $75,000.

December 17. The strike declared against the Union Traction Company by the Amalgamated Association of Street Railway Employees was inaugurated. Cars were run during the morning on most of the Company's lines, especially the lines of the People's Division, where almost the regular service was maintained. Disorder and rioting began early in the morning, and was continued until late in the afternoon. Motormen were pulled from their cars, windows broken and cars disabled. Mayor Warwick issued a proclamation requesting citizens to observe peace and order, and in the evening quiet was restored but no attempt being made to run cars.

December 21. Two passenger trains running in opposite directions on a single track on the Frankford branch of the Reading Railway, collided near Orthodox Street. Daniel Hart, seventy years old, and George Anderson, aged sixteen, passengers on the train from Frankford were killed, and nine others were injured.

December 25. There was a tie-up on the Girard Avenue line of the Union Traction Company, because the employes who had been on strike claimed that in starting the cars early in the morning preference was given by the company to men who came here from other cities to take the strikers' places. A committee of dissatisfied employes was sent to the Company's office at Eighth and Dauphin Streets, and after a conference with officials, the trouble was adjusted and cars began running regularly again early in the afternoon. Several cars in charge of non-union men were attacked by rioters, and one motorman and one conductor were wounded and several cars were wrecked. Ten men, charged with inciting to riot, were arrested near Second Street and Girard Avenue during the afternoon.

December 26. A bronze tablet inscribed "Joseph Jefferson, the actor, was born here 20th February, 1829. Here's your good health and your family's, may you all live long and prosper," was placed on the house at the southwest corner of Sixth and Spruce Streets.

December 31. The Bourse was dedicated. Addresses were delivered by Mayor Warwick, Cyrus Borgner, Chairman of the Building Committee, President George E. Bartol, Dr. William Pepper and John F. Lewis.

1896

January 4. The handsome club house of the Merion Cricket Club at Haverford, with all its contents was destroyed by fire of unknown origin. The Casino building, adjoining, was also burned. The loss was estimated at $75,000, nearly covered by insurance.

January 30. The third floor of 132 South Third Street was discovered to be ablaze, and a fireman found the charred body of Dr. Alfred L. Kennedy, formerly a widely-known physician and scientist, who occupied the apartments. It is supposed the fire was caused by an explosion of chemicals with which the doctor was experimenting. He was in his seventy-eighth year.

February 2. A fire in the Haseltine Building, on Chestnut Street above Broad, destroyed the structure as well as that of the American Baptist Publication Society adjoining. The rear of the Hotel Lafayette and the dry goods store of Homer, LeBoutillier & Co., and the Wistar mansion were also damaged. The total loss was nearly $1,500,000. A number of firemen were injured.

February 20. The four-story building, 36 South Second Street, owned and occupied by A. J. Widener, lamps, china and glassware, was destroyed by fire. Mr. Widener estimated his loss at $50,000, on which there was about $40,000 insurance.

March 9. The first train crossed the new bridge over the Delaware River. It carried President Roberts and many other officials of the Pennsylvania Railroad.

March 11. A fire in the basement of Crew, Levick & Co.'s lubricating oil warehouse, 113 Arch Street, caused a total loss of about $120,000. Of this amount L. Bomberger & Co., tobacco merchants, 111 Arch Street, $50,000 and Julius Vetterlein & Co., also tobacco dealers, 115 Arch Street, nearly $70,000 their stocks being greatly damaged by water and smoke.

March 28. The battleship Iowa was launched at Cramps' shipyards, Vice-President Stevenson, Secretary of the Navy Herbert and other distinguished men came from Washington to witness the launch.

March 31. Ira Gibson, a florist and truck farmer, residing near Woodbury, shot and killed Sallie March, proprietor of a farmers' hotel near Second and South Streets, and then fired a bullet into his own head, inflicting a mortal wound.

April 8. Trustees of the Jefferson Medical College bought the northwest corner of Tenth and Walnut Streets, 118 feet 6 inches on Walnut Street by 107 feet 5 inches on Tenth Street to Medical Street, and will erect thereon commodious hospital buildings.

April 13. The Pennsylvania Railroad Company celebrated the fiftieth anniversary of its incorporation.

April 18. The old passenger station of the Pennsylvania Railroad Company, at Thirty-second and Market Streets, was destroyed by fire, causing a loss of nearly half a million dollars, of which more than $300,000 was on rolling stock. Assistant Chief Engineer William Staiger and Hugh McGranigan, a tillerman of Truck F, were killed, and a dozen firemen were injured by falling walls.

May 18. By the explosion of benzene, with which the contents of the parlor of 2013 North Twelfth Street had been sprinkled, preparatory to the departure of the family for the summer, Rosie Griggs was fatally burned and the house destroyed. The explosion is ascribed to spontaneous combustion.

May 30. The Garfield Monument, in Fairmount Park, was unveiled with impressive ceremonies.

June 7. The new Methodist Episcopal Church of St. Luke, at Broad and Jackson Streets, was dedicated by Bishop Foss.

June 21. Archbishop Ryan laid the cornerstone of the new Catholic Protectory for Boys at Fatlands, Montgomery county, in the presence of about 25,000 people.

September 3. Viceroy Li Hung Chang, the Special Ambassador of the Emperor of China, spent six hours in Philadelphia.

September 23. The property of the Philadelphia and Reading Railroad Company and the Philadelphia and Reading Coal and Iron Company was sold at auction under the decree of the United States Circuit Court in the foreclosure suit brought by the trustees of the general mortgage bonds. The total of the bids was $20,500,000. The properties were purchased for the reorganization managers, represented by J. P. Morgan & Co., of New York, who were the only bidders.

November 10. The Fairmount Park trolley road was formally opened, a party of three hundred guests being taken over the completed portion of the line in the West Park.

November 13. The battleship Iowa returned from her builders' trial trip. In a two-hours' burst of speed the vessel averaged 16.27 knots per hour, and in other respects the runs were satisfactory.

November 17. The Philadelphia and Reading Railway Company, the successor of the Philadelphia and Reading Railroad Company, organized with Joseph S. Harris as President, and these Directors: George F. Baer, of Reading; Charles H. Coster and Francis Lynde Stetson, of New York; Thomas McKean, George C. Thomas and J. Lowber Welsh.

November 25. A sub-committee of Councils' Committee on City Property agreed to recommend a plot of fifty-four acres in the Twenty-fifth Ward, fronting on the Delaware River, north of Pennsylvania Railroad's new bridge, as a site for a municipal hospital. The price asked for the property was $200,000.

November 27. President Isaac A. Sheppard sent to the Board of Judges his resignation as a member of the Board of Education.

December 11. Henry McMillan's box factory, at Frankford Avenue and Harrison Street, was almost destroyed by fire. Several adjoining properties were slightly damaged by the flames. The loss was estimated at from $15,000 to $18,000.

December 19. The revenue cutter Hugh McCullogh was launched at Cramps' shipyard.

1897

HAPPENINGS IN YE OLDE PHILADELPHIA

January 4. The Board of Education reorganized and elected Simon Gratz, President, and Samuel B. Huey, Vice-President.

January 26. Fire which was discovered in the basement of the grocery store of Hanscom Brothers destroyed nearly all the buildings in the block bounded by Market, Filbert, Juniper and Thirteenth Streets, including those occupied by Hirsch & Brothers, Blum Brothers, Hanscom Brothers and S.W. Dennett. The clock tower of John Wanamaker's store was burned, and only the most strenuous efforts of the firemen saved the building from destruction. The establishment of the Dunlap Printing Company sustained about $50,000 damage. The losses aggregated nearly $1,125,000 and in most cases were covered by insurance.

Fire in the upholstery department of John & James Dobson's carpet warehouse caused about $50,000 damage.

February 4. The breaking of a water pipe in Lit Brothers' store damaged goods to the extent of $15,000.

February 12. A fire in the meat and provision warehouse of Swift & Co., Ninth Street and Girard Avenue, caused a loss of about $45,000 of which amount $25,000 was sustained by F. Gutekunst, who occupied the third floor as an electrotyping and photo-engraving establishment.

March 3. The large power house of the Union Traction Company, at Thirteenth and Mount Vernon Streets, was destroyed by a fire that was started, it is thought, by the chain of a traveling crane touching the armature of a generator. The roar of steam escaping from a bursted supply-pipe caused a stampede of spectators and frightened the horses attached to a chemical engine, which knocked down and fatally injured Aug. A. Binder, aged 30 years, and William P. Brown, aged 26 years. A score of people were injured. About a dozen lines of street cars were blocked for almost four hours. The loss on buildings and machinery was estimated at $400,000.

March 8. The Northwest Public School building, on Race Street below Fifteenth, was badly damaged by fire, the loss being estimated at from $10,000 to $15,000.

March 22. The breweries of John Roehm, Spaeth, Krautter & Hess, Welde & Thomas Company, Excelsior Company, John C. Miller & Sons, and the Mutual Company, consolidated, under the title of the Consumers' Company, with a capital of more than $5,000,000.

March 23. By a collision with the tugboat Asa W. Hughes, the tugboat Fidget was sunk in the Delaware River, opposite Gloucester. The crew of the Fidget was saved.

April 8. The new building of the Apprentices' Library Company, at Broad and Brandywine Streets, was thrown open for public inspection.

May 6. Lincoln Park on the Delaware was sold at auction to E. D. Savage, of New York, for $4,400, subject to encumbrances aggregating $119,500.

May 15. President McKinley unveiled the Washington Monument in the presence of a vast assemblage, and the remainder of the official programme was carried out in a highly successful manner.

May 20. The bronze statue to Stephen Girard on the plaza west of the City Hall was unveiled with impressive ceremonies. James M. Beck delivered the oration. Addresses were delivered by Mayor Warwick and Governor Hastings.

June 8. The Land Title and Trust Company awarded the contract for the erection of its new 16-story building on the southwest corner of Broad and Chestnut Streets, to be completed May 1, 1898, to Charles McCaul.

June 12. The steamboat John Ericsson, built for the Baltimore and Philadelphia Steamboat Company, was launched from Neafie & Levy's shipyard.

June 21. The National Sængerfest of the Northeastern Sængerbund opened in the new Sænger Hall, in the presence of 10,000 people. Mayor Warwick delivered an address of welcome to which Major Carl Lentz, of Newark, N. J., President of the Northeastern Sængerbund, responded. A concert concluded the day's programme.

July 5. While James Seebeth, 65 years old, was dozing on a chair in front of the club house of the William Penn Volunteer Hose Company, Girard Avenue above Frankford Avenue, a cannon cracker in his coat pocket was ignited and exploded, causing injuries which proved fatal.

July 16. The Philadelphia tugboat A. R. Gray was burned to the water's edge off Andalusia while coming to this port from New York by way of the Raritan Canal.

August 4. During a fire at the Jayne Chemical Works, Frankford, two employes and thirteen firemen were burned, some of them seriously. Several explosions of highly inflammable oils made the work among the flames exceedingly hazardous. The loss did not exceed $10,000.

August 16. William C. Wilson, aged about 60 years, proprietor of Wilson's Circulating Library, 1117 Walnut Street, was brutally murdered on the first floor of his library between 6 and 7 P. M. His head was beaten into a jelly. No clue to the murderer was discovered.

September 6. Warehouses Nos. 128, 130, 132 and 134 North Delaware Avenue and Nos. 121, 123, 125 and 127 North Water Street destroyed by fire. Many firemen overcome by smoke and several injured, but none dangerously. The total loss estimated at $250,000 fully covered by insurance.

September 20. The sixtieth anniversary of the laying of the cornerstone of the Boys' High School was celebrated at the school. Addresses were delivered by Dr. Robert Ellis Thompson and Professor Zephaniah Hopper, who was a member of the first graduating class.

October 2. Fire damaged the tanning and finishing works of the Quaker City Morocco Company, at Second and Oxford Streets, to the extent of $80,000.

November 12. Mayor Warwick signed the ordinance leasing the Gas Works to the United Gas Improvement Company and made public a statement giving his reasons therefor.

November 14. The Cramp Shipbuilding Company was awarded the contract for building four steamships, each 290 feet in length, for a syndicate, which chartered them to the Boston Fruit Company to be run in the West India trade.

November 18. The new building of the Kensington Hospital for Women, on Diamond Street opposite Norris Square, was formally opened.

November 28. Apt Brothers' dry goods store, 39 and 41 North Eighth Street, was almost destroyed by fire. The firm estimated the value of its stock at $75,000, on which there was an insurance of more than $50,000. Adjoining properties were damaged by water. Three firemen were injured, but none seriously.

December 6. The Board of Judges filled vacancies in the Board of Education caused by the resignation of Avery D. Harrington, Second Section, and the death of A. M. Spangler, Fourteenth Section. George M. Lowrey, Secretary of the Second Sectional Board, was elected to succeed Mr. Harrington and Joel Cook to succeed Mr. Spangler.

December 11. Fire of unknown origin destroyed the building of John & James Dobson, carpet manufacturers and retailers, on Chestnut Street above Eighth. Falling walls and water damaged the building and stock of Sharpless Brothers, adjoining on the east, and the building of the Commonwealth Title and Trust Company and the establishment of William H. Hoskins on the west. The total loss was estimated at $750,000 fully covered by insurance.

December 15. The building at 1025 Market Street, owned by ex-Judge Hare, and occupied by Conway Bros., dealers in novelties, china and glassware; Gately & Fitzgerald, dealers in installment goods, Henry J. Bartle, manufacturer of blank books, and F. W. Klinger, manufacturer of leather goods, was badly damaged by fire, the total loss being about $75,000. A fireman came in contact with an electric light wire and was hurled to the pavement from the fifth floor, sustaining dangerous injuries. Three other firemen were severely injured and one was overcome by smoke.

The road jury in the case of the projected League Island Park, bounded by Eleventh and Twentieth Streets, Pattison and Government Avenues, filed its report, awarding $399,670 to property owners who claimed $1,502,529.

December 20. George D. Widener was elected President of the Philadelphia Traction Company, to succeed the late D. W. Dickson.

The Chestnut Street National Bank, of which William M. Singerly was President, was closed for business and put in the hands of United States Bank Examiner Hardt. The publicity announced cause of the closing was an impairment of the capital. The capital was $500,000 and surplus $150,000.

December 24. The Chestnut Street Trust and Saving Fund Company made an assignment for the benefit of creditors to George H. Earle, Jr., and Richard Y. Cook.

December 30. The number of school children in this city between the ages of 6 and 16 years was reported by the Real Estate Assessors as 196,375.

1898

January 3. At the annual meeting of the Board of Education, Samuel B. Huey was chosen President, to succeed Simon Gratz, who declined a renomination and Henry R. Edmunds was elected Vice-President.

January 14. The Trustees of the Northern Liberties Gas Works announced a reduction in the price of gas from $1.25 to $1 per 1,000 cubic feet.

January 29. George F. Ott's copper, brass finishing and machine works sustained $100,000 damage by fire.

February 1. The Union Traction Company took possession of the property of the Hestonville, Mantua and Fairmount Passenger Railway Company.

February 16. The steamer Ericsson, of the Baltimore and Philadelphia Steamship Company (Ericsson Line) was capsized by the high wind in the Delaware River near Wilmington, and sunk. Her sixty passengers were rescued by the tug Laura B.

February 18. E. L. Beeler. who is said to have escaped from the County Prison in 1867, after serving one month in a five years' term, was arrested at the Betz Building, where he had gone to appear as a witness in a proceeding in which a well-known politician and contractor who married Beeler's wife in 1882, sought divorce.

February 19. The United States torpedo boat Mackenzie was launched at

Hillman's shipyard.

February 20. Fire destroyed the barrel factory of Christopher Koch, at McKean and Swanson Streets, causing about $14,000 damages, on which there was $11,000 insurance. Six horses were suffocated.

February 21. A freight engine jumped from the track at Beach and Ball Streets, stove a hole through a thirty-inch wall of Cramps' machine shop, and, falling over, crushed Engineer Isaac Quigley.

March 3. The Seventh National Bank, at Fourth and Market Streets, went into voluntary liquidation, and transferred its business to the Fourth Street National Bank, which several months before absorbed the National Bank of the Republic.

April 9. The Commercial National Bank closed its doors and transferred its books, accounts and business to the Fourth Street National Bank.

The South Jersey Railroad was leased to the Atlantic City Railroad Company, controlled by the Reading Railway Company.

April 23. Mines were placed in the Delaware River, near Fort Delaware, under the direction of Major C. W. Raymond, United States Engineer, to increase the effectiveness of the system of defenses. They were removed at the end of the war.

May 9. The Philadelphia tug-boat Thomas G. Smith foundered off the Delaware Capes. Her captain and crew were rescued by a schooner.

May 11. A fire destroyed the toy and fancy goods store of McCadden Bros., 619 Market Street, and a number of adjoining buildings were badly damaged by fire and water, and caused a loss of $200,000. Three persons, William McCadden, aged 58 years; Charles S. Richardson, 35 years, and Evelyn G. Caldwell, were burned to death.

May 13. The old monitor Jason was placed in commission at League Island.

May 18. The battleship Alabama was launched at Cramps' shipyard at 12.49 P.M. Miss Mary E. Morgan, daughter of the Alabama Senator, christened the battleship. Only a few persons, mainly members of Congress and naval officers, were present, owing to a request for privacy from the Government.

May 27. The gunboat Princeton was placed in commission at League Island.

June 18. On her builders' trial trip the Japanese cruiser Kasagi, built at Cramps' yard, made twenty-three knots an hour, half a knot more than her contract called for.

June 22. The Public Buildings Commission agreed to contract with the Johnson Temperature Regulator Company, of Milwaukee, for a tower clock for the City Hall, for $27,960.

June 25. Fire destroyed the oilcloth manufactory of Thomas Potter Sons & Co., causing a loss of half a million dollars.

June 30. The John Dickinson Square, at Fourth and Tasker Streets, which had been equipped as a public playground under the auspices of the Culture Extension League, was formally opened.

July 10. The five-story brick factory building, at the northwest corner of Diamond and American Streets, owned by Thomas J. Holton and John Shoemaker, was destroyed by fire. The Philadelphia Linen Company, Champion Machine Company, Olner, Lupton & Company (Women's coatings), and the Franklin Silk Mills, carried on business in the burned structure, and each sustained a heavy loss. The total damage was about $100,000.

July 12. The Board of Education elected J. Monroe Willard, principal of the Normal School for Girls, and Andrew J. Morrison to succeed Mr. Willard as principal of the Northeast Manual Training School.

August 7. Over 100 survivors of Pickett's division of Confederate soldiers arrived in the city from Richmond, Virginia, and attended a Low Mass at the Cathedral, where Archbishop Ryan presided and made an address. The sermon was preached by the Rev. James F. Loughlin, D. D. In the afternoon they were taken to Washington Park.

August 20. A yawl, in which there were five young men, was run down by the Wilmington Line steamer Brandywine, at the mouth of the Schuylkill, and three occupants of the small boat were drowned. They were Harry J. B. Smith, aged 22; James Barr, 20; James G. Lynch, 21. Hugh Coyle and James Bradley were rescued.

August 22. The auxiliary cruiser St. Paul arrived at Cramps' to be refitted to re-enter the service of the International Navigation Co.

August 24. The auxiliary cruiser St. Louis arrived from New York to be restored to her former condition, so that she might resume her trips between New York and Southampton.

August 31. The auxiliary cruisers Yosemite and Yankee, and the monitor Jason, arrived at League Island.

September 8. The officers and crew of the Japanese cruiser Kasagi, nearing completion at Cramps', arrived from Japan and took up quarters on the vessel.

September 11. What is believed to have been an explosion of gasoline in the grocery store of Samuel Schottenstein, 1444 South Street, caused the destruction of that and the two adjoining stores and dwellings, the loss of five lives and injuries to sixteen persons.

September 13. Peter Schemm, the brewer, committed suicide by jumping from the Goat Island bridge into the rapids at Niagara Falls.

September 17. Fire of unknown origin destroyed the four-story grain and storage warehouse of J. T. O'Rourke & Co., 2229-33 American Street, causing a loss of $40,000, on which there were $27,000 insurance.

October 4. The will of Colonel Joseph M. Bennett, deposited with the Register of Wills, contained a bequest of the Chestnut Street Opera House and adjoining properties, as well as three properties at Thirty-fourth and Walnut Streets, to the University of Pennsylvania to aid in the co-education of women and girls. Colonel Bennett made a number of bequests to relatives and friends, gave $2,000 each to five charitable institutions, and devised his large residuary estate to the Methodist Orphanage. The will was contested by Imogene E. Bennett-Wellens, whom he refused to recognize as his daughter.

October 24. The Admiral Schley, one of the four vessels being built for the American Mail Steamship Company, was launched from Cramps' shipyard.

The cruiser Kasagi was transferred by her builders, the Cramps, to the Japanese Government.

November 23. John W. Keely, inventor of the Keely Motor, was buried at West Laurel Hill.

December 9. Harmonie Hall, Eleventh and Brandywine Streets, owned by the Harmonie Singing Society, was damaged by fire to the extent of $40,000.

1899

January 2. The Board of Education reorganized and re-elected Samuel B. Huey, President; Henry R. Edmunds, Vice-President, and Andrew F. Hammond, Secretary.

January 9. An illicit whisky still, between fifty and sixty gallons of whisky, and fourteen barrels of mash, were seized in an establishment on Germantown Avenue below Venango Street. Four alleged proprietors were arrested and held in bail for a hearing.

February 3. A fire which started in the building at the northwest corner of Thirteenth and Hamilton Streets, occupied by William S. Cooper, manufacturer of brass goods, destroyed that structure and the Stewart Building, extending from Hamilton Street to the Reading Railway crossing on Thirteenth Street. This building was occupied by the Stewart Cracker Company, the DeKosenko Manufacturing Company, makers of gas and electric fixtures; P. P. Mast & Co., agricultural implements; B. Hooley & Sons, silk yarn manufacturers, and the Philadelphia Novelty Company, manufacturers of stationers' hardware. Shops of Hoopes & Townsend, machinists, and the lithographers' establishment of Hoover & Co., 450 North Thirteenth Street, were also damaged. The total loss was estimated at $465,000. One fireman was slightly injured by a falling wall.

February 4. T. B. Rice's box factory, near Mifflin Street Wharf, Delaware River, was damaged by fire to the extent of $75,000.

February 15. The keel plate for the new battleship Maine was laid at Cramps' shipyard on the anniversary of the destruction of the Maine in the harbor of Havana.

February 16. Fire destroyed the three buildings, 1224, 1226 and 1228 Market Street, and the parochial building of St. John's Roman Catholic Church. The total loss was estimated at $700,000, of which $320,000 was on the drug house of William R. Warner & Co., 1228 Market Street, and $245,000 on No. 1226, owned by John Wanamaker and occupied as a laundry upholstering establishment, and for the storage of carpets, etc. Fernberger Bros.' liquor store, No. 1230 Market Street, was badly damaged, as was the Emerson Shoe Store, No. 1224.

February 17. More than two hours after it was believed that the fire at Thirteenth and Market Streets was under control, Hugh Duffy, aged 45 years; William J. Chance, aged 25 years, and George W. Steinle, aged 35 years, hosemen, were killed by the fall of floors of the building, 1224 Market Street. Eight other firemen were injured, but not dangerously. At five o'clock in the morning it was found that St. John's Roman Catholic Church was on fire, and despite the utmost efforts of the fire department it was damaged to the extent, it was estimated, of $60,000. Several valuable paintings were saved.

February 19. Fire in the spinning department of George Campbell & Co.'s Continental Worsted Mills, Twenty-first and Ellsworth Streets, caused about $25,000 damage, covered by insurance.

February 23. Stockholders of the Camden and Philadelphia Steamboat Ferry Company and the West Jersey Ferry Company voted in favor of the adoption of a joint agreement of consolidation and merger of the two companies, both of which are controlled by the Pennsylvania Railroad Company.

March 13. The charter of the Philadelphia Protectory for Boys, of which Archbishop Ryan and a number of Roman Catholic clergymen were incorporators, was approved by President Judge Biddle, of Court No. 1.

The plant of the Charles Scott Spring Company, manufacturers of car springs, occupying about one-half the block bounded by Germantown Avenue, Hancock, Mascher, and Pollard Streets, was destroyed by fire. The loss was estimated at $90,000.

March 16. George C. Boldt purchased the minority interest in the Hotel Stratford, and announced his purpose to erect on its site a hotel of a design similar to that of the Waldorf-Astoria, New York City.

April 4. The Ward Line steamer Mexico was successfully launched at Cramps' shipyard.

April 5. As to the right of the Board of Education to select school sites, the City Solicitor declared that its discretion in such matters is not in any manner under the control of any other body whatsoever; nor can such power and duty so imposed by law upon it be by it delegated to others.

April 10. A jury was obtained and the taking of testimony was begun in the trial of ex-United States Senator Quay on charges of conspiracy with the late John S. Hopkins, cashier of the People's Bank, to misuse State moneys on deposit in that institution.

April 21. M. S. Quay was acquitted by the jury in the Court of Quarter Sessions of the charge of conspiracy under the indictment upon which he was tried.

April 27. The heroic bronze equestrian statue of General Grant, erected at Fountain Green by the Fairmount Park Art Association, was unveiled by Miss Rosemary Sartoris, a granddaughter of the General, in the presence of a distinguished assemblage, including President McKinley, Mrs. U. S. Grant, General F. D. Grant, General Miles, members of the Cabinet, Governor Stone and officers of the Army and Navy.

May 3. Fire destroyed the clothing store of Bacharach & Co., which covered the triangular block bounded by Ridge Avenue, and Thirteenth, Green and Mount Vernon Streets. Sixteen buildings on Thirteenth Street, five on Green Street and three on Ridge Avenue were damaged by the flames. A number of firemen were overcome by the intense heat or injured, but none fatally. The total loss was estimated at about $150,000.

June 9. A. J. Cassatt was elected President of the Pennsylvania Railroad Company, at a special meeting, to succeed the late Frank Thomson. James McCrea, of Pittsburgh, was chosen a Director to fill the vacancy caused by Mr. Thomson's death.

June 14. The statue of Benjamin Franklin, erected on the south plaza of the Post Office building as a gift to the city by Justus C. Strawbridge, was unveiled by Miss Margaret Hartman Bache. Postmaster General Smith made the speech of presentation, and Mayor Ashbridge accepted the memorial for the city.

June 19. Eight or ten masked men entered the office of the Fairmount Park Transportation Company, near Belmont, after the cars had ceased running for the night, and after overpowering the receiver and five other employes, whose hands and feet they bound with wire, threatening them with death if they resisted or made any noise, forced open the safe with powder or dynamite, and abstracted $3,355.57, the receipts of Saturday and Sunday, with which they escaped. The robbers took the precaution of cutting telephone wires. Three men were arrested in the Park on suspicion of being implicated in the robbery, and were held for a further hearing.

June 22. Fire destroyed the storehouse and badly damaged the factory building of the glazed kid works of Charles J. Matthews & Co., northwest corner of Willow and American Streets. Two factory buildings at 209 and 211 Willow Street were slightly damaged by the flames. Loss estimated at $50,000.

July 1. The New York Ship Building Company purchased the property of the Manufacturers' Land and Improvement Company, in South Camden, above

Newton Creek, and commenced the erection of its big plant.

July 27. The Board of Education removed its executive offices to the City Hall.

August 22. While Harney R. Ward, a Bustleton plumber, was repairing an iron pump in the basement of the Lower Dublin Baptist Church, the pump came in contact with an overhead iron gas pipe, which seems to have been charged with electricity. Ward was killed by the shock, and a fellow workman was severely stunned.

August 26. Gill & Co.'s glass works, East York and Thompson Streets, were destroyed by fire. The loss is estimated at between $75,000 and $100,000, partly covered by insurance.

August 28. The battleship Alabama left Cramps' shipyard on her builders' trial trip.

September 2. Five vessels of the North Atlantic Squadron— the battleships Indiana, Massachusetts and Texas, and the cruisers New York and Brooklyn— anchored in the Delaware River.

September 5. Thousands of persons viewed the electric illumination of the vessels of Admiral Sampson's squadron.

September 8. Encampment week was practically ended with the naval parade, which was a most successful and imposing demonstration. A long line of crowded river craft passed in review around the ships of the North Atlantic Squadron, and to the firing of cannon and screeching of steam whistles was added the cheering of many thousands of people afloat and ashore.

September 12. By a vote of 26 to 9 the Board of Education adopted the report of its Committee on Property recommending that the lot at Twenty-eighth and Huntingdon Streets, selected by Councils as a school site, be purchased, if the owner will accept $22,000 instead of $25,000 the price first asked.

September 19. The Board of Education Property Committee was advised by William D. Price that he is willing to accept the Board's offer of $22,000 for the lot at Twenty-eighth and Huntingdon Streets, on condition that settlement be made as of January 2d last, when the ordinance for the purchase was signed by the Mayor. The lot was accepted, and settlement left to the City Solicitor.

September 27. The building 1707 and 1709 Filbert Street, occupied by the Reliance Storage Company, and the one adjoining, 1711 Filbert Street, were damaged by fire to the extent of about $70,000.

September 29. The matter of the purchase of a school site at Twenty-eighth and Huntingdon Streets again came before the Board of Education, the owner having requested that body to adopt a resolution accepting the ground for $22,000 and accrued interest and taxes from January 2d, amounting to $1,200.

October 12. Some four hundred representatives of trade and commerce from every quarter of the globe, members of the Diplomatic Corps and National, State and municipal officials, were present at the opening of the International Commercial Congress, at the National Export Exposition.

October 14. Harmonie Hall, Eleventh and Brandywine Streets, dedicated.

October 19. Select Council adopted a resolution instructing Congressmen and members of the Legislature to vote and work for the repeal of the Civil Service Reform laws.

November 29. A fire which started in the stores of Partridge & Richardson, Eighth Street above Market, destroyed those buildings, the establishments of J.

B. Lippincott Company, publishers, Filbert Street below Eighth, and Partridge & Son, and Bailey & Co., Eighth Street below Filbert, and damaged the stores of Lit Brothers, Strawbridge & Clothier, P. T. Hallahan, P. J. Hallahan, H. Mosebach Sons, Samuel D. Long, F. W. Bean & Co., Artman & Treichler, and others. The total loss was estimated at $1,250,000. Eight firemen were injured, but none dangerously. Nearly 2,000 persons were deprived of employment.

December 4. The Board of Judges appointed James Pollock as a member of the Fairmount Park Commission to succeed the late James McManus.

December 7. P. A. B. Widener purchased thirty-six acres of land, fronting on Old York Road, near Logan Station, on which he established the Widener Industrial Home for Crippled Children. Mr. Widener spent $2,000,000 in improving the property and endowing the institution. An ordinance was introduced in City Councils, and subsequently passed, to strike from the city plan streets which would intersect the tract.

December 29. It was learned that the recently announced gift of $250,000 to the University of Pennsylvania was from the estate of H. H. Houston, who shortly before he died contributed a like sum to the same institution.

HAPPENINGS IN YE OLDE PHILADELPHIA

REGATTAS—DELAWARE RIVER

1872

May 13. Regatta of the Philadelphia Yacht Club. Forty-six boats entered. The prizes were won by the yachts, B. Akins, Louis Scheer and John J. Hare, Jr., of the first class; Charles Able, John F. Brewer and Geo. K. Wise, Jr., of the second class.

June 13. Regatta of the Delaware Yacht Navy. First prize for cabin yachts, thirty to thirty-seven feet long, won by the Col. J. M. Davis; second prize by the Bessie Garsides; distance, 13 miles; time, 4 hrs., 35 min.

Race for first class fifteen foot yachts (tuck-ups) won by the Lizzie Ardis; second prize won by the Eggleton; third prize won by the Kate Aiken; distance, 11 miles; time, 3 hrs. First prize for second class fifteen foot yachts won by the John B. Brewer; time, 3 hrs.

1873

May 19. Regatta of the Philadelphia Yacht Club on the Delaware River. Sixty-two boats entered. The prize for cabin yachts was won by the Eliza; other prizes were not awarded, in consequence of violation of rules by the boats, and the race, as to them, decided to be a draw.

June 23. Second regatta of the Philadelphia Yacht Club on the Delaware. Prize for first class boats won by the George Hoff; second class prize won by the Enchantress. The wind was very heavy; several boats "carried away," several boats upset. Course, from Shackamaxon Street, Kensington, to Delanco and return—thirteen miles. Time, first class, four hours and two minutes; second class, four hours and four minutes.

October 7-8. National amateur regatta upon the Schuylkill. Prizes for pairs and double sculls won by Crescent Club, of Philadelphia. Prize for four-oared shells won by the Argonauta, of Bergen Point, New Jersey. Prize for single scull won by Chas. Myers, of the Nassau Club, of New York.

1874

May 18. Regatta on the Delaware River of the Philadelphia Yacht Club. Course from Shackamaxon Street Wharf to the Block House (below Gloucester) and return. The prizes for first class yachts were won by the following boats: 1, Willie Kleinz, time, 3 hrs. 15 min.; 2, Albert Dager, 3 hrs. 18 min.; 3, Albert Edwards. Second class yachts: 1, Richard F. Riddell, 2 hrs. 45 min.; 2, John B. Brewer, 2 hrs. 52 min.; 3, Dollie Tilton.

June 15. Annual regatta of the Philadelphia Yacht Club on the Delaware River. Course, from Shackamaxon St. Wharf to Torresdale and return. Contestants, nineteen first class and twenty-six second class yachts. Prizes for first class boats won by Alfred F. Eggleton, time, 6 hrs. 26 min.; second class yachts, Richard F. Riddell.

1876

June 19. Annual regatta of the Philadelphia Yacht Club. Course, from Shackamaxon Street Wharf to Delanco and return, twenty-five miles. Prizes for first class boats won by the yacht Kate F. Kennedy, time, 3.24; second class, Sallie Cox, 3.10; third class, Wm. J. Thompson, 2.52.

114

1877

June 4. Regatta of the Quaker City Yacht Club on the Delaware River. Course, from Shackamaxon Street Wharf to Chester and return. Prize for first class yachts won by the Minerva; time, 5 hours. First prize, second class, won by the Lillie, time, 5 hours and 4 minutes.

June 11. Annual regatta of the Philadelphia Yacht Club. Course from Kensington to Delanco, N.J., and return. All the boats were 15 feet, 3 inches in length. First class, 6 feet, 3 inches beam; second class, 5 feet beam; third class, 4 feet, 7 inches beam. Prizes won: Kate F. Baisly of first class, Ida May of second class, and J. W. Scholz of third class.

1878

May 20. Annual regatta of the Delaware River Yacht Club. Course, from Kaighn's Point to Chester Buoy. Race won by the Adelphi in 3.15, said to be the quickest time ever made by a sailing yacht on the Delaware.

May 22. Fourth annual regatta of the Southwark Yacht Club (Smoky Hollow). Course, from Washington Avenue Wharf to Chester Buoy and return. Yachts of the first class, prize won by the Spirit in 4.18; second class, by the Korbin, in 4.24; third class, by the Lenvir, in 4.38.

May 23. Third annual regatta of the Quaker City Yacht Club. Course from Kensington to Chester and return. Prize for first class won by Yacht Minerva in 4.36; second class, Lillie in 4.43; third class, Bianca, in 5.011,4.

June 10. Sixth annual regatta of the Philadelphia Yacht Club. Course from Shackamaxon Street Wharf to Delanco and return. Prizes for first class boats won by Geo. Hoff and Mahlon H. Thomas; second class, Charles W. Meekie and David H. Geary; third class, Christian Farne and David H. Schuyler.

First regatta of the Schuylkill Yacht Club. Course from Ellsworth Street Wharf, Schuylkill, to Chester Buoy and return. First class prize won by the F. B. Doyle; second class, the Bently; third class, the Vindex.

June 24. Annual regatta of the Southwark Double End Yacht Club. Course, from Dickinson Street Wharf to Chester Buoy and return. Prizes for the first class won by the Mitchell in 4.21^{1}/$_{2}$, and the Spurt in 4.23; third class, by the Dav. H. Schuyler (of Fishtown) in 4.09, and the Powell in 4.141^{1}/$_{2}$.

1879

May 26. Annual regatta of the Southwark Yacht Club. Prizes: First class won by yachts Lawrence and Maud; second class, Emma and S. H. Oliver; third class, Thomas Ledyard and Hugh Boyle.

June 12. Fourth annual Spring regatta of the Quaker City Yacht Club, on the Delaware River. Course, from Market Street Wharf, Camden, to Chester Buoy and return. Prizes for first class cabin sloops won by Clara, 4.32; Minerva, 4.32^{3}/$_{4}$; Comet, 4.41; Selim, 4.52. Second class, cabin sloops and thirty feet; Minnie, 4.45^{3}/$_{4}$; Gallagher, 4.51; Stella, 4.54. Third class, open yachts between twenty and thirty feet: Adelphi, 4.13; Eddie, 4.27; Bianca, 4.29.

June 16. Seventh annual regatta of the Philadelphia Yacht Club. Course, from Shackamaxon Street Wharf to Delanco and return, twenty-six miles. Prizes, first class won by Willy Kleinz and Anna, time, 2.37 and 2.43; second class, Enchantress and Abel, time, 2.35 and 2.42; third class, Crawford and Wm. Flick, 2.17 and 2.18^{1}/$_{2}$.

1880

May 17. Fortieth annual regatta of the Cooper's Point Yacht Club. Course, to Chester Buoy and return. First prize won by the Cohill; second prize by the Norcross; third prize by the Shack. Time, 4.32.

First regatta of the Independent Yacht Club for fourth class tuck-ups (mosquito fleet); twenty-three boats entered. First prize won by the I. G. Iddies; second, by the G. W. Smith; third, by the Sarah A. Nield. Course, from Kensington to the Block House and return.

May 31. Fifth annual regatta of the Quaker City Yacht Club. Course, from opposite Market Street to Chester and return. First prizes, first class, Minerva, 3.25; second class, Lillie, 3.38; third class, Eddie, 3.41.

June 7. Eighth annual regatta of the Philadelphia Yacht Club. Course, from Shackamaxon Street Wharf to Delanco and return. First prize won by the Geo. Hoff and Anna; second class, Richard Mengert and J. T. Martin; third class, Robert Ledyard and Alex. Crawford.

June 14. Sixth annual regatta of the Southwark Yacht Club. Course, to Chester to return. Prizes for first class boats won by the Emma Brougan, 3.53; second class, by John H. Hagan, 4.02^{3}/4; third class, by Thomas Ledyard, 3.44.

June 21. Second annual regatta of the Independent Yacht Club for fourth class tuck-ups. Course, from Marlborough Street Wharf to Delanco and return; 16 boats entered. First prize won by the Thomas M. Seeds; second, by the Joe and Willie Smith; third, by the Chris. Ulmer.

1881

Annual regatta of Philadelphia Yacht Club. Course, from Allen's Slip, Kensington, to Delanco and return. First prizes as follows: First class won by the Anna; second class by the John Robbins; third class, Geo. C. Flick. Shortest time, 5.37.

June 20. Seventh annual regatta of the Southwark Yacht Club; 30 entries. Course, to Chester and return. Prizes to boats of first class won by the Emma Brougan, 5.28; second class, John H. Hagan, 5.47^{1}/2; third class, Thomas Ledyard, 5.06.

July 25. Annual regatta of the Pennsylvania Yacht Club. Course, from Allen's Slip, Kensington, to Wheat Sheaf Buoy, opposite Andalusia, and return; twelve entries. First prize awarded to the yacht Joe and Willie Smith, 3.53; second prize to yacht Albert Murray, 3.56.

September 5. First fall regatta of the Pennsylvania Yacht Club; eleven entries. Course, from Allen's Slip, Kensington, to Delanco and return. First prize, Minerva, 2.44; second prize, Willy Graham, 2.44^{1}/2; third prize, Leonhard Stadtler, 2.45.

1882

May 30. Third annual regatta of the Pennsylvania Yacht Club on the Delaware River. Course, from Kensington to Delanco, twenty boats started. First prize won by the Joe and Willie Smith, 3.14; second prize, Bessie, 3.17; third prize, Leonard Stadtler, 3.171^{1}/2.

June 5. Seventh annual regatta of the Quaker City Yacht Club; twenty-two boats entered. Course, from Market Street Wharf, Camden, to Chester Buoy and return. First prize, first class, won by Minerva, 4.33^{3}/4; second class, won by N.E. Morgan, formerly the Stella, 5.14; third class (A) Minerva, of Trenton,

5.14; third class (B) G. W. Hasse, 5.22.

1883

June 4. Fourth annual regatta of the Pennsylvania Yacht Club, composed of fifteen foot boats, carrying not over fifty yards of sail. Course, from the Delaware Water Works Wharf to Delanco and return, 28 miles. Sixteen entries. First prize won by the Thos. M. Seeds, 4.55; second prize, Joe and Willie Smith, 4.56; third prize, Sarah A. Nields, 4.59$^{1/2}$.   June 11. Eighth annual regatta of the Quaker City Yacht Club; twenty-two boats entered. Course, from Market Street Wharf, Camden, to Chester and return, 32 miles. Wind strong from southwest; boats under double reef. Prizes: First class won by Minerva, 4.03$^{1/2}$; second class, Florager, 4.21$^{1/2}$; third class, Lily, 4.40; fourth class, Pierson, 4.46$^{1/4}$; fifth class, Chris. Gallagher, 4.54.

June 12. Eighth annual regatta of the Southwark Yacht Club; twenty-seven boats entered. Course, from Dickinson Street Wharf to Chester Buoy and return. In consequence of little wind and adverse tides, none of the boats were able to sail over the prescribed course within seven hours, the time limit, and no prizes were awarded.

June 25. Ninth annual regatta of the Southwark Yacht Club. Course, from Dickinson Street Wharf to Chester Buoy and return, a distance of about 30 miles. Twenty-seven entries. Nine boats capsized during the race. Prizes, first class, J. Bright, 4.00$^{1/2}$; second class, a tie between three boats; third class, Hugh Boyle, 3.52; fourth class, Joe Nobre.

Annual regatta of the Philadelphia Yacht Club; twenty entries. Course, from Shackamaxon Street Wharf to Delanco and return. A severe storm was encountered on the way up, during which fourteen boats upset or "carried away" their rigging. Prize for first class boats won by Mary A. Black; second class, Geo. Hanna; third class, Geo. Flick.

July 24. Second attempt to sail the eighth annual regatta of the Southwark Yacht Club; thirty-three boats entered. In consequence of light wind the race was a failure, no boat succeeding in making the course within the prescribed allotted time, 7 hours.

1884

June 2. Ninth annual regatta of the Quaker City Yacht Club. Course, from Market Street Wharf, Camden, to Chester Buoy and return; twenty-one entries; wind light from south. Prizes, first class, won by Sunbeam, 7.21.47; second class, Minerva, 7.30.53; third class, M. S. Thomas, 6.35.20; fourth class, Thos. J. Pratt, 6:50.29; fifth class, Richmond, 7.07$^{3/4}$. The Pratt won the first general prize and the commodore's challenge cup.

June 9. Fourth annual regatta of the Pennsylvania Yacht Club. Course, from Kensington Water Works to Delanco and return. Fourteen entries; wind light from southwest. First prize won by Bessie, 5.30; second prize, Leonhard Stadtler; third prize, Joe and Willie Smith; fourth prize, Mediator.

June 16. Tenth annual regatta of the Southwark Yacht Club; twenty-five entries. Course, to Chester and return. Prizes, first class, double enders, won by James Mitchell; second class, double enders, Laura; third class, tuck-ups, Chas. Benton, the latter making the shortest run, 5.05; fourth class, tuck-ups, Amanda C.

July 14. Race by yachts of the Quaker City Yacht Club of the third class for commodore's challenge cup between the yachts Mamie S. Thomas and Mahma. Course, from Market Street Wharf, Camden, to Chester Buoy and return. Wind strong from northwest; sails under double reef. Won by the Thomas, 2.11$^{1/2}$.

Sweepstakes regatta between tuck-ups; six entries. Course, from Kensington Water Works to Chester Buoy and return to Mifflin Street Wharf. Won by the Ledyard, 2.35.

August 12. Sweepstake regatta of the fourth class boats of the Quaker City Yacht Club. Course, from Market Street Wharf, Camden, to Chester Buoy, and return, five entries. Won by the yacht F. J. Pratt, 4.40.

1885
June 7. Tenth annual regatta of Quaker City Yacht Club.

June 8. Tenth annual regatta of the Quaker City Yacht Club. Course, from Market Street Wharf, Camden, N. J., to Chester Buoy and return. Twelve entries. Prizes: First class, won by Venitzia, 3.52; second class, Nahma, 5.14; fifth class, Au Revoir, 5.27.

June 22. Eleventh annual regatta of the Southwark Yacht Club. Course, from Dickinson Street Wharf to Chester Buoy and return. Twenty-six entries; wind from northwest, very strong. Prizes: First class, J. Mitchell, 5.22; second class, Gertrude; third class, Thomas Ledyard; fourth class, V. P. Dorp.

1886
June 7. Twelfth annual regatta of the Pennsylvania Yacht Club. Eleven entries. Course, from Kensington Water Works Wharf to Delanco and return. First prize won by yacht William A. Birch, nicknamed the "Candy Boat," time, 5.00; second, David Bennett, 5.03; third prize, Little Tycoon, 5.05.

June 7. Twelfth annual regatta of the Southwark Yacht Club. Course, from Dickinson Street Wharf to Chester Buoy and return, 36 miles. Twenty-five entries. Prizes, first class, J. Mitchell, 5.01$^{1/2}$; second class, H. D. Boardman, 5.24$^{1/2}$; third class, Thomas Ledyard, 4.16; fourth class, J. Nobre, 5.01.

June 9. Eleventh annual regatta of the Quaker City Yacht Club. Course, from Dickinson Street Wharf to Chester Buoy and return. Thirteen entries.

1887
May 30. Seventh annual regatta of Pennsylvania Yacht Club. Course from Kensington Water Works Wharf to Chester Buoy and return. Thirteen entries. First prize, Frank and Willie Playford, 5.45; second, George Kilroy, 5.46; third, Bessie, 5.52.

June 13. Twelfth annual regatta of the Quaker City Yacht Club. Course, from Gloucester Point to Marcus Hook and return. Fourteen entries. Prizes, first class, sloop Venitzia, 5.17; second class, Leda, 5.30; third class, Minerva, of Trenton, 6.03; fourth class, Comfort; class B, open yacht Hurley, 6.10.

Thirteenth annual regatta of Southwark Yacht Club.

GLIMPSES OF YE OLDE TIME PHILADELPHIA

The Philadelphia that is "typical" is rapidly disappearing—the insatiable maw of the business efficiency expert has wrought havoc with the city of old associations.

Of the glory that was once "Early Philadelphia" barely a vestige has survived.

A delightful picture of this "greene countrie town" is given in Horace Mather Lippincott's "Early Philadelphia," published by J. B. Lippincott Company. We are afforded a fascinating glimpse of the notable dwellings and the habits of their occupants. It gives too, a graphic idea of what the city looked like and did during the early days of its existence, when it staged many distinguished events in the nation's history. Not the least interesting is the manner of birth of so many well-known institutions, so solidly founded that they in the complexities of modern business life are serving as useful a purpose as when they were started.

Indeed, the remarkable development of these venerable institutions from their lowly origin form a curious and important chapter in the history of this country's progress.

Thus we read that the Library Company of Philadelphia, the mother of all North American subscription libraries, dates back to the Leather Apron Club founded by Franklin in 1728 "for the mutual improvement of its members." An offshoot of that body, the American Society Held at Philadelphia for Promoting and Propagating Useful Knowledge, also founded by Franklin, gave us the now famous American Philosophical Society.

"Two young men, a chemist and a dentist, called together a few friends in their own walk of life, rented a little room over a little shop, placed in it with infinite pride a dozen stuffed birds and a jar or two of reptiles and met there at night to discuss the operations of nature." From this modest beginning sprang the Philadelphia Academy of Natural Sciences, the oldest of its kind in America.

That interesting establishment, the Bank of North America, which, curiously, is the only national bank in the United States which does not have the word national in its title, originated in a patriotic endeavor to sustain the feeble credit of the early Congress. The bank, under the capable administration of Robert Morris, began business in 1780 in Front Street, two doors above Walnut Street.

At a noon gathering of business men at the old Merchant's Coffee House on Second Street, where now stands the bonded warehouse of the United States, on a day in December, 1809, was born the first trust company in the United States, formed by a group of business men for the insurance of lives and granting annuities, under the name of the Pennsylvania Company for Insurances on Lives and Granting Annuities.

Problems of fire protection naturally attracted early attention, and in February, 1752, a little body of subscribers convened at the courthouse and organized the Philadelphia Contributionship for the Insurance of Houses from Loss by Fire, familiarly known as the "Hand-in-Hand," which is today not only the oldest fire insurance company in America, but also one of the strongest active fire insurance companies in the world.

The well-known Philadelphia Saving Fund Society, at Seventh and Walnut Streets, which boasts of a hundred thousand more depositors than any other bank in the United States, owes its conception in 1816 to Colonel Raguet, whose colored waiter, Curtis Roberts, had the honor of making the first deposit.

One of Philadelphia's greatest claims to antiquity perhaps is that it harbors the oldest business concern in America, the Francis Perot's Sons Malting Company, which is older than the Bank of England and has descended from father to son for eight generations.

Early Philadelphia was located in 1682, "having a high and dry bank next to the water, with a shore ornamented with a fine view of pine trees growing upon it." In this bank, the early settlers made caves to shelter their families and belongings while they went out into the wilderness with a warrant to survey and choose their lands. Pastorius, the founder of Germantown, says he was often lost in the woods and brush in going from his cave along the river's bank to the house of the Dutch baker, Bom, at the southeast corner of Third and Chestnut Streets, where he procured his bread. The cave-dwelling period was brief, however, for sixteen years later, according to that observant traveler, Gabriel Thomas, there were 2,000 houses, stately and of brick, generally three stories high after the mode of London.

Front Street was the principal street of the city for a long time, first as a residence street, when all the houses were built on the western side, and afterward as a place of trade. On the arrival of ships from England in spring and autumn the pavements from Arch Street to Walnut Street were covered with boxes and bales from foreign shores, consigned to the warehouses and stores of old-time merchants like Robert Morris, Stephen Girard, Thomas Willing, Jacob Ridgway, the Walns, Whartons and many others. Penn's design, according to Mr. Lippincott, was to have a promenade on the high bank of the river front the whole length of the city, intending Front Street to have an uninterrupted view of the Delaware River scenery. Had it not been for the trickery and deceit of some of the people during his absence this wonderful plan would have given us the most beautiful city in America.

The little center of colonists of that time, bustling with self-importance, was hardly less busy than that neighborhood of today, which bristles with ghostly memories and historic traditions. Among the residents of "Society Hill," so named because of the location there of the office of the Free Traders, were Samuel Powell and Joseph Wharton. The former lived at 244 South Third Street and was distinguished as Mayor of the city and as a lavish entertainer in his handsome house built in 1769. Nearby lived Thomas Willing and William Bingham. Bishop White, the first American bishop in America, lived at 402 South Front Street and later in Walnut Street above Third.

On the square running from Front Street to Second and fronting on High (Market) Street was the large lot and house built for the proprietor before his first coming, afterward on Letitia Street, named for his daughter. The house now stands in Fairmount Park and

presents much the same appearance as it did when Penn resided in it. Samuel Carpenter had the first "Coffee House" in the neighborhood of Front and Walnut Streets. He also had a crane, bakehouse and wharf. At the southeast corner of Norris Alley and Second Street, where now stands the main office of the Keystone Telephone Company, the same active citizen built the "Slate Roof House," noted as the city residence of Penn and his family when on his second visit to the city in 1700. The large house at 321 South Front Street sheltered Henry Hill, of Madeira wine fame, in 1786, and later the McCalls and

Dr. Syng Physick, the father of American surgery. The fine old house at 422 South Front Street, now occupied by the Pennsylvania Seamen's Friend Society, was built by John Barclay, Mayor of the town in 1791. Its spiral stairway, running to the lantern in the roof, is a famous piece of architecture. On Pemberton Street near Front and south of Bainbridge there is a high wall with two quaint little houses facing each other at each side of a gateway through which one gets a glimpse of a courtyard and trees. In the bricks of the wall are blockheaders forming the letters "G. M." and the date 1748. This little settlement was built by George Mifflin, father of Governor Thomas Mifflin, who afterward left it to his son. It is now used by the Octavia Hill Association for housing betterment.

OCCURRENCES OF THE EARLY SETTLEMENT

In the early period of Philadelphia it was very common for the good livers to have malt-houses on their several premises for making home made strong beer.

Professor Kalm, a Swedish traveler, who visited Philadelphia in 1748-49, related that red cedar was so abundant that all fence posts were made of it, even the very rails.

He speaks of minks living in the docks and hollow trees along the shore, destroying numbers of the rats.

A primitive story of much interest is accredited to a pious lady of the Society of Friends, Deborah Morris, of Philadelphia. She made the codicil of her will peculiar by some of the memorials she perpetuated, by connecting the history with the gifts which she there wills to her descendants. "The large silver old fashioned salver, I give to my nephew, Thomas Morris, was given to my dear parents by my mother's aunt, Elizabeth Hard, a worthy good woman (she being the first orphan ever left in charge of George Fox's Society of Friends in England), whose sweet innocent deportment used to give me high esteem and regard for the ancient people. She came from England with William Penn and other Friends. My grandfather and wife came two years before her, and settled in the Jerseys; but when she heard her sister designed to Philadelphia they removed thither also, and just got settled in a cave on the bank of the river, where now is called the Crooked Billet wharf (so named from a tavern on the wharf, about 100 feet northward from Chestnut Street, having a crooked billet of wood for its sign) when my dear aunt (Hard) arrived; which she esteemed a divine providence thus to find her sister, whom she had not seen for some years, thus ready to receive her in the cave. They there dwelt together until they could build."

The first prison was "the hired house of Patrick Robinson, in Second Street, a few feet north of High Street." The first prison that the city owned was below High Street, a little eastwardly from Second Street. Nearby stood Wm. Penn's two-story house, in Letitia Court; before which was the "Governor's Gate," where the proclamations of the day were made by "publick outcry."

The "Coffee House" belonged to Samuel Carpenter, and was situated on Front Street, near Walnut.

THE BRITISH BARRACKS

These barracks were on a plot of ground extending from Second to Third Street, and from St. Tamany (Buttonwood) to Green Street. Originally this was a field of buckwheat, which was cut off and the barracks built. The region thereabouts was called Campingtown.

THE LONDON COFFEE HOUSE

William Bradford, the Colonial Job Printer, tiring of setting type and pulling the lever of his hand press, applied to the Governor for a license to conduct a coffee house in the year 1754, upon the declining of the Widow Roberts, who until then kept a coffee house in Front Street below Blackhorse Alley. His petition for a license read: "Having been advised to keep a coffee house for the benefit of merchants and traders, and as some people may at times be desirous to be furnished with other liquors besides coffee, your petitioner apprehends it is necessary to have the Governor's license."

The then Governor was a frequent visitor at the coffee house.

Alderman John Baker often shot partridges on a large grass plot, extending from Sassafras (Race) to Vine Street, from Third to Fourth.

The northeast corner of Fourth and High Streets was a cow-lot, which was offered for rent at an annual rental of £10 ($50.00).

"The Great Meeting House" of Friends was originally located at the southwest corner of Second and High Streets.

Christ Church. In Gabriel Thomas' publication of 1698, it is stated "the Church of England built a very fine church in this city in the year 1695."

Blacksmiths were located in the neighborhood of Third and High (Market) Streets. William Bissel was located at the northeast corner of Third Street and Elbow Lane. John Roase had his smithy at the northeast corner of Third and High Streets; adjoining the prison, southwest corner of Third and High Streets, extending along Third Street stood blacksmiths' and wheelwrights' sheds.

Centre Woods. That portion between High and South Streets, and west of Broad Street to the Schuylkill was a body of forest trees. The young folks usually went there to frolic and gather berries.

Hudson's Orchard extended from Fifth to Sixth Street and from High to Arch Street. About sixty feet from the northwest corner of Fifth and Market Streets.

The first shipyard was located at Vine Street, which lay along "a vale" causing that street to be called "Valley Street." The shipbuilder was Charles West, who came out with Penn: In close proximity was an inn and landing, "Penny Pot House."

The first lumber merchant was William Rakestraw, who advertised his board yard, on Water Street near Vine.

Water Street was the main street for shopping, as the earliest newspapers show by their advertisements. It was a matter of surprise to the good people when John Warder built at north Third Street opposite Church Alley, for going *so far out of town.*

Coates' Woods, consisting of about 5 acres, were situated in the vicinity of Third and Brown Streets. Some of the boys would, with dogs, tree raccoons there.

Bath Town. In the year 1765 John White and wife advertised their mineral springs in Bath Town, located in the neighborhood of the present Third and George Streets, on the banks of the Cohocksink.

Northwest corner Second and High Streets, now occupied by the Columbia Spa, was the drug store of John Speakman, Jr., a Friend, whose domicile was above the store. Here on January 25, 1812, the Academy of Natural Sciences was organized.

The building at the southwest corner of Third and High was erected in 1722 and used as a prison. The first prison was in the middle of High Street below Second.

The Pennsylvania Hospital was originally located on the south side of High Street above Fifth.

The Morris house, 225 S. Eighth Street, with its old time garden, was built in 1786 by John Reynolds.

An oyster cellar was kept by a man named D. McClain, on Third Street west side below Vine. Over the doorway was a sign with the following thereon:

> "Oysters opened or on the shell,
> Of the best I keep to sell;
> Walk down and try them for yourself,
> That D. McClain may gain some pelf."

HAPPENINGS IN YE OLDE PHILADELPHIA

A lad living in Germantown, by the name of Anthony Klincken, in the fall of the year, when he desired to go duck shooting, would come to Fourth and High (Market) Streets. There filled with spatter ducks was the proper head of Dock Creek, an alluring body of water for migrating fowl.

Another deep pond existed at the northeast corner of Eighth and Arch Streets.

Evans' Pond was on the north side of Sassafras (Race) Street, extending to Branch Street.

Hudson's Pond lay at the northwest corner of Fifth and High (Market) Streets.

Broom corn was introduced into this country by Benjamin Franklin, who planted a single seed which he obtained by accident, and from it he raised enough of the plants to make brooms for his own use, and was able to give away seeds which were planted in other portions of the country.

Benjamin Franklin died in 1790 in his own house, in a court leading south from Market Street, between Third and Fourth (now called Hudson Alley).

Front Street was soon superseded in importance by High Street, as Market Street was originally called, the familiar name of the principal street in nearly every English town. The markets, which from very early in the city's history were characteristic of the High Street, caused the inhabitants to refer to the latter as Market Street, just as the arch over Mulberry Street at Front involuntarily led Philadelphians to allude to the street as Arch.

The earliest recorded date of a market house is 1683, when a "market-place was established where butchers have movable stalls." The most famous, perhaps, was the building which we know at Second and Pine Streets, designed after the courthouse at Second and High Streets. It constitutes a historical evidence of past custom, the last of a type intimately associated with the early history of the city. Not only the fairest of Philadelphia's prominent families patronized it and did their purchasing here, but President and Mrs. Washington, Dolly Madison, Stephen Girard, Joseph Bonaparte and other notables are said to have frequented this old market. The markets were generally very crowded, and as there were no side aisles a good deal of difficulty was experienced, especially when the women began wearing hoopskirts. Tradition has it that the men bought frogs from the farmers to frighten the ladies in crowded aisles a little bit and make them fall back so as to let the men through.

Old Market Street is rich in historic associations. It was past the old courthouse and the Market Square that General Howe and his army made their triumphal entry into the city when the throngs of citizens, clad in their best arrays, lined the sidewalks to see the grenadiers march by steadfast and composed and splendidly equipped. What a contrast, says the author, to the little patriot army which Washington had led along the same street not so long before, a sprig of green in the men's hats forming the only sign of uniformity.

On the site of the building now numbered 110 the English Bible was first published in America by Robert Aitken, and at the southwest corner of Second and Market there stood until 1810 the Meeting House of the Society of Friends. Here the prominent Quakers of our early Colonial history worshipped and here, it is said, the tired lad Benjamin Franklin wandered after his arrival in 1723 and fell asleep on one of the benches. On the same side of the street to the westward were the Royal Standard and Indian King taverns, in both of which the lodge of Free Masons was accustomed to meet. John Biddle kept the latter for many years. Matthew Corley began business on Front below Market Street in 1784, where he published the *Pennsylvania Herald*. John Dunlap, one of the founders of the First City Troop, associated with David C. Claypoole, published the first daily newspaper in this country in a printing house near Second and Market. This neighborhood became the printing house center of Philadelphia until the beginning of the last century. At what is now 135 Market Street Franklin started his first printing house, and here began the publication in 1741 of the first monthly magazine in this country. It is thought that William Bradford, the first printer in the middle colonies, had his shop near Front and Market Streets, and his descendants continued the trade in the neighborhood for a full century or more.

At 43 Water Street dwelt the famous Stephen Girard, "merchant and mariner," and here were entertained Talleyrand, the Duke of Orleans, later Louis Philippe, and his brother and other famous French émigrés. The vicinity of Fifth and Sixth Streets and Market was the scene of many historic events. At the site now numbered 526, 528 and 530 was a noble old mansion, regarded as the finest in the city. During the British occupation it was taken by General Howe for his headquarters, and on its grounds was quartered the Fifteenth Regiment of Foot. Here Benedict Arnold lived, followed by Robert Morris, the financier, and later by President Washington. Charles Biddle, the president of the Second United States Bank, the father of Nicholas Biddle, lived at what would be No. 611 Market Street, and on the north side between Sixth and Seventh Streets Dr. Joseph Priestley, the discoverer of oxygen, dwelt.

No history of Philadelphia would be complete without a record of the early inns and theatres, and interesting reading it makes. Philadelphia, very fittingly, had the honor of seeing the first Shakespearean presentation in America in 1749. The little company was managed by Murray and Kean, but there is no authentic record of just where they gave their performance. Lewis Hallam's English company came to the city in 1754 and gave as an "opener" "The Fair Penitent" in a large brick warehouse of William Plumsted, situated in King or Water Street, between Pine and Lombard Streets. Eventually a theatre was built for them at Cedar or South and Vernon Streets, on Society Hill, just outside the town limits, as in Shakespearean days. Like the history of all early theatrical enterprises, this met with great protest on the part of religious organizations and sensitive citizens, and only on promising programs of a "harmless" nature were they allowed to continue. The word play was always avoided, and "Hamlet" and "Jane Shore," are described in their announcements as "moral and instructive tales." The first American play ever publicly acted in the colonies was by Thomas Godfrey, Jr., "Prince of Parthia," recently revived by the students of the University of Pennsylvania. It was produced in 1767 by Hallam's company at a new theatre built for them at South and Apollo Streets the previous year. The theatre was called the Southwark Theatre, and Hallam, with his "American Company," played during the winters of 1768, '69, '70, '72 and '73. It was destroyed by fire in May, 1782, but its walls remained to house a distillery until a few years ago.

Where the United Security Life and Trust Company building now stands was the Chestnut Street Theatre, opened in February, 1794. Joseph Jefferson the elder made his first Philadelphia appearance here in 1803. As often happened, the building fell victim to fire and was destroyed seventeen years later, but was immediately rebuilt and reopened with "The School for Scandal" in 1822. Here Booth made his appearance on February 17, 1823, unknown, and, it appears, with little success. There was a theatre on Locust Street (then Prune Street) between Fifth and Sixth in 1820, named the Winter Tivoli Theatre and later the City Theatre. The Walnut Street Theatre, the oldest in America at the present time, was fitted up in 1811 by Pepin and Breschard, who combined stage and ring performances in what they had built for a circus. This theatre had only a moderate success for a while, but its first season is memorable on account of the appearance on November 27 of "a young gentleman of this city" as Young Norval. This was no other than Master Edwin Forrest, who was born at 51 George Street, and was then fourteen years of age. It was here also that he made his last appearance in this city. Edmund Kean also played at this theatre.

Many important events and illustrious personages are connected with the old inns and not a little of early history was made in them. All the earliest innkeepers, we learn, were Friends, and the most   famous inn, the Blue Anchor Tavern, situated at what is now the northwest corner of Front and Dock Streets, is supposed to have been not only the first house erected in Philadelphia, but appropriately the first tavern. It was subsequently called Boatman and Call. The present Blue Anchor Tavern, near this spot, is according to the author the third of the name.

Other famous inns were the Penny Pot House, noted for its beer at a penny a pot; Clark's Inn, opposite the State House, famous for its cooked meat; the Indian King Tavern, on Market Street near Third Street, the meeting place of the "Junto Club," and the old Coffee House, situated at the corner of Second and Market Streets, where most of the early business of the city was transacted. An interesting and only survival of tavern days is to be seen in the remains of the Black Horse, on Second Street near Callowhill, which goes back to 1785. It is hardly recognizable as an inn on the front, but the arched entrance, which leads into the old yard, and the quaint old balcony still suggest the busy times of its early history. In 1845 it was still used by teamsters and farmers, "who used to take their beds and lodge on the floors."

DEED HELD IN THE FAMILY 163 YEARS FINALLY PRESENTED FOR RECORDING
(PUBLIC LEDGER, APRIL 2, 1924)

More than 160 years after its execution, a deed to property at the northeast corner of Fifth and Market Streets was placed on record in the office of the Recorder of Deeds.

The instrument, still in an excellent state of preservation, was brought to light when search was made of title to the present property, which includes not merely the corner but the lots 437 to 443 Market Street and 5 to 7 North Fifth Street. In tracing back the title it was found that no public record had ever been made of the conveyance of the northeast corner of "High and Fifth Streets," on May 9th, 1761, by Thomas Wharton, merchant, and his wife, Rachel, of the province of Pennsylvania to Jacob Barch shopkeeper. The lot in this conveyance was 30 feet 6 inches front by 100 feet deep. The consideration was 800 pounds which is approximately equivalent to $4,000.

The old deed reached the Recorder's office when members of the Graff family, in Kennett Square, recently sold the entire property for $300,000. They delivered the old Wharton-Barch deed, which had been in their family since their ancestor, Barch, had acquired the property nearly 163 years ago. The deed is a large and substantial sheet of fine old parchment, and bears in addition to the signatures of the granter and grantee those of the two witnesses.

The deed shows that the ground at the northeast corner of Fifth and High Streets was granted by the proprietary Government of Pennsylvania on July 12, 1736, to William Hudson. Upon his death Hudson left the property to two granddaughters, Rachel and Susanna Medcalf, the former of whom later was married to Thomas Wharton. Subsequently Susanna conveyed her one-half interest in the property to her sister, retaining a ground rent of £15 a year. This ground rent later was extinguished and the property was conveyed to Barch free from that encumbrance.

The entire group of properties in the recent sale is assessed at $240,000. Of this amount, $135,000 is the assessed value of the corner alone.

DOCK STREET

FROM *THE EVENING BULLETIN,* JANUARY 27, 1919.

BY PENN (WILLIAM PERRINE).

Within the old incorporated city of Philadelphia—the city-proper as it was once called—every street is laid out at right angles with another except one. The visitor who comes to Philadelphia for the first time and walks through the central district seldom fails to remark something about our topographical checkerboard. But if he goes down toward the river region of the Fifth Ward, he finds he seldom sees the one exception to the rectangular arrangement. This is Dock Street, which takes a curving or irregular course, from south east to northwest, between the vicinity of Spruce Street and comes to an end at Third Street, in front of the old Bank of the United States. It is not a handsome street; it is, old, full of crude commercial bustle in the hours of the day, and after night-fall or in the early hours of the night until the nocturnal preparations for the next day begin, it is almost wholly deserted. Wholesale traders in provisions and fruits and other such activities as mark the nearby parts of Front Street give the street its characteristic aspect. Perhaps not one Philadelphian in fifty, outside of those who are interested in the daily buying of produce, and fish and oysters, has occasion to go through it once in a year. But in some respects it is a peculiarly interesting bit of old Philadelphia in what it has been and in what it still suggests.

The area which Dock Street now covers was once a stream or indentation of the Delaware River and was sometimes described as a spacious cove or "harbor." The choice of the site of Philadelphia was doubtless due to the favorable impression which this stream or creek made upon the original planners of the city. The reason why the name of Dock Creek was given to it was that they expected it to become a capacious and permanent dock. The Indians, to whom it was a convenient inlet and outlet for their canoes, called it Coocaconoon, and doubtless its shore at the mouth had been places of rendezvous for them long before white men first came up the Delaware. It was familiar to the Swedes and other whites who were here before Penn took possession of his province, and near it was born one Drinker, whose life lasted more than a hundred years or until after the Revolution, Franklin once saying, when asked how long people lived in Philadelphia, that he could not tell until "old Drinker" died.

There were three branches of Dock Creek in the early days of the city. One of them extended northwestward from Third Street, between Walnut and Chestnut, and terminated between Fifth and Sixth above Market. Another extended from Third Street, between Walnut and Chestnut, to the vicinity of the present Athenaeum Building on Sixth Street, opposite Washington Square. Still another flowed southward toward the present Second Street Market and in the vicinity of Society Hill—a region where the Free Society of Traders had special privileges from the founder of the city for carrying on their commercial operations. At the mouth of the creek, or on its northern side, where the upper corners of Front and Dock Streets now are, the first tavern in Philadelphia was built—one of a row of houses known as "Budd's Long Row"—and it was here, when the tavern was not yet finished, that William Penn is supposed to have set foot for the first time on the soil of Philadelphia. This public house was called the Blue Anchor Inn; it was also known later on as the "Boatman and Call," and it was there that Penn established one of the two earliest public landings, the other being the Penny Pothouse at the foot of Vine Street. Until the other day a Blue Anchor sign with "1682" on it was affixed, as it had long been, to the premises at the northwest corner of Front and Dock, where many of the sons of bibulous cheer have delighted to refresh themselves, and near Walnut Street there has been for many years another Blue Anchor sign which would create the impression among the patrons of the tavern that Penn must have sailed up Dock Creek. As a matter of fact, the Blue Anchor at Front and Dock Streets marked the true place of the tradition; that is, it was there that the first Blue Anchor—the Blue Anchor of the landing—existed, although not the slightest trace of it is now to be found.

Along or near the shores of Dock Creek some of the most prosperous of the early citizens of Philadelphia erected their homes. The soil was grassy, the water clean, and in the summer time the view was pleasant. But trade and industry also promptly took advantage of the opportunities which this waterway gave them. Anthony Morris had a notable brewery there, and William Frampton another, and members of the Society of Friends had so little thought that there was anything undesirable in the making of good beer that Penn himself had a little brew-house on his manor estate in Bucks county. Tanneries and lumber yards were added to the industries of Dock Creek, and in the course of time it ceased to be a wholesome stream. This deterioration had probably begun when Penn came to the city for the second and last time. It was then that he lived in the Slate Roof House, on Second Street, where his American son was born, and from its windows he could easily see Dock Creek. Doubtless the barge in which he would sometimes come down the Delaware from Pennsbury to the city would be rowed into the creek and landing made at the Blue Anchor. Nor is it difficult to imagine how the first Edward Shippen, from the windows of his mansion on Second Street, looked out over the creek and enjoyed the breezes which came across it from the Delaware.

It was so difficult, in even the earliest years of the city, to keep Dock Creek clean that citizens who owned property along its shores or slopes were almost always urged to the duty of maintaining it in an orderly condition. The breweries and tanneries could not be prevented from discharging their refuse into the stream, and the residents made use of it as a receptacle for their household sweepings and rubbish. Forty years after Penn, in the city's charter, had named the Blue Anchor as a public landing, the creek was commonly charged with having become a nuisance. When Benjamin Franklin was a member of the Common Council of the city and active as editor of the Pennsylvania Gazette, he served on a committee which had been appointed to inquire into the question of what should be done with the creek. One of the earliest visitations of the yellow fever in Philadelphia was supposed to have had its origin in the filth of the stream. There seems to have been a conflict between public interests and private interests in the course of the inquiry, and some citizens subscribed money to clear out the creek, wall it, and improve the sewers which led into it, but this was not in accord with the official view, and the creek continued to be regarded as a nuisance to public cleanliness and health.

But the land at and about the original Blue Anchor Tavern from the time of George Guest, who was the first of the landlords at that abode of hospitality and refreshment, was a favorite place for the comings and goings of ship captains, traders and other enterprising citizens of Philadelphia in its infancy. The Water Bailiff of the harbor could be found there; boats carried passengers from its wharf to other points on the Delaware, or to Windmill Island, or to ships that were anchored in the stream; and for more than two centuries men have made the cannikin clink there, although in modern times they have done so in chiefly the plain way of tippling and certainly without that sturdy and large capacity for punch which marked the daily habits of the patrons of the Blue Anchor. The tradition that William Penn had his first glass of ale there after he came ashore did not serve to injure either his public or his private reputation in the slightest degree among even the most pious or the most censorious of Philadelphians; and indeed the Blue Anchor, as the Public Landing, was related to the municipality itself. What would be the astonishment of George Guest, the landlord, who was a member of the Society of Friends, and of the great founder of the city, if they could now come back and contemplate not alone the disappearance of Dock Creek, but the preparation for the extinction of all the taverns in Philadelphia, such places to them having been essential works of rational pleasure and prime necessity.

In the region where the creek crossed Third Street, halfway below Chestnut Street, there was at one time, or when the main portion of the population of the town lived on or near Front Street and Second, a mansion which was regarded as an example of opulent life. With its grounds and garden it was known as Clarke Hall, the name having been derived from William Clarke, who was a rich member of the bar and who built the house probably not long before Penn's second and final visit to Philadelphia. It occupied the lot on which the Mariner and Merchant Building of the Stephen Girard Estate now stands, and it was viewed by the people at the close of the seventeenth century as an evidence of Clarke's prosperity and importance. For a while it was occupied by James Logan, John Evans, Roger Monpesson and William Penn, Jr., in common. Evans was appointed as Governor, although he was not more than twenty-six years old, and the son of the Founder was still younger; and they gave great scandal by going on an all-night spree at a public house in Pewter Platter Alley and in beating the watchman who quelled the tumult. Clarke Hall must have been as pleasant a place as could then be found in Philadelphia for merry gentlemen who wanted to rest up quietly or to entertain their friends in seclusion. Not only was the brick house perhaps the largest in the city, but the garden was modestly laid out in a style which had been much imitated in England after the advent there of the Prince of Orange as William the Second. There were trees and plants which seemed to have given a slight suggestion of a bit of Dutch landscape, and the ground sloped down gently with the effect of a terrace to the waters of Dock Creek, seemingly at the site of the edifice which is now known as the Girard National Bank. This was built for the first Bank of the United States when Washington was President and when Clarke Hall, then nearly a hundred years old, was used as a United States Government office. Half a century after the Bank of the United States was opened, the press which printed the Evening Bulletin, was situated in the soil where Dock Creek had once flowed along the edge of the grounds of Clarke Hall.

In the early days of the city, when Captain Kidd and other freebooters in the West Indies and along the American coast were well known, it was not uncommon for those of them who were not under the ban of the law to make their appearance on the river-front when seeking diversion. King Street, which afterward became Water Street, and the vicinity of Dock Street, were full of hospitable taverns and coffee houses for seafaring men. It was said that one of the most famous of pirates, the enterprising and fearless Teach, known everywhere as "Blackbeard" and not yet forgotten as such, was at times a familiar figure in these resorts, and, therefore, almost undoubtedly he was also a denizen of the Blue Anchor. On Second Street, in after years, where the waters of Little Dock Creek crossed Spruce Street in the direction of Society Hill, Captain Benjamin Loxley had his abode in what was long known as the Loxley House, and it was there that the Revolutionary legend of Lydia Darragh and the British officers and her journey of warning to the outposts of the Continental army near Whitemarsh had its initial scenario. Nearby was situated, on Second Street, the Bethsheba Bower and Bath, and it is to be supposed that the waters of this resort and spring were not unconnected with those of Little Dock Creek.

What was considered as one of the great improvements after the Revolution took place when all of the discontents and agitations of more than half a century over Dock Creek came at last to a head, and it was decided that the stream should cease to exist. It had become stagnant and ill smelling; there was no doubt that it had often bred pestilential disease, and lawless characters found places on its banks for hiding from constables and watchmen, while tipsy men at night sometimes fell into the foul water. After much controversy over the question as to what should be the policy of the city in dealing with the nuisance, recourse was had to the Legislature for relief. It appears, however, that a large proportion of conservative citizens did not favor such action, and especially the measure which the friends of public improvement finally agreed upon. This was nothing less than the abandonment of the creek and the creation, in its place, of a street or avenue.

It was provided that the stream should be confined within stone walls and arched with substantial brick and that the top of the upper part of the creek should be filled in with earth or dirt so as to enable a level of a street to be formed. This new street extended as far as the drawbridge at Front Street and in later years the portion of the creek between Front Street and the Delaware was included in the operation. Everything was so changed for the better with marts and shops and sidewalks and a broad highway that public sentiment came to be loud in its approval. A quarter of a century afterward Dr. James Mease, who was a resident of the neighborhood, congratulated his fellow citizens on the fine improvement when he wrote his "Picture of Philadelphia," and on the displacement which had been effected in much vice, poverty and filth.

Dock Street it then became, and so it has been to this day. Still some of the waters of the creek could be seen in the big archway, or culvert, at the outlet, and at one time, after the Bank of Stephen Girard had replaced the Bank of the United States, on Third Street, a story was told of a plot that was said to have been formed by some desperadoes to the end of kidnapping Girard by going through the archway in a boat, excavating a way into the Bank, seizing him and hurrying him into their little craft and thence down to the Delaware, where he would be put on board ship and held for a ransom. In the course of time the erection of the Stock Exchange, at the upper end of Dock Street, gave the street great distinction, and there, in connection with the omnibuses which began or ended their routes at the Exchange or at the Post-office on the opposite side, it became the chief point of the active life of the city proper, Dock Ward once comprising all the area adjacent to the creek, and the greater part of the present Fifth Ward.

At one time, too, most of the newspaper offices and printeries were nearby; even now men who are still active in journalism can readily recall the existence of a major portion of the Philadelphia press at or near Dock Street or within a stone's throw of it. Oysters and fish at its foot had been there from the days when it was a creek, and in later times these and the produce of the "commission merchant" overshadowed everything else. In the days when the Hibernia Fire Company No. 1 was situated at Pear and Evelina Streets, its followers would sometimes meet their aggressive enemies, like those of the Good Intent or the Hope, on the spacious arena which Dock Street afforded for a strategic fight to a finish; and on election nights, when big bonfires were kept agoing until the early hours of the next morning, "gangs" would seize furniture wagons or other such vehicles that were tied up along the curb of the warehouse for the night. Filling a wagon with boxes, crates and barrels, the rowdies would rush it to a bonfire and burn wagon and all in either defiance of the police or with their good-natured connivance at the exploit.

The last time when Dock Street and the site of the old Blue Anchor Tavern were highly conspicuous in the public eye—although it was not wholly forgotten when the Founder's Week celebration took place more than ten years ago—was on the occasion of the Bi-Centennial celebration in the autumn of 1882, when Samuel G. King was Mayor. The series of commemorative events, lasting for several days, began with the ceremonies at the foot of Dock Street in honor of the landing of the Founder—a scene which was not unlike the Mardi Gras custom at New Orleans when the Mayor and the rest of the city government go to the foot of Canal Street, welcome Rex in his supreme role and sovereignty as King of the Carnival, and tender him the keys of the city. What a time there was that morning when the modern "Welcome" appeared in the Delaware with William Penn on board and "Commodore" James M. Ferguson, one of the most popular of printers and men-about-town, came into view as commander of the fleet, and all hands got ashore at Dock Street amidst a crush of Swedes, Dutchmen, Quakers and Indians—most of them the products of the picturesque art of Van Horn as a costumer— and the mighty Tammanend or Tammany coming forward on behalf of the red men to hold out the hand of peace to the great pale-face brother! How the "big spring" in the Blue Anchor Tavern flowed as probably it never did before under the ancient roof-tree, and certainly not since under the modern one! How Governor Hoyt, standing at the point where the great Quaker is supposed to have made his landing, and a dense crowd of citizens were almost swept off their feet in the midst of the glorious excitement and enthusiasm as the aborigines and pioneers shouted their greetings, and the Founder was put into the line of the procession, and the archway of the old Delaware Avenue Market House resounded to the echoes of the joyous music, while the guns of the fleet in the harbor roared and boomed!

RIDGE ROAD
By Miss Jane Campbell

Extending from Montgomery Avenue north almost to Laurel Hill, on either side of Ridge Road were two farms, owned respectively by William Warner and Jacob Esher. Two children of these farmers, Henry Warner and Rebecca Esher, played hide and seek in the hay mounds and wove daisy chains together. Their courtship terminated in a happy marriage, which ended after their golden anniversary had been celebrated, and now they lie side by side in Laurel Hill overlooking the scenes of their childhood's days and lovers' dreams. It is because of this courtship and this marriage that I am here today, for they were my paternal grandparents.

Ridge Road—along most of its city course we usually call it Ridge Avenue—is a mart, a popular promenade, and a highway, in part urban, in part suburban and in part rural. It is one of the oldest of the "great roads," as they once were known, that led out from Philadelphia into the inland, and it is the only road, or avenue, if we except Passyunk and Grays Ferry, that touches the boundary line of the old city proper. It has long been one of the most important as a "short cut" in our rectangular system of streets, as Moyamensing, Woodland, Lancaster and Germantown also are, and beyond our city it passes into two of our counties through some of the most delightful landscapes in Eastern Pennsylvania. Almost everywhere along it may be traced some landmark or memory of the Indians of Tammany or Tedyuscung, of the Welsh Quakers, of the colonists of the Revolution, of the German settlers in not only the eighteenth, but the seventeenth century, and of the thrifty and substantial population which spread through either side of it in what was once the District of Spring Garden and Penn Township.

Even a stranger, when passing over it in the city, may easily see that it was not expressly designed for the municipality. Its turns and bends every now and then readily denote its original use as a country road. Its name betokens the high backbone, as it were, of the land which separates the valley of the Schuylkill from the valley of the Wissahickon, and even to this day there are some Philadelphians who keep up the habit of calling it the "Ridge Road." For mile after mile it consists of almost continuous rows of retail stores or shops, in which usually a small or moderate business is done and in most of which the storekeeper or shopman has dwelling or living quarters for himself or his family. It is a busy rather than a bustling thoroughfare, is well ordered rather than spick and span, and is marked for the most part by a simple, unaffected respectability. I do not know of any highway of its length and type which has a higher average of sobriety and decency in its habits and its habitat, despite a good deal of the flotsam and jetsam of town life that flows through it. In nowise is it a sensational or a showy street, but in most of its atmosphere there is something which suggests an honest one.

The Ridge Road or turnpike that ascends from the Wissahickon to the region behind Manayunk, and thence into Roxborough, and on to Manatawna and Barren Hill, and to the White Marsh country and over to Norristown, and thence up to the Perkiomen, is pleasant and peaceful in its domestic comfort. Some touch of ancient simplicity or historic quaintness may be noted there time and again. A good American sometimes feels, when going over it and seeing Valley Forge in the distance, as he does when he goes out on the road that leads from Boston to Lexington and Concord. Old Charles Thomson Jones, whose paternal grandfather was the Rev. David Jones, the "Fighting Parson" of the Revolution, used to say that no one could live on the Ridge from boyhood without becoming a sound American, because the battle of Germantown and the march to Valley Forge would be sure to become a part of his very being. In recent years Roxborough has largely been taken out of the sort of semi-isolation in which it once existed by reason of the peculiarities of its topography, and although it is in need of more modern transit, it is now comparatively easy of access, and electric service has conquered the former terrors of its steep approaches. It has gradually become much more urban, but it still retains some of the old-fashioned American rural habits that have been inherited in not a few of its thrifty homes.

HAPPENINGS IN YE OLDE PHILADELPHIA

In the city the shops and the shoppers, and the double tracks for the trolley cars, and the crowds of big trucks and wagons that go to or from Manayunk or Conshohocken often make Ridge Avenue look too narrow for its business and traffic. If we should ever have a Baron Haussman here to do what was done in Paris, he would make Ridge Avenue a hundred feet wide. Some day it may figure largely, too, in our schemes of transit as well as those processes of reconstruction which are followed by adornment. Directly upon it, that is in the city, churches of importance have always been few, and, for that matter, so have important houses of amusement. The National Theatre, at the Tenth and Callowhill Streets intersection, has become a thing of the past, and Israel Fleishman's Park, at the Fairmount Avenue intersection—it was built by him more than a quarter of a century ago in high expectation—never could quite get its roots into the soil. But for many years in the Twenty-fourth and Columbia Avenue quarter the Philadelphia Base Ball Club provided an abundance of good sport on the grounds which had once been the Doerr horse market, although poor Harry Wright, who had been so famous in Cincinnati and in Boston, labored in vain to repeat here his great achievements as one of the cleanest and manliest of sportsmen of his time. Then, too, the simple joys of the catfish and waffle suppers in the little inns and wayside houses near "the Falls" have become almost archaic. Even Laurel Hill and the rest of the cemetery region to which countless funerals along "the Ridge" have passed for more than two generations, is no longer the area of silent seclusion it once was, while the advance of population everywhere along the boundary line of the East Park is sometimes suggestive of the value of extending the domain at some points into new territory. Moreover, the mill district of the Dobsons and the rest of the captains of industry is no longer so cheerless as it used to be. One may now ride past them on the old road without feeling that sort of dreariness which depresses him when he is in the midst of the Down East severeness of Fall River.

But I must pause in recounting these rather random impressions and reflections of my own and recur for a moment to the little paper of the Monday Morning Class, which serves as our text today. As its author remarks, the most famous and enduring landmark along Ridge Road—although it ought not to be so enduring that provision may not be made some day for its removal, at least, in part—is Girard College, which was dedicated seventy years ago on what had been the Peale Hall farm in a quiet region of farms and villages of the Penn Township far beyond the city's frontier. A study of this alone would give rise to not a few curious, entertaining, and also practical sources of local knowledge, such as the ladies of the Current Events Class would appreciate and enjoy, for it is by knowing the past, and knowing it by the small as well as the great affairs of life that they may understand better both the present and the future. For example, if in the studies of Ridge Avenue they were to picture what it was in its early days as a turnpike at the point where it begins at Ninth and Vine Streets, and where Oliver Evans had his Mars Iron Works, they would find their inquiries into the life of that Quaker inventor, promoter and maitre de forge, carrying them into various fields of city lore. Or again, a few yards further on, where the Fairmount Fire Company had its origin among the butchers of Spring Garden when that district was still young, and where, in later days, David M. Lyle, the most noted of the Chiefs of the Volunteer Fire Department, made his headquarters—for as the church is the bride of the priest, so was "the company" to him—the haunts, and habits, and exploits of the "Fairies" from the days of "Mose" and "Jakie" to the last of the red shirts, would furnish many a clue to the changes and the peculiarities that have come about in that quarter.

During Franklin's time the Quakers owned a tract of land located on what is now Ridge Avenue and Thirteenth Street. A place for pasturage for the Quakers who came from outlying points to attend meeting. Considered by all the inhabitants as a Common.

Here it was that Franklin accompanied by his son William, came to fly a kite, previous to a threatening storm. A kite-flying that was chronicled in the history of the world.

VINE STREET
FROM *THE EVENING BULLETIN*, NOVEMBER 1, 1923

Probably no point in Philadelphia has drawn the fire of ministerial denunciation so heavily as did Vine Street, between Franklin and Eighth, in the latter eighties and the early nineties of the past century. Pulpiteers mustered their most stirring invective in picturing Applegate's carrousel, at the northwest corner of Franklin and Vine, as a place of sin and temptation out-rivaling Sodom and Gomorrah, and no parental injunction was so strongly impressed upon the youth of respectable households as the admonition to shun this spot as a plague. Applegate, by the way, was also the proprietor of noted photographic establishments, one on Eighth Street nearby and another in Atlantic City when the tintype was at the height of its popularity, and it is amusing today, when bathing beauties display their physical charms so widely on the printed page, to recall the days when women, covered from neck to ankle in the voluminous bathing suits of the period, thought it quite daring to have their pictures taken in that garb at the shore.

The Lyceum Theatre, as a home of burlesque when tights were still considered shocking,—though they would now be regarded as the least objectionable feature of the performances staged—made the south side of Vine Street here impassable to moralists who wished to keep their skirts free from the contagion of vice. Jerry Donoghue's saloon, a popular rendezvous for sporting men of all sorts—with its side room fitted up like a Pullman palace car—was another target for critics of the neighborhood.

This condition, however, had not been of long standing. Previously the section about Franklin Square had been a quiet residential one. Indeed until about 1880 the First Moravian Church stood at Franklin and Wood Streets, and the north side of Vine, below Eighth, was graced by the beautiful Episcopal church of St. Philip's, built in 1841, and afterwards located on Spring Garden Street, below Broad, before removal to West Philadelphia. The same site, according to Watson, had previously been occupied by an old tavern, of wood and red painted, which had served as a busy rendezvous for enlistments during the Revolution and the succeeding Indian wars, afterwards becoming a headquarters for drovers when Franklin Square and the territory around it were still extensive green commons upon which sheep and cattle grazed.

The worst days of Eighth and Vine Streets were over by 1888, when the Brooks high license act and the vigorous enforcement of the dictum "Beer and music don't mix" by Stokley under the Fitler administration put an end to the "free and easies" which radiated from the intersection, dives which even the lowest of the present day "cabarets" do not approach in viciousness.

At the northwest corner of Eighth Street, in the large second floor hall which had frequently been the scene of boxing bouts under the supervision of "Johnny" Clark, who kept a saloon below and who at one time managed the Lyceum, the Salvation Army made its advance base for rescue operations among the erring and fallen, a work in which the Galilee Mission nearby actively participated. Across the street, at 810, William Boothby laid the foundation of a fortune in an oyster house noted for the excellence of its viands. There has been little change in the block during the past generation. There are the same old pawnshops, the same Turkish bath house, the same shabby "hotels" and restaurants now flaunting such up-to-date names as "The New Bridge" and "The Pershing," and the pavements swarm with the same old down-and-outers, ready to tell, at the slightest encouragement, the same old tale which has so often in the past proved serviceable in extracting dimes from sympathetic listeners "to buy a cup of coffee."

A similar atmosphere pervades the next block of Vine Street, though it takes on something of the nature of a back eddy, the main current being diverted by the Ridge, which at its beginning is largely monopolized by second hand furniture and old clothes men, a newcomer in the region being that paradoxical "institution," the Hobo College. A century ago the intersection was distinguished as the site of the Mars Iron Works, owned by Oliver Evans, who here probably— though he was interested in like enterprises elsewhere in the city— constructed his curious dredging machine, the Oruktor Amphibolis, which created quite a sensation on the day when it trundled out Market Street from Centre Square and into the Schuylkill.

Just above at a later day, Arthur Chambers kept a public house which, as "The Champion's Rest," was the favorite resort of the devotees of Fistiana. On the north side of Vine Street nearby for many years was the shop of an old German watchmaker named Wolf, one of whose sons had more than local repute as a wrestler.

From Tenth Street westward Vine Street was, not so many years ago, lined for the most part with three-story brick houses, with the inevitable white marble steps and trimmings, and occupied by substantial families. Like Arch Street, however, it was disrupted as a domestic habitat by the blighting effect of the Reading viaduct. At the northwest corner of Tenth Street, Dr. Eliza Pettingill lived for many years, and built up a practice, even before the prejudice against women physicians had been entirely worn away. As a young man, the late Judge Morris Dallett lived at No. 1010 with his widowed mother. Rooming houses, whose occupants comprise a number of foreign strains, including Armenians and Greeks, now predominate to the Reading crossing.

From Twelfth westward to the very shadow of Broad Street lies the motion picture exhibitors' rialto, blazing with strikingly colored posters of the latest features. Until noon, the thoroughfare is almost deserted. Then the proprietors of the moving picture palaces arrive to shop for the next attractions. In their talk one may find the explanation of that oft-repeated interrogation, "What's wrong with the movies?" Each exhibitor, as he returns his reels, makes a report of how the film "took" with his audiences. That is the way Main Street makes its choice of stars and stories, for the motion picture people take these reports very seriously, and when the mass of opinions is thoroughly digested, the conclusions drawn are forwarded to Hollywood for guidance in the preparation of the next releases.

HAPPENINGS IN YE OLDE PHILADELPHIA

The two eastern corners of Broad Street are familiar to the present generation, one as the site of the Catholic High School and the other, until the recent erection of a loft building, used for years as a lumber yard, justly regarded as an anachronism on a corner so prominent in the central section, and constituting a dangerous fire hazard.

Just above Vine, on the west side of the street, Industrial Hall was long a landmark on the site on which the new home of the Elks is rising. In the auditorium on the second floor, which also contained a popular banquet hall, was held many a local political convention, some quite tempestuous. In the hall on the first floor, in latter days used as Nicholas' Horse Bazaar, were held a variety of exhibitions, such as prize fights, in one of which Kid McCoy received a lacing at the hands of Rid Carter. Theatrical performaces, includes three in which the eccentric "Count" Johannes did Hamlet behind a net stretched at the footlights to intercept the expected barrage of vegetables and eggs beyond their prime; cycling contests, walking matches and the like, dot the record of this spot.

At Vine Street, too, the first out-croppings of Automobile Row, which now extends far along Broad Street, made their appearance, and much of the block between Broad and Fifteenth Streets is now given over to accessory shops. Here dwellings long ago disappeared. Indeed business had made considerable inroads up to and beyond Seventeenth Street, where a fine row of marble-faced and brownstone fronts—one of the latter housing a bureau of the Department of Welfare—still defy its advance. At the southeast corner of Sixteenth Street Robert C. Davis, whose skill in analyzing handwriting made him a figure in many a sensational trial, had his drug store, while across the way was Christian Einseler's bakery, a popular resort for superior pastry and ice cream.

Emerging at Eighteenth Street into Logan Square—famous as the site of the Great Sanitary Fair during the Civil War and previously a commons which was the scene of many a hanging—a Philadelphian returning after an absence of ten or twelve years would be completely at sea, were it not for the continued presence of the Cathedral, the Wills Eye Hospital and the Academy of Natural Sciences on its further borders. The Square is now a Circle, and the precise lines of its formal landscaping strike strangely upon eyes accustomed to its former simplicity as a preserve of grass and old shade, broken only by the tulip bed which bisected "Jim McNichol's front yard" from east to west. The residence of that Napoleon of local politics, together with that of his friendly enemy, the late Mayor Blankenburg, and the homes of Martin Malony, of the Van Dusens, the Claghornes, the Smuckers, the Bonbrights, the Dunglisons, the Philbins and many another family of substance, have disappeared in the extension of the Square westward to Twentieth Street.

On Vine Street similar destruction has been visited upon the mansions which stood on the site prepared for the Convention Hall that is to be and of the Public Library, now advanced to a stage giving some idea of its impressive, yet not severe, dignity. Possibly the most distinguished resident of the 1800 block was the late William Sellers at No. 1819. Ex-Congressman J. Washington Logue lived around the corner at 308 North Eighteenth Street in his youth and later occupied a house in the 1900 block on Vine, which numbered among its residents such men as R. L. Brownfield, a Delaware Avenue commission merchant; Dr. Thornton Barnes, E. K. Nichols, well known at the bar; William C. Carrick, the cracker man; W. H. Palmer, another prosperous baker; S. V. R. Hill, railroad freight agent, and Gustavus C. Ralston, well-to-do fish merchant.

After the razing of these properties for Parkway purposes, it will be recalled that the lot was hurriedly graded for the erection of the great Tabernacle in which Billy Sunday exhorted sinners to hit the Sawdust Trail.

West of Twentieth Street, the industrial district along the Schuylkill has made encroachments here and there which have served to blight the domestic atmosphere of the street, though the residents nearest the course of the invasion, in the section between Twenty-second and Twenty-third Streets, are putting up a valiant fight. Here the well-scrubbed white marble steps and attempts to keep a spark of life in a few grass plots and stunted trees stand out as symbols of the redemption that yet may come when the Parkway fulfills the promise of its projectors and a start is made on the Schuylkill Embankment. Perhaps the headquarters of the Municipal Court, shorn of the extravagant features which have halted the project, and the Administration Building of The Board of Public Education will be the first physical evidence of the regeneration of Vine Street, west of Logan Square.

CALLOWHILL STREET
FROM THE EVENING BULLETIN, SEPTEMBER 14, 1925

Callowhill Street, or "Callow Hill," as it used to be called— although it was understood it bore the name of William Penn's second wife, Hannah Callowhill—has two wide places, one east of Second and the other west of Fourth Street, which occasionally arouse curiosity as to their original use.

In the case of the latter, which extends from Fourth to Marshall Street, and which makes the street wider than at any other part of its run from river to river, if the market houses and street sheds of old Philadelphia, and such as we still have on Second Street, are kept in mind, it is not hard to determine why this great open plaza was provided. Spring Garden Street, Girard Avenue, South Eleventh and lower Bainbridge Streets have similar spaces showing where market places formerly furnished neighborhood shopping centres.

But in the case of the smaller plaza, east of Second, at the point where New Market Street crosses, it is not so easy to determine just why the deep inset in the curb line of the northwest corner occurs. Only one corner of this intersection is set back and from its appearance it is hard to tell whether that was the desire of the owners of the corner properties or the design of the city surveyors at some time past.

That plaza, small as it is, however, is the last landmark of one of the oldest markets in Philadelphia and probably the first to be established north of the city line at Vine Street. By right of gift it might have been the first Penn Square. There, at one time, was a larger square, forming the shopping centre of "the town of Callow Hill."

Here and there in local histories of the Colonial and Revolutionary days one finds passing mention of this "town," which deserves to be counted as one of the city's earliest and nearest suburbs. Prior to the Revolution much of the land in that part of the Northern Liberties was owned by the Penns, and Thomas Penn, son of William Penn and Hannah Callowhill Penn, was particularly concerned with selling off the lots around Front and Callowhill. That they were choice lots goes without saying. They were the first across the city line, near the water front and, with the road improvements promised, easy of access from all parts of the old city. Furthermore the proprietors had provided for what was then a good-sized market square or plaza at the point where a new thoroughfare, New Market Street, was to cross Callowhill, between

Front and Second. By the time of the Revolution a settlement had grown up around this square, that, in popular parlance, although not officially so designated, was known as "the town of Callow Hill" and the "town" extended from Pegg's Run, about where Willow Street now crosses, to Vine Street, and from Front Street west to the Old York Road, on the line of Fourth Street.

At the northeast corner of Front and Callowhill there is still standing an old residence that is a reminder of this Colonial suburb. Used now for business, and shabby and worn with age, the three-story red and black brick structure, half-screened in front by the Frankford elevated, shows, in its construction and design, that it was once a notable residence. How old it is no one seems to know, although by the style of architecture, the method of construction and its conformity to the classic design of other Colonial mansions in Philadelphia, there is little difficulty in classifying its period.

Here, a century ago, dwelt the Brittons, a well-to-do family of social connections. Next door there then dwelt the Dewees and, a short while after the close of the Revolution, Captain Charles Biddle was one of the residents of Callowhill. The property, which in 1832 passed into the possession of Samuel Stevenson, the grocer, had been conveyed to the Brittons, on the eve of the Revolution, by the Penns shortly before the confiscation of their lands by the State.

Along Callowhill, west of Front, on the north side of the way, there also are some other examples of old-time Philadelphia dwellings, smaller in size, but showing almost equal marks of age, although, for the most part, the structures round about are of a later date. In surveying the old landmarks of this section, one has to keep in mind the fact that, in July, 1850, it was swept by one of the greatest fires Philadelphia has ever known, a conflagration that began in a warehouse on Water Street below Vine, filled with hay and molasses and saltpetre and brimstone, and which spread west to Second Street, north to Callowhill and east to the river before it was checked, and which brought Newark and New York firemen on the scene. How small and how numerous were the buildings then about the old Callowhill Street Market Place can be judged from the record that between Vine and Callowhill and Delaware Avenue and Second Street two hundred and eleven houses were burned.

The selling of lots, the grading of streets and the building of houses in this section had preceded the Revolution. In 1770 a petition addressed to the Courts, asking for the opening of Callowhill Street, from Fourth to Front, speaks of the number of residents thereon. It was still on the edge of open country. Campingtown, the military camp, was just across Pegg's Run. It was largely settled by Germans, as shown by the remark of one of the Colonists that when he took Baron Steuben to "Callow Hill," during the Revolution, the Baron thought he was back in his native land.

Presumably the market square provided by the sons of the Founder proved serviceable, for before the Revolution was over a number of the residents of the neighborhood asked the permission of the Legislature to provide a permanent market house or houses thereon. In the petition for the right to erect these buildings and rent the stalls, the applicants recited how shipbuilding and commerce and other occupations had flourished in "the place called Callowhill;" how a new ferry had been started at the foot of the street and how Jersey's farmers had found it a convenient crossing. So they asked, and secured, the right to erect a market house, of four sections, with the understanding that this square was to remain "forever" as a public market place, and that when the subscribers to the building program had been reimbursed, with interest, for their civic contribution, the property was to pass to the ownership of the local authorities.

Isaac Coates, of the Coates family after whom Coates Street, now Fairmount Avenue, was named, David Rose, George Forepaugh, George Leib, Peter Brown and John Britton were named as Superintendents of the Market, which, for some unknown reason, was named "The Norwich Market." In the archives of the Historical Society of Pennsylvania there is the old receipt book of that market company in which one can see how faithfully, year after year, for more than two generations, the accounts of the company were kept. On the plaza provided by the Penns its subscribers built the four houses, "covered with cedar shingles and tiles," as stipulated in the enabling act, with Callowhill and New Market Streets cutting through between the buildings and open spaces of twenty feet kept on each side between the markets and the adjoining properties. Business, however, was not as good as expected at the start and, as evidence of the pull of the promoters, there is the strange statute of March 18th, 1789, which imposed a penalty on any one who tried to peddle fruit or poultry, meat or butter and eggs, from door to door anywhere in the Liberties, or who sought to sell food of any kind, save vegetables, outside the market. Any one so doing had to pay double the amount received for the sale, one half of which went to the Superintendents of the market and the other half to the private prosecutor.

Even with this monopolistic control, the market did not pay and finally the stockholders were glad to sell out to the municipal authorities. For many years, however, the market square furnished a local business centre for the Northern Liberties and was partly the reason for the presence in that section of the city of a number of old inns and taverns like the White Horse, the Black Horse, the Bald Eagle, the Red Lion and the Camel, and for the early extension of Second Street's shopping centre northward to the city line at Vine.

Meanwhile, growing steadily to the West, the Liberties, with Callowhill as one of the main thoroughfares, found need of other markets and even the old privilege which the farmers had of parking their market wagons on north Second Street did not serve. A little more than a century ago, another market on Callowhill Street came into existence, almost over night, in the larger open space left west of Fourth Street.

The little square to the east continued to decline in importance, although within the memory of the present generation it has come to new import as one of the chief wholesale food markets of the city, that entire district about the plaza at New Market and Callowhill, being given over now almost entirely to the sale and handling of foodstuffs. At the back of one of the buildings, on the southwest corner, one may note, in the apparent corner placement of the structure in the rear, how the square probably extended in that direction in times past, while the opposite corner, now used again for market purposes, was once the home of the Gaul Brewery and previously had been the property of the Hares. Later it became the first of the Betz breweries and the place where that enterprising resident of old Callowhill laid the foundation for his fortune.

BETHLEHEM PIKE
FROM *THE PHILADELPHIA INQUIRER*

The Bethlehem Pike is probably the oldest road in the country, for it antedates the discovery of America. When William Penn came to Pennsylvania the primeval wilderness lay before him, unmarked save by the foot of the savage. But the savages had already laid out certain trails, not from Philadelphia, then unborn, but from the tidewater to the North and West. The North route was known as the "Minsi Trail," trodden out of the forest along the waterways of the Wissahickon, the Saucon and the Lehigh.

It was along this trail, now become a well-defined path, that David Nitschman and his party came on foot to Bethlehem and Nazareth, in December of 1740, the servants leading pack-horses with all the worldly goods of the little group strapped upon their backs. In December, 1741, a second party joined the first, traveling over the same road. The second party included Count Zinzendorf and his suite, who visited the pioneers in the log cabin on the banks of the Monocacy, and on Christmas Eve conducted the famous love-feast service which christened the new settlement "Bethlehem."

With the rise in the number of settlements along this route came a constantly increasing use of the road. From an indefinite Indian trail it became a Colonial highway leading from the capital to the frontier, and was known as the "King's Road."

Over this road the first trip by "stage wagon" was made by George Klein on September 10, 1763. After that he ran regularly between Bethlehem and Philadelphia, making the round trip weekly.

He started on Monday mornings from the Sun Inn, Bethlehem, and on his return he set out from the "King of Prussia Inn," Race Street, Philadelphia, on Thursdays. The "King of Prussia" was at Second and Race Streets, not far from Benjamin Franklin's printing shop, and the Bethlehem stage rattled away at a very early hour, turning up Front Street, then a beautiful river road. Crossing Poole's bridge over Pegg's Run, it went on by Isaac Norris' country house and garden.

Crossing the Northern Liberties, as the settled country north of the city was then called, the little hamlet of Rising Sun was reached, where the Old York Road branched off. Legend says that at this cross-roads, Tammany, the great Indian chief, presented all lands within vision to the young Germans, of whom his tribe had become very fond. The gift was from the tribe "until the Great Spirit shall call them to the 'Eternal Wilderness.'" As the three stood there concluding this arrangement the sun rose superbly and the young men named the spot "Aufgehende Sonne" or Rising Sun. The inn of that name was opened in 1746.

From this inn the stage went to Stenton, the home of James Logan, secretary of William Penn. Beyond Stenton lay Germantown, boasting one long street, then Main Street, now Germantown Avenue. Up through Market Street and past Pastorius' Green Tree Tavern, the road stretched away to the north. Green Tree Tavern was built in 1748 by Daniel Pastorius, and old-time driving and sleighing parties gathered there for the meals which made the hostelry famous.

At the foot of the long hill near the beginning of the present pike, is the Wheel Pump Inn, where British officers frequently gathered in the days when their army faced the Colonials at Whitemarsh. Further on is Church Lane, leading up to Old St. Thomas' Church. The hill on which this church stands was one of the hills in the Whitemarsh Valley where Washington held Howe at bay, and became famous in history as Church Hill.

This entire section is filled with memories and souvenirs of the patriot army, which encamped here until December 11, 1777, when Washington moved on to Valley Forge. The story of Lydia Darragh is a typical anecdote brought down from the early dwellers in Whitemarsh. Lydia lived in Philadelphia, and on the evening of December 2, 1777, a group of British officers used her house for a consultation. She hid in a closet and overheard the details of their plan for a surprise attack on Washington's army. Lydia obtained a pass out of the city to visit a flour mill at Frankford. She went to the mill, but hurried thence on to Rising Sun Tavern, where General Boudinot was dining. Fearful of spies, she did not try to speak with the general, but secretly passed him her old needlebook, in which she placed a piece of paper containing her information. Boudinot realized its importance and hurried with it to Washington. When Howe advanced according to plan, he found effectual preparations against him and was compelled to fall back on Chestnut Hill.

Fort Washington lies just around the hill from Camp Hill, and the earthworks of 1777 can still be distinguished along Fort Hill. The road runs on to Ambler. Beyond, near Springhouse, is the Foulke mansion at Penlynn, where Sally Wister wrote her vivacious journal.

A few miles beyond is Montgomery Square, originally called "Baptist Meeting." Montgomeryville, beyond Montgomery Square, possesses the Walker Inn, a house more than a century old.

The list of old stage stations gives "Benjamin Davis" as the next stop. The weather-beaten old tavern here has helped to make history. During the Fries Rebellion in 1709, when Bucks to Northampton and adjacent counties were completely disorganized by the excitement stirred up by John Fries in opposition to the house tax law, this tavern was the headquarters for the militia.

From here the pike crosses the upper corner of Hilltown and enters Rockhill township, where the combined armies of Pennsylvania and New Jersey militia in 1799 listened to Judge Richard Peters, a member of the Colonial Assembly, who accompanied them to rule on legal questions which might arise. At Sellers' Tavern, now Sellersville, they camped. This was a place of considerable importance, and Samuel Sellers, who established the tavern, was the leading citizen and aided in the search for Fries, leader of the rebellion.

As the stage driver of old drew near the end of his journey, he whipped up his horses and rounded the end of South Mountain, crossing the stone bridge over the Saucon at Iron Hill. The Bethlehem Ferry now lay before him, a difficult matter in unfavorable weather. But the Moravian brethren who operated the ferry were brawny of arm and strong of back and generally contrived to get coach and horses and passengers safely to the other side. The run was finally completed with a flourish at the Sun Inn, on Bethlehem's main street.

During the Revolution the pike and the ferry saw busy times, for Bethlehem was crowded with the delegates to Congress, with officers and civilians, with soldiers and prisoners of war, and the heavy baggage and wounded of the army. The Marquis de LaFayette arrived this way by carriage from Bristol in September, 1777, and drove directly to the inn, where he lodged in the infirmary, to care for his wound, later moving to the residence of George Frederick Beckel, the farmer-general. Here Sister Beckel and her daughter were his nurses for six weeks.

On September 13, 1777, there was great excitement in Bethlehem because of the retreat of the patriot army from Philadelphia. Then a letter came by express courier from David Rittenhouse announcing that all the military stores of the army, in more than 700 wagons, were being sent north over the Bethlehem Pike. Even the church bells were sent away for safekeeping, and also the bell that has since become a sacred relic, the State House bell, known now as the Liberty Bell.

The farm wagon bearing the Liberty Bell broke down in Bethlehem. The entry in a diary under date of September 25, 1777, says: "The bells from Philadelphia brought in wagons. The wagon with the State House bell broke down here, so it had to be unloaded. The other bells went off."

The breakdown occurred on Seminary Hill, two blocks below the Sun Inn. The exact spot was somewhere between the entrance to the Moravian Seminary campus and Luckenback's flour mill. Eventually the wagon was repaired, and the bell went on to Allentown, where it was hidden in the cellar of Zion Reformed Church, on Hamilton Street, until all danger was over. The broken wagon was repaired by the Moravian wagonmaster, Frederick Beitel, whose descendants are still living in Bethlehem today.

OLD CONESTOGA ROAD

The Old Lancaster Road was the original stage coach road from Philadelphia to Lancaster. It branched off from Market Street as far as Hestonville, and then turning to the right at Fifty-second Street, and then again turned somewhat to the left.

Running up a long hill it passed on the left the Longstreth property, where Horace J. Smith and his wife, who was a Miss Longstreth, lived for many years. This property has been destroyed, the railroad company's excavations on the southerly side and rows of houses on the side next to the road, having changed the fine old farm into a mass of hideousness.

The next point of interest was where the old road crossed City Line, and entered Lower Merion township. At the corner stood a somewhat notorious hostelry, called the Black Horse Tavern.

Then the road continued in a northwesterly direction, passing on the left, the properties of William Simpson and his son-in-law, Lincoln Godfrey, while on the right was the old homestead of the Latch family, whose name is given to one of the neighboring branch roads known as Latch's Lane.

The next point of interest was the village of Merionville. When the broad highway called Montgomery Avenue was laid out, it joined the old Lancaster Road at this point, and the two roads were identical up to the vicinity of Haverford.

The country between Merionville and Cynwyd, which began its existence as an unimportant station on the Schuylkill Valley Railroad, has been so covered with houses of recent years that the two places have become one, and now are generally known as Cynwyd.

In the early days near Merionville, the first road reached, after passing Merionville, was Merion Avenue, which runs off to the left, and reaches City Avenue at Overbrook. Between Merionville and Merion Avenue on the footpath of the old road there were to be seen marks of the old Columbia Railroad, which preceded the Pennsylvania Railroad. These marks were the stones to which the rails were fastened before the days of wooden ties. They have all disappeared from this place, but are still to be seen in Wister's woods, about a mile further west.

About 1874, a new road was opened east of Merion Avenue, and called Bowman's Avenue, General W. P. Bowman's family home lying on the corner, where this road starts from the old road. Next to this is the home of Nicholas Thouron. The house was built by one of the George family, probably about the beginning of the nineteenth century, and was one of several built by different members of the same family between Hestonville and Merion, all of them in the same style of architecture. It passed through a marriage to Dr. John W. Lodge, who was for many years the well-known family physician of the neighborhood. After his death and its purchase by Mr. Thouron, it was altered into its present shape.

The next objects of interest are the General Wayne Tavern and immediately above, the Merion Friends' Meeting House, where William Penn is said to have worshipped. It is also noteworthy as departing from the usual Friendly simplicity of architecture, the present building being in the form of the Greek cross.

About a quarter of a mile above, the old Gulph Road starts off to the right. The spelling of this name is now said to be derived from a Welsh word, Guelph, meaning a gorge; so that the change to "Gulf," which is frequently made, is improper.

After passing through the village of Libertyville, now a part of Wynnewood, and the picturesque old Jones cottage, where Penn is said to have stayed on his visits to Merion Meeting, the road turns sharply to the right at Wister's Corners, as it was called by the old-timers. Here a branch road runs to the left over to the Lancaster turnpike. It used to be called the Church Road, as it led to the Lutheran Church on the "pike."

The "Old Road" then continues along what is now called Montgomery Avenue to a point a short distance above Haverford Station, where it turns to the left, crosses under the tracks of the Pennsylvania Railroad, and immediately turning sharply to the right reaches the Turnpike. This is its first contact with the Turnpike since the two roads separated at Hestonville. It continues with the Turnpike for a few hundred feet, and then leaves it, bearing to the left.

After leaving the Turnpike, the road curves again to the right, and reaches "Henderson's Store," south of Rosemont, where it is joined by the Haverford Road, about the point where the Roberts Road and the road marking the old tracks of the Pennsylvania Railroad crossing. It passes under the tracks of the Philadelphia and Western Railroad, and then climbs "Methodist Hill," as it used to be called, from the church of that denomination which stands at the top of the hill. The Sorrel Horse Inn was on the right, as the road reaches the village of Ithan, and the Radnor Friends' Meeting House. It continues on to a point nearly south of Strafford Station, where it again joins the Turnpike, which it follows for a short distance, again leaving it on the right, and passing the Eagle Tavern runs north of Berwyn to the corner where now stands the large Easttown and Tredyffrin High School building.

At the High School corner there is a road which looks like a continuance of the Old Road, and which soon merges with the Turnpike, and does not separate from it until Warren Tavern, north of Malvern, is reached, where the two roads again follow different paths.

At the High School corner, above mentioned, Cassatt Avenue, running from the Turnpike down into the Chester Valley, crosses the road, and at a short distance from the crossing, forks the avenue bearing to the right, and the other fork to the left. This is now known as the Howellville Road. It passes through the village of that name, and then connects with the Swedesford Road. This road, starting at the Schuylkill River, runs up through the middle of the Chester Valley to a considerable distance west of its junction with the Howellville Road. According to this view, the Old Lancaster Road followed this Howellville Road, and the Swedesford Road ran from it eastwardly to reach the river at the well-known point called Swedes Ford; the Old Road proceeding towards the west on its way to Lancaster. After the building of the Turnpike, the Old Road lost its usefulness in this part of its course, except as a local road, and in many places became entirely disused.

With regard to the name, the writer has within the past few years, in driving up the valley, seen a road marked Conestoga Road, running out of the Swedesford Road, or the Chester Springs Road, and I believe this name, as applied to the Old Lancaster Road, is a very modern use. Signboards with the latter name are still to be seen where the road passes north of Wayne.

R. FRANCIS WOOD.

THE NECK

The Neck, generally speaking, comprised all of Philadelphia between the two rivers south of Moore Street. And thirty years ago, half a mile south of this was still, in the eastern section, covered more or less with marsh lands, drained by dikes that had been cut generations ago by the first settlers in this section.

East of Broad Street—which, by the way, was little more than a trail wide enough for a single wagon, and terminated at the navy yard at League Island—was a waste brightened near the Delaware by several old road houses. There was "Bub" Rivels about on the line of Moore Street, which was also known as the Yellow Cottage, on account of its ocher hue; and there was the old Point House at Greenwich Point, one of the ancient ferries between Philadelphia and Gloucester. It was a ferry in the days before the Revolution, and the British troops passed over the river at this point.

In this neighborhood on a Sunday afternoon the Neckers assembled in groups at the old road houses and amused themselves at quoits. These were the extent of the Neckers' excesses There were men who became something of importance in their neighborhood on account of their success at quoits.

The country all around rejoiced in odd names for different neighborhoods. Thus there were Martinsville, or Frogtown, the Eleven Gun Battery and Greenwich Point. Everything had its nickname, There was a tavern at Old Second Street and Ferry Road, which was known by no other title than Catfish Tavern. In this neighborhood also was the Deering Farm, noted for a terrible tragedy which happened there fifty years ago.

West of Broad Street sportsmen took their way toward Penrose Ferry, in which vicinity there were probably more than 100 roughly made cabins, called by courtesy boathouses. During the gunning season, and at other times, these were occupied by a large colony.

Even so recently as thirty years ago, the adventurer in the Neck would come upon numerous gunners on their way, with their setters at their heels. Both setters and pointers are unfamiliar sights in the lower part of the city now.

Across Penrose Ferry stood Cannon Ball Farm, with its historic farmhouse, which was seemingly proud of the three holes in its walls through which shots passed during the battle of the Delaware in 1777.

On the first day of September the Neck used to be overrun with gunners paddling their way through the dykes in their flat-bottomed boats and taking a shot now and again through the tall reeds as a flock of reedies hove into view.

Only the old-timers know where the Neck was, for it defies detection in these times, and, as for reedbird hunting, that sport has disappeared from this immediate vicinity forever.

FISHTOWN

That portion of the extreme northern or rather northeastern section of the Northern Liberties lying close to the river front was formerly called Camptown, and was principally inhabited by fishermen and boat builders. But Camptown gave way to Fishtown.

The original Fishtown is that section lying between Palmer Street and Ash (now Fletcher) Street, and the Delaware River and Thompson Street.

Those born or residing in this jurisdiction are very proud of their Fishtown and will not tolerate any other portion of Kensington as belonging to it.

The first settlers of Fishtown were the Bakers, Bakeovens (or Backoven as the name was originally), Bennets, Collars, Cramps, Faunces, Potes, Tees and Tuttles.

These families intermarried and there is not a long-time resident here, that is not of the posterity of one of the above. Speak to one or the other of one of these inhabitants concerning any of the other folks, he will give their family history.

A great many after acquiring wealth, in the later days, removed to other sections of the city, notably to the northwest, but they do not forget their Fishtown, they are not too proud to disown it.

They were a clannish set, but good natured. The men were nearly all fishermen, plying their vocation on the Delaware River and neighboring creeks. Each had his "gillen skiff" or sloop, which when in port was moored to the docks adjacent to the Kensington Water Works (foot of Otis Street, now Susquehanna Avenue), with a "live-box" afloat astern, nearly filled with "catties." The live-box was a boat-shaped box, about three feet long, closed all around, with a hinged door on top, perforated with numerous holes in the sides through which the water percolated, keeping the catfish alive until wanted. The docks were a veritable fishmarket with numerous skiffs and cat-boats. Purchasers would come to the wharf and make their purchases, the "catties" and eels being skinned in their presence, thus guaranteeing fresh fish. The catches of fish would be trundled home in a wheelbarrow, and early the next morning, by name generally Sal or Mag, would start out with a tray of fish on her head, and a basket on her arm, gowned in a blue, clean and ironed wrapper, and peddle her fish, crying as she perambulated from street to street "Fresh C-a-t-t-i-e-s." These women were always well received by their customers especially in the Spring Garden district. If by chance you called at the house of one of these women, you would be astonished at the tidiness and cleanliness of their homes. Their dwellings were mostly built of wood, with a large yard, containing a garden. The fences freshly white-washed, and the walls of their kitchens bedecked with tinware; not the cheap kind, but utensils made of imported block tin, shining as if it were silverware.

In nearly every square there resided a "smoker" whose business it was to smoke the shad or herring brought to him by the fishermen, to be stored for winter use. Snappers were very plentiful at this time in the tributaries of the Delaware; there was seldom a function in the Northern Liberties or Spring Garden that the first course was not snapper soup or stewed snapper. Snappers are nearly all extinct in the tributaries of the Delaware now, the most of them

146

brought to the Philadelphia market being caught in the Mississippi River and shipped here.

The girls of Fishtown could all swim, row or sail a boat as well as a man. For pastime they would sail over to Pea Shore in the cove back of Petty's Island and have a shore party. The men would build a camp fire, there was always sufficient dried driftwood along shore, put on an immense coffee pot and make a "hot pot"—black coffee, sweetened with sugar, a lump of butter, together with a dram of good liquor added to each cup. The women in the meantime getting the necessary ingredients together for a snapper soup or "cattiehead stew," baked potatoes and onions, baked in the hot embers, fried beefsteak, ham or flitch (at that time bacon was not in their dictionary). When the tide was high men and women donned old clothes of a light texture and a glorious swim was had by young and old. At twilight camp was struck and they sailed for home, again refreshed to take up their various vocations.

At that time fishing was profitable. Shad in the spring were numerous, being sold generally at retail for 25 cents apiece. Sturgeon were so numerous that the meat was peddled and sold two pounds for five cents. But sturgeon was not to be "sneezed at." Sturgeon properly stewed with a piquant gravy, or a la vinaigrette, or smoked for sandwiches were always appetizing.

The spring of the year was always a busy time for the fisherfolks, for during the winter the seines and nets were repaired, and the toms (buoys fastened to each end of a seine or net) painted. Now the buddies banded together to fish for shad in common, for it required some brawn to row a gilling-skiff and pay-out or haul in the seine with fish; nor was there much comfort connected therewith when fishing off shore, standing in the water up to the hips in the months of April and May.

Eventually the fish in the Delaware became scarce, the old fishermen died off or accepted employment in spar and shipyards. Shipbuilding is now the main industry in Fishtown.

Fishtown had quite a few noted characters as Rudy Bowers, who had a boat shop adjoining Allen's Slip at Otis Street Wharf. He bought any kind of a boat, no matter in what condition, but always at his price. If one wanted to see a variety of boats, he had them. It certainly was humorous to see Rudy attired in a long coat and a naval officer's cap, set sail in his sloop, accompanied by a goat and sail up the river to his bungalow on the banks of the Rancocas.

Another character known to all was Tom Swan, who pretended he had an elixir, that would impart one with vigor. It is said numbers of women called on him for a bottle of his elixir of life. Tom always dressed as a Beau Brummel of the fashion of 1860. For 60 years or more always dressed in the one fashion, a long cutaway blue coat, lavender trousers and patent leather shoes. It was his pride to walk out Girard Avenue, paying no attention to anyone, unless greeted, which greetings he courteously returned, but woe to the rowdy who insulted him. Tom always came out a victor after a few minutes "discourse" with the insulter. He was never insulted a second time by the same person or his accomplices, once was sufficient, for Tom was very handy with his knuckles. It did not make any difference to Tom if the man that insulted him was alone or with a group of men, he would go right in to a group and get his man.

Fishtown had its own volunteer fire company, namely Kensington Hose, commonly called Shad Hose, which was instituted on January 11th, 1842. The quarters were on Richmond Street, below Otis, this was the town hall, for here the male portion assembled and gave out all the news, especially during the stirring times of 61-65.

For pastime on a Sunday morning for the young men of Kensington, and some old ones too, was to take a stroll to Allen's and Faunce's boat slips adjacent to Otis Street Wharf and watch the amateur yachtsmen bring out a fifteen foot boat with square stern, or double-enders (fifteen foot boats with pointed bow and pointed stern), and rig them up. This was easily performed by stepping the mast, (as the mast, spars and sail were attached), haul the boat down the slip to the water's edge, making the sheet fast to the boom, and running same through sheaves and traveller; then all it required was for the crew to board her, step the rudder, the man forward to pull on the throat and peak halyards, make fast, and according to the direction of the wind, step the centre-board in the well. The helmsman would take the sheet in the one hand, and with the other hand guide the helm, and they were off. Boats rigged with a sprit sail were rigged in a jiffy. There was always more or less excitement before the whole mosquito fleet was off—good pastime for the onlookers. Perhaps it was the Sunday preceding a regatta, then could be seen various crews "black-balling" their boats, putting a mixture of plumbago on the hull of the boats that they would slide through the water easier. Other yachtsmen would be painting their craft, or repairing minor defects, the onlookers going from boat to boat, until ten o'clock, when amateur yachtsmen and onlookers would adjourn to the saloon at the head of the slip—in those days the saloons would be open on Sunday—kept by Harry Whiteside and later on by "Dad" Flick, the father of the noted oarsman "Bill" Flick. Then it would be constantly "Bill," "Sam" or "Eels" bring us a couple of bowls of snapper soup and some beer. This would continue until all of the snapper was devoured. This barroom certainly was crowded every Sunday morning. The yachtsmen would then embark in their boats for a spin to Schiller Heights, Fisher's Point, Plum Point, "Bull Pens," Cinnaminson or perhaps up the Pensauken, Rancocas or Neshaminy Creeks. The stiffer the wind would blow the better the yachtsmen would like it, and these boats carried some sail; there were very few boats that could "stand up" with their rigging on, sails unhoisted, without any ballast being in the boat.

That was certainly a fine sight to a yachtsman who stood on the wharf on the morning of a regatta, as the gun gave the signal— the crews hoisting sail, the sail furled to the wind, and if a stiff breeze off the quarter, whew! how they did fly. This was sport, sport which cannot be had with a motor boat. "It was highly exhilarating," as "Brother Bill" remarked.

CHURCHES

The first Presbyterian church to be erected was in 1704, at the corner of Whitehorse Alley and High Street (now Bank and Market Streets) by Rev. Jedediah Andrews. This church was called "Old Buttonwood" from the number of these trees growing near it.

Later on this congregation (1825) erected a new church, "the First Church" in Washington Square and Seventh Street. It was built on what was known as "the old cow-yard."

The second Presbyterian church was erected at Third and Mulberry (Arch) Streets.

The Baptists established their first church at Pennypack in 1687.

The North Baptist Church was in the middle of what is now called Girard

Avenue, on the line of Sixth Street. This church was originally established in Elizabeth Street above Parrish. The reason why the church was put on Girard Avenue was that Franklin Ave. (now Girard Avenue) which ran from Germantown Road west, extended no farther than Sixth Street, the ground beyond being in Penn Township. When Girard Avenue was laid out the church building was taken down. Girard Avenue, when originally laid out, extended only from Broad Street west. It was not open from Broad Street to Sixth Street until after 1848.

The Lutheran Church was transplanted in America by that patriarch, Heinrich Melchior Muehlenberg, who instituted St. Michaelis Kirche (St. Michael's Church) in 1742 at the northeast corner of Fifth and Appletree Alley, extending to Cherry Street. They paid £200 for the lot.

The second church (Zions) of the same congregation was built on Cherry Street below Fourth. In this church, under the auspices of the Congress of the United States, the memorial services for General George Washington were held. Here, from the pulpit of this church, in his address General Henry Lee coined the now historical phrase "First in war, first in peace, first in the hearts of his countrymen."

In 1759 this congregation bought the lot at the northeast corner of Fifth and Cherry Streets for £915, currency, for a burial ground.

In 1777 the British used St. Michael's for a garrison church and Zion for a hospital. After the British evacuated the congregation returned and increased very fast. They then bought another burial ground, the square from Race to Vine Street between Seventh and Eighth Streets. In 1793 the congregation lost through yellow fever 625 members.

The last person to be christened in St. Michael's Church was John C. Geuther, born in 1841, a man well known in building association circles. Mr. Geuther later lived on a farm, above Sixth Street and Girard Avenue, and attended Sunday school in the church standing on Sixth Street opposite Franklin Street (now Girard Avenue). On the day of this writing Mr. Geuther related to the writer many incidents that occurred in the '50s, also stating changes, etc., that since occurred.

In 1809 the English-speaking members of this congregation desiring to have their services in English, left the German church and built St. John's Church, Race Street below Sixth.

Later on, in 1829, another church was built by the English-speaking Lutherans, in New Street below Fourth, St. Mathew's.

Zion Church eventually left their property at Fourth and Cherry Streets and built on Franklin Street below Vine.

An offspring of this church is St. Michael's, corner Trenton Avenue and Cumberland Street.

It appears by a record in Harrisburg "that a Calvinistic Reformed Church was begun in 1763 in Fourth Street north of Sassafras (Race), but that the parties not being able to finish it, it was ordered, by a law passed February 18, 1769, to be sold for the payment of its debts." It was sold and purchased by the Methodists and is now St. George's, Fourth Street near New.

OLD SCHOOL

The first public school for instruction was founded by William Penn in 1689. This grammar school was conducted by the Monthly Meetings Committee, incorporated in 1701, now known as William Penn Charter

School. The school was originally located on Fourth Street between Chestnut and Walnut.

There were several "Corporation Schools" throughout the city, instituted under Penn's charter, which in 1873 were consolidated into the William Penn Charter School, located on Twelfth Street between Market and Chestnut until 1925, when it removed to Queen Lane.

This school is known as one of the best educational institutions in the United States, its graduates being prominent in all walks of life. This, no doubt, is due to the untiring and successful management of its late headmasters, Charles Roberts, Richard Mott Jones and Frederick L. Smith, a very capable and efficient assistant to the latter, and who succeeded Mr. Jones upon his death.

UNIVERSITY OF PENNSYLVANIA

The house at the southwest corner of Fourth and Arch Streets was built in 1760 by the University of Pennsylvania for the residence of its provost, Rev. Dr. Smith.

The peaceable progress of the institution was interrupted during the Revolution. An act was passed annulling the charter and creating a new institution with Dr. Ewing at its head as provost, and taking possession of the property. This later was declared illegal in 1789 by the Council of Censors and the Legislature restored the franchises of the college. The university carried on in new quarters for two years, but the two were again united September 30, 1791, by act of Legislature, and were henceforward known as the University of Pennsylvania. The trustees purchased, in July, 1800, the elegant mansion built for the President on Ninth Street, west side, the lot extending from Market to Chestnut Street.

From Current Topics of the Town—*PUBLIC LEDGER*.

Provost William Smith in 1758 proudly flaunted before readers of the American Magazine the fact that there were five professors in the faculty, and that "six other persons are continually employed in this institution, making eleven in all." And they shepherded a flock of 266.

And what medicines there were in those times! Most of the popular herb-lore came from the Indians.

Goldenrod was the specific for dysentery. Alder buds and dittany purified the blood. Boneset was the sure cure for consumption.

People could understand dosage, with black, horrible concoctions. But anatomy, such as Morgan and Shippen practiced, was a devilish thing.

There was one place to which the wayfaring man on a dark night gave a wide berth. That was a building close to a stone bridge over the Cohocksink, on North Third Street (Third Street, below Girard Avenue, formerly called Canal Street, now Cambridge Street), which was professedly a place for boiling oil and making hartshorn.

But the town busybodies and rumormongers knew better, and told ten times as much as they knew. They said the body-snatchers, at dead of night, deposited gruesome burdens there, and when, once in two weeks, a column of pungent black smoke rose skyward, the human fiends within were boiling and burning cadavers for the use of Morgan, Shippen and their blasphemous confederates.

So a quaint folk-song came into being, anonymously, as such ballads have often originated in all lands and times, and the boys of the town "vociferated" it, though only the boldest spirits dared venture anywhere near the place where the caldrons of the hell-brew were bubbling.

> "The body-snatchers, they have come
> And made a snatch at me;
> It's very hard them kind of men
> Won't let a body be.
> Don't go to weep upon my grave
> And think that there I'll be—
> They haven't left an atom there
> Of my anatomy."

Faith, courage and persistence in the cause of science had their reward, and in 1765 the trustees of "The College of Philadelphia" named Morgan as professor of the theory and practice of physic— the first chair of the kind in America.

Presently they raised Dr. Shippen to a seat of the mighty beside the stalwart pioneer as professor of anatomy and surgery.

Such initiative took courage, in a day when people discussed anatomy, pro and con, as in these passing hours they debate evolution.

The medical faculty was far from venerable in age. Morgan, the patriarch, was 34. Shippen was 83, Adams Kuhn (materia medica and botany) was but 28, and the brilliant Benjamin Rush, professor of chemistry, was the youngest of the quartet, being only 28. Notes made by Rush at the age of 17, on the yellow-fever epidemic of 1762, are the sole scientific record we have of that "visitation."

The latter days of the school in which they were zealous docents have been worthy of the heritage of courage and personal sacrifice.

ONE HUNDRED YEARS AGO
(FROM THE *DEMOCRATIC PRESS* OF MAY 6, 1824)

Wood is now selling at very reasonable prices at our wharves— oak at $3.50 and hickory at from $5 to $5.50. This is one, and but one of many advantages which must flow into this city from the working of our coal mines.

Best shad were selling on the 28th ult. in the Potomac at from $1.75 to $2 per hundred, and excellent herrings at from 50 to 75 cents per thousand.

HUNTING PARK

Forty-five acres of ground at the intersection of Nicetown Lane and the Old York Road were for many years the "Hunting Park Race Course." In 1854 a number of gentlemen joined together to purchase the ground with the intention of presenting it to the city, to be used as a public park.

On the 29th of January, 1855, Councils adopted a resolution accepting the ground, in trust, for the use of the public as a park. The enclosure contains about forty-three acres. On July 10, 1856, the ground was dedicated "free of access for all the inhabitants of the city, and for the health and enjoyment of the people forever, under the name of Hunting Park."

FAIRHILL SQUARE

The heirs and trustees of the estate of Joseph Parker Norris held for many years after his death a large tract of land, embraced in what was called the Fairhill and Sepviva estates, in the district of Kensington. The Fairhill estate was on the east side of Germantown Road, and extended over almost to the Delaware, crossing the Frankford Road. The eastern portion of the ground which lay to the east of Frankford Road was called Sepviva. The western portion was known as Fairhill. The original Sepviva plantation was one hundred and fifty-five acres, and the Fairhill estate five hundred and thirty acres. This plot of land, six hundred and eighty-five acres, was derived from Isaac Norris, of Fairhill, who obtained title to some of it as early as 1713. After the death of Joseph Parker Norris, June 22, 1841, the members of the family made arrangements to bring the plot of ground into the market in the shape of building lots. In so doing they generously determined to devote two considerable pieces for public use. By act of Assembly, passed April 6, 1848, the trustees and parties in interest were authorized to convey to the commissioners of Kensington district in fee-simple for such consideration as they might think proper "and to be held for public use as a public green and walk forever, the plot or square of ground now called Fairhill Square, part of the said Fairhill estate, bounded by Lehigh Avenue on the north, by Huntingdon Street on the south, Fourth Street on the east, and Apple Street on the west."

NORRIS SQUARE

By the act of Assembly of 1848, which authorized the conveyance to the district of Kensington of Fairhill Square, the commissioners were also authorized to accept Norris Square, part of the Fairhill estate, bounded by Susquehanna Avenue on the north, Diamond Street on the south, Howard Street on the east, and Hancock Street on the west.

MARKET SHEDS AND HOUSES

Dr. James Mease, in his Picture of Philadelphia, states that the first markets were held at the corner of Front and High (Market) Streets, and that a bell hung on the shed was rung when anyone brought provisions there from the country for sale. These were a range of wooden stalls from Front to Second Street.

Councils, on July 4, 1720, resolved to erect a new building "the building to be the width of the court-house, in height ten ffoot to the joice, the length of the stalls joining to be sixteen ffoot, to have an alley of ffour ffoot betwixt them and the next two stalls. The shelter at the back of the stalls three ffoot and a half on the outside, the Breadth of the stall three ffoot and a half within, the clear Walk ffourteen ffoot, and the stalls to be eight ffoot Distance from the court-house, but the Roof to join to the court-house. That the whole be paved with Brick at the Height of the court-house ffloor in the Middle, and to be painted without on both sides."

In the market house the following regulation was posted: "No person be suffered to Smoak Tobacco in the market or Market House or in any of the stalls," by order of Councils.

When a boat with produce made fast to the wharf a bell located at Front Street was rung.

In May, 1745, the residents of the southern part of the city petitioned to erect a market house on South Second Street, from Pine to Cedar (South) Street. The market house erected there is an exact reproduction of the court house or town hall and market house as stood on High (Market) Street in Colonial times.

In 1759 the market house on High Street was extended to Third Street. In 1810 the sheds were continued to Sixth Street, and finally to Eighth Street; then from there to Fifteenth Street; the farmers stood with their wagons at the street-curb and on the pavements around Centre Square at Broad Street (the site of the present Public Buildings). From Fifteenth to Seventeenth Street was another series of market houses; these were demolished in April, 1859.

The market sheds in the Northern Liberties, on Second Street, from Hickory Lane (Fairmount Avenue) to Poplar Lane were built in 1763.

Later sheds were erected on Callowhill Street, from Fourth to Seventh; Girard Avenue, westward from Marlborough Street to Frankford Road, and again from Howard to Third Street, from Apple (now Lawrence) to Eighth Street, and from Tenth to Twelfth Street, the intervening plots being curbed, but otherwise open, and used by the children in the immediate neighborhood as playgrounds. There were also market sheds on Shippen (Bainbridge) Street from Third to Fifth Street. Moyamensing Avenue and South Eleventh Street.

In 1852 a movement was instituted to abolish the market sheds belonging to the respective municipal corporations that were all in public streets. A company was incorporated under the title of "The Broad Street Market House Company," which erected a suitable building on the east side of Broad Street, below Race, in 1854. But the public could not be induced to do its marketing there, and it became a failure. The city eventually becoming the possessor of the building, and using it as the city armory. Another market house was erected on the south side of Race Street, at the corner of Juniper, which also proved a failure. The city also acquiring this property, and later using it for the headquarters of the fire department.

In 1859 the subject of the entire removal of the markets from Market Street was warmly agitated. The stalls from Front to Eighth Street were commenced to be removed November 25, 1859. This was at the instance of the Pennsylvania Railroad which wanted Market Street as an avenue to the Delaware River, and they ran their tracks alongside of the market houses and turned down Third Street to Dock Street to the river. The freight depot being at the southwest corner of Thirteenth and Market Streets, until 1874, when, the city having decided to erect the City Hall at the intersection of Broad and Market Streets, the railroad tracks below Fifteenth Street were taken up, and the freight depot removed to Market Street above Fifteenth.

Individual corporations, composed mostly of farmers, erected closed market houses as follows:

The Western, northeast corner of Sixteenth and Market Streets, opened in 1859, was later disposed of to the Pennsylvania Railroad, and another erected on Market Street between Sixteenth and Seventeenth. The Eastern, opened on November 26, 1859, corner of Fifth and Merchant Streets (now the site of the Bourse); the Farmers', north side of Market, between Eleventh and Twelfth; the Franklin, at the corner of Twelfth Street, adjoining the above. This market was originally built on Tenth Street above Chestnut, where the Mercantile Library now stands; the Southwestern, southeast corner Nineteenth and Market Streets; the Lincoln, southwest corner Broad and Coates Streets; the Globe, Tenth Street and Montgomery Avenue and Nineteenth and Oxford Streets; the Norris, at Third and Norris Streets; the Centennial, at Twenty-second and South Streets; the Federal, Seventeenth and Federal Streets; the

Northwestern, Ridge Avenue below Girard Avenue; the Girard Avenue Farmers' Market, Ninth Street and Girard Avenue; Keystone, Third and Girard; Phoenix Market, Sixth and Columbia Avenue; Kater, Nineteenth and Market Streets and Broad and Columbia Avenue.

The smallest market shed was at Newmarket and Callowhill, adjacent to Gaul's Ale Brewery.

Curbstone farmers' markets are still in vogue on South Street on Fridays and Saturdays. Wagons, minus their horses, and automobile trucks laden with fresh produce, closely packed, line the curbstone on South Street from the Delaware River to Fifth Street.

OLD-TIME DRINKING PLACES IN PHILADELPHIA
BY JOHN IRVING DILLON

Back in the early eighties tippling among men of prominence was comparatively common. Moderate drinking was not frowned upon, as later it came to be. Men in all walks of life indulged to some extent, and the saloon was looked upon as a kind of unofficial club, where kindred spirits were wont to meet and pass an hour or two in genial fellowship.

Each of the drinking places of that day had its own individual clientele. One learned instinctively to know at which one of the several taverns one might find certain well-known men, as loyal in their preferences in this respect as diners of the present day are to fixed places for eating. The lawyers, one learned to look for, at Louis Lesieur's. Lesieur was a Frenchman who kept a quiet, very respectably-conducted and unassuming place at the southeast corner of Seventh and Sansom Streets. He had the reputation of keeping excellent cognac. And his wines, sherries, madeiras, burgundies and sauternes were rated highly by local connoisseurs.

At Lesieur's, just after the adjournment for the day of the Courts, then at Sixth and Chestnut Streets, one could be sure of meeting the celebrities of the local bar; such men as Colonel William B. Mann, Lewis C. Cassidy, "Chris" Kneas, James H. Heverin, "Joe" Bonham, "Ned" Perkins, John McKinlay, "Max" Stevenson, John H. Fow, "Mat" Dittman and a host of others of the class known as "gentlemen drinkers;" men who were keen judges of good liquor and who indulged temperately and with discretion. Many a case, involving big stakes, was compromised at French Louis' over a round or two of cognac or a special bottle of burgundy.

The political element one looked for at Steve Walker's, on Fifth Street below Market. Walker's, back in the eighties, was a local institution. It was not the garish, gaudy thing that the saloon of a later era came to be, there was no bar. A huge, elaborately-carved sideboard held the decanters. The habitués of the place seated themselves on brandy casks, or on wine cases. Walker served the tipples, expensively garbed, and wearing a silk hat. "Bill" Leeds, "Ham" Disston, "Johnny" Hill, "Bill" Douglass, George Fairman, Theodore F. ("Plunger") Walton, and men of that class were among Walker's regular patrons.

At the ale vaults of Dick Penistan, on Chestnut Street below Fifth, one met the theatrical and sporting element. Penistan had been an actor, and his saloon attracted men of the stage, together with a goodly sprinkling of men about town. The piece de resistance at Penistan's was old English ale. On Sixth Street, just above Sansom, was a little saloon, kept by a Democratic politician of some prominence in those days—one "Sam" Josephs. Josephs was a pudgy little man who affected a white plug hat. His place was the pet rendezvous for aspiring Democrats and for Court hangers-on.

Canfield's, "The Cabinet," on Seventh Street above Chestnut, famed for many years for its collection of framed cartoons of public men, on the other hand was the favorite resort for Republican politicians of the smaller calibre and for the newspapermen of that day. The first of October of each year, the anniversary of the opening of Canfield's "The Cabinet," was eagerly looked for by the clientele. On this day, all day a free lunch was served, consisting of anything imaginable in the eating line from roast turkey to ice cream, including chicken, lobster and herring salads. It goes without saying, that on this day "The Cabinet" was overflowing.

155

HAPPENINGS IN YE OLDE PHILADELPHIA

On Fifth Street above Chestnut stood one of the most elaborately-fitted saloons and restaurants of the period, Philip J. Lauber's, among the first of local drinking places to serve imported beers, such as Hofbrau, Muenchener, Wurzburger and the like. Every year in the fall there would be a large display of game in front of Lauber's, consisting of bear, moose, buffalo, deer, the various species of duck, geese, swan and birds and fish in general. This would lure the gunner and the angler.

"Bob" Steel's, subsequently a landmark for many years at Broad and Chestnut Streets, was then located on the north side of Chestnut Street, just west of Eighth. His place was by long odds the most elaborately fitted drinking place of the town and was rated a show place of some note. Steel's, Finelli's and Dooner's were among the exclusive drinking resorts of the early eighties. Finelli had two places, one on Tenth Street above Chestnut, and another on Chestnut east of Broad. At Peter Dooner's one met the epicure element, les bon vivants of the town. Tom Green created quite a stir a few years later by fitting up, at Green's Hotel, Eighth and Chestnut Streets, a, for that day, very showy barroom. One of its novel features was a ceiling effect suggestive of the Arctic, with tapering icicles and vistas of shimmering snow and frost.

At just about this time "Andy" Moore, a millionaire distiller, remodeled the barroom of the old Girard House, at Ninth and Chestnut Streets, on a scale of garish magnificence that threw every rival establishment into the shade. Heavily carved and massive mahogany fixtures, velvet fittings and paneled paintings of nymphs, somewhat scantily arrayed, entered into the Moore decorative scheme.

Visitors to Philadelphia counted a visit to the Girard bar one of the things, on no account, to be missed.

Down on Walnut Street, just west of Eighth, was Poulson's, adjoining to the east the old Central Theatre. Poulson's was also noted largely for its paintings, the character of the subjects being such that, when the Brooks License act went into effect in 1889 a remonstrance filed against renewal of the Poulson license, by Lewis D. Vail, the Gibboney of that day, was based upon the supposed indecency of these pictures. Also famous for its works of art was "Charlie" Zeisse's, on the south side of Walnut Street, in the same block. Zeisse's was favored extensively by the theatrical element, chiefly those playing in burlesque, and what was then known as "variety." The Zeisse pictures, however, ran to still-life subjects and were not objectionable to the Josiah Leeds, morally straight-laced, of that day.

On Eighth Street below Walnut, on the west side, stood Campiglia's, a resort famous in those days for its spaghetti, chianti and Neapolitan cookery. Around on Ninth Street above Walnut, on the west side, was a place very much similar to Steve Walker's, kept by George De Waele. De Waele's was, essentially, a resort for the elect. It was managed along very strict lines and was frequented only by the very best class of drinkers.

At the northeast corner of Seventh and Chestnut was the old Guy House, kept by Charlie Murray, another resort for men-about-town, as was the Continental bar at Ninth and Chestnut, then under the control of the Kingsleys.

A few paces below Chestnut, on Eighth, was the saloon of E. T. Dillon, a brother of the "Tom" Dillon, whose saloon on Tenth Street was, for many years, a landmark in the city's centre. On Chestnut Street, west of Tenth, under the old Chestnut Street Opera House, was the saloon of "Billy" McGonegal, a

156

favorite tippling-place for the journalistic and sporting element, and on Eleventh, just below Chestnut, the widely-known bar of "Billy" Morris.

"Joe" Bowes, famous for his old ales, kept at Eighth and Sansom, and "Tom" Bowes, his brother, at Eighth and Locust. "Charlie" Soulas, in those days, was at the northeast corner of Eighth and Sansom. Later he fitted up and opened the Rathskeller, in the basement of the Betz Building, made notable by "Lew" Megargee, Old Commodore Betz, Count O'Neill and about everybody of any prominence in local politics.

At Thirteenth and Sansom Streets was Henry Hornickel's, noted for stewed snapper, and at Fifteenth Street, on the present site of the Union League, the place of Dennis McGowan, famed far and wide for the excellence of its shore dinners. Back in Drury Street was the quaint, old ale house of "Billy" McGillin, and around on Penn Square the cafe of Otto Fuchsluger, a cafe and bar much favored by working newspapermen. On Broad Street, midway between Walnut and Locust Streets, was Doerler's, a quiet, German saloon whose chief claim to note was that it was the meeting place, for many years, of the Pegasus Club, numbering among its members such local litterateurs as "Dan" Dawson, "Billy" Walsh, Charles Henry Luders, C. H. A. Esling, Melville Phillips, Morton McMichael, 3d, and "Tom" White.

Among the pug element of that period, notable places were those of Dominick McCaffrey, on Eighth Street; Fogarty & Ryan, on Vine Street; Arthur Chambers, on Ridge Road and Wood; Walter Campbell's, "Long Branch Phil Daly's," at Second and Pine Streets, "Billy" McLean's, Girard Avenue below Tenth, and Charley Devere's, Fourth Street above Girard Avenue.

Other popular saloons were John Welde's, at Broad and Christian Streets; "Squire" McMullen's Randall House, at Ninth and Bainbridge Streets; the place of "Gil" Ball, negro leader, on Lombard Street; Dalmedo's, on Girard Avenue; Dennis Considine's, at Second and Walnut Streets; Wm. Lindig's and Gus Seitz's, at Fourth Street and Girard Avenue; John Hahn's, on Girard Avenue and Randolph, where the Quail Club covied.

Clustered about the old financial district, at Third and Walnut Streets, where the White House, owned by ex-City Commissioner "Bill" Douglass; the English Chop House, back of the present Bourse, where "Larry" McCormick, afterward of the Bellevue, tended bar; "Jim" Gosch's, behind the Custom House in Library Street, and "Corny" Haggerty's, at Fourth and Spruce Streets.

Wine and music mixed amicably at Bob Tagg's Mænnerchor Garden, northeast corner of Franklin and Fairmount Avenue; Thron's Broadway Garden, at Broad and Locust Streets, on the site of the present Hotel Walton; Tirsot's and Turf Villa, on the River Drive, and at Seney's Garden, at Eighth and Vine Streets. Tony Wagner's "Punch Bowl," which sat on a hill on North Broad Street below Susquehanna Avenue, and Lamb Tavern Road in the rear; "Fred" Stehle's and "Dick" Patterson's, at the Falls, were favorite resorts with horsemen, as was also Tagg's Belmont Mansion, in the West Park.

No article assuming to deal with the drinking places of Philadelphia could be complete without a mention of "Bill" Long's Museum, on Third Street below Fitzwater, and of "Joe" Malatesta's, on Eighth Street at Lombard. Long's saloon was a museum, fitted with cases containing curios and wax reproductions of notorious criminals. Here could be seen the cart which Anton Probst, the murderer of the Deering family, down the "Neck," used in hauling the bodies. This murder created quite a sensation among the residents of Southwark.

Then there was Pat. Gaffney's Museum at 321 W. Girard Avenue, with its

Irish relics, notably the large lock taken from Dublin jail, portraits of the Irish martyrs, blackthorn canes, pictures of pugilistic events, etc.

Malatesta's, like Campiglia's, was noted for its Italian cooking, and was the scene of many a gay party of gourmets, with a penchant for the vintages of the land of grapes and olives. One of the oddities of saloon-keeping was the Cobblestone Saloon, Thirteenth Street and Moyamensing Avenue, for years a show place in the southern section of the city. The entire barroom was fitted up in cobblestones, set in cement, and was well worth a visit.

HISTORIC OLD TAVERNS

Historic old taverns that kept alive historic traditions were the Jolly Post and Seven Stars, in Frankford; the old Blue Anchor, in Dock Street; the King of Prussia, the Wheel Pump, the Anthony Wayne and the Blue Bell.

Thousands of other drinking places are no more that deserve a line or two of mention in deference to ties that connect them with the past growth and progress of the town. There was "Paddy" Carroll's, for instance, dear to the dog-fighters and rat-terrier fanciers of another day, and Arthur Chambers, on Ridge Avenue above Wood Street, locally noted as the stopping place of the mighty John L. Sullivan when, as a champion, he hied himself to Nicholl's handball alley, on Carpenter Street near Ninth, to indulge in his favorite pastime.

"Jerry" Donohue's, at Eighth and Vine Streets, for years the most remunerative saloon in Philadelphia; George Dasch's, on Market Street; George Concannon's, "Pat" Bunce's, Gibbons, and "Two-for-Five" Moran's, are all worth a line. At "Two-for-Five's" the tippler of limited means could purchase two hummers, of a fluid with a kick like whisky, for a solitary nickel.

TAVERNS

Philadelphia, previous to the enactment of the Brooks High License Law, had a large number of saloons or taverns, and previous to the war of the rebellion it was a custom of these taverns to have a large sign in front of the premises, mostly illustrated, and some with quaint sayings, as:

The "Yellow Cottage," on the east side of Second Street, near Greenwich. The sign swinging in front had the following invitation:

"Rove not from sign to sign, but stop in here
Where naught exceeds the prospect but the cheer."

On Thirteenth Street above Locust there was "McDermott's Inn," who announced his business as follows:

I, William McDermott, lives here;
I sells good porter, ale, and beer;
I've made my sign a little wider
To let you know I sell good cider.

On Shippen Street (Bainbridge) between Third and Fourth there was a tavern having a swinging sign representing a sailor and a woman, separated by these lines:

"The seaworn sailor here will find
The porter good, the treatment kind."

"The Three Jolly Sailors" was the sign of a tavern on Water Street above Almond. On this sign was a tar strapping a block, and the motto below made him say:

"Brother Sailor! please to stop,
And lend a hand to strap this block;
For if you do not stop or call,
I cannot strap this block at all."

In Frankford Patrick Keegan presided over the Bee-Hive. On his sign he had this inviting inscription:

"Here in this hive we're all alive,
Good liquor makes us funny;
If you are dry, step in and try
The flavor of our honey."

The "Lemon Tree," also called the "Wigwam," was the headquarters of butchers, situated on Sixth Street, Noble to Buttonwood, extending westward to nearly Seventh Street.

The Bull's Head Inn, Second Street above Poplar. In the yard of this tavern was exhibited the plan of the first railroad in the United States.

A place much frequented by farmers was the Black Bear Tavern, on the southeast corner of Fifth and Merchant Streets, with a large yard containing wagon sheds extending eastward on Merchant Street.

The "Butchers' Arms," connected with the drove-yard on the north side of Vine Street, Franklin and Eighth Streets.

The Washington Tavern, at the corner of Sixth and Carpenter (Jayne) Streets. Later on this became known as the Falstaff Inn.

The "Yellow Cat," corner of Eighth and Zane (Filbert) Street.

The "Harp and Crown," corner of Third Street and Elbow Lane.

"The Sorrel Horse," at the intersection of Frankford Road and Shackamaxon Street, where dancing was the most popular entertainment.

"Shooting the Deserter," Boon's Tavern, at the foot of Shackamaxon Street.

"Landing of Columbus," Beach Street above Laurel.

"The Mansion," Frankford Road and Manderson (below Richmond) Street.

Daniel O'Connell's Inn, west side of Second Street above Thompson.

The "Bird-in-Hand," Fourth Street below Callowhill.

On Third Street above Shippen (Bainbridge) "X-10-UX."

The "Adam and Eveses" Garden, on Sixth Street below Norris, with a sign picturing Adam and Eve in Eden. Later on this was called "The Rosengarten" conducted by Fred. Schwamb.

The "Cock and Lion," at the corner of Second and Coates Streets. The sign was later on removed to a tavern on Fourth Street above George.

The "Shakespeare Hotel," northwest corner of Sixth and Chestnut Streets.

"The Robin Hood Tavern," a popular dance house, on Poplar Street below Fourth.

"The Richmond Hotel," at Port Richmond. Charles J. Wolbert, who occupied it in 1821, announced that in addition to his large stock of catfish he had received about fourteen hundred others from the cove opposite Richmond.

"The Decatur Inn," on Carpenter (Jayne) Street below Seventh. Originally known as the German Hall, frequented by quiet loving people. It gave its name to Decatur Street, which was formerly called Turner's Alley, now Marshall Street.

"Our House," on Library Street above Fourth, later on known as "Military Hall."

"The Wasp and Frolic," at the corner of Vine and Garden Streets.

"The Old White Bear," corner Fifth and Race Streets.

"The Pewter Platter," Front Street above Market.

"The Red Lion," Second and Noble Streets, noted for selling dressed hogs.

"The Rising Sun," at the intersection of Germantown Road and Old York Road.

"The Wheat Sheaf," Richmond Street and Wheat Sheaf Lane.

"The Jolly Post Boy," Main Street (Frankford Avenue), Frankford.

"The Seven Stars," Main Street and Bustleton Pike, Frankford.

"The Golden Swan," Third Street above Arch.

"The Stetson House," Third Street above Willow.

"The Merchants' House," Third Street above Callowhill.

"The Green Tree," Race Street below Third.

"The Wagon and Horses" (later on Ladner's Military Hall) 528-532 North Third Street.

"The Bald Eagle," west side of Third Street above Callowhill.

"The Black Bear," Third Street, east side, below Willow.

"The Tiger," northeast corner Fourth and Vine Streets.

"The General Montgomery," northeast corner Sixth and Willow Streets.

"The Seven Presidents," Coates Street above Ninth.

"The Barley Sheaf," Fourth Street below Vine.

"The Sheaf," Second Street below Vine.

"The Kensington Black Horse," Frankford Avenue, east side, below Palmer Street.

"The White Horse," Frankford Avenue, west side, below Palmer Street.

"The Bull's Head," Front Street above Poplar

"The Delaware," Second Street, east side, below Lombard.

"The Eagle," 227 North Third Street.

"The Fleece Hotel," 1120 Frankford Avenue.

"The Pennsylvania Farmer," Third Street below Callowhill.

"The Seven Presidents," Seventh and Germantown Road.

"The Sorrel Horse," Fourth Street below Vine.

Northern Liberties Town House, Second Street above Coates.

"The Green Tree," corner Marlborough Street and Girard Avenue.

"The Thomas Jefferson," corner Fifth and Poplar Streets.

Keystone Hotel, Third Street above Girard Avenue (adjoining the Bible Christian Church, which had nails driven through the bricks in the sidewalk) now the site of Louis Burk Abattoir.

"The Bull's Head," later on Montgomery Hotel, northeast corner Sixth and Willow Streets.

"The Red Lion," corner Fourth and Wood Streets.

"The Two Bulls," Germantown Road below Girard Avenue.

"The Hornet and Peacock," Fourth Street below New.

"The Falstaff," Carpenter (later on Jayne) Street above Sixth.

"The White Bear," southwest corner Fifth and Race Streets.

"The Spread Eagle," Sixth Street above Diamond.

Phoenix Tavern and Garden, between Fifth and Sixth Streets and Camac's Lane (Oxford Street) and the present Columbia Avenue. Joseph Knox, an Englishman, kept this place, once the resort of the elite of the city. Camac's Lane ran from Turner's Lane in a southeastwardly direction to Germantown Avenue, passing the Phoenix Tavern on the south. Cohocksink Creek flowed through the garden, with a fancy bridge over it. Later on this property was purchased by the firm of Powers & Weightman, who erected chemical works there, later on removing to Ninth and Parrish Streets. The buildings for a long number of years were used in the manufacture of furniture, notably chairs, by D. B. Slifer, and Hall. Eventually these factories were torn down by the Weightman estate, and neat and commodious dwellings erected.

Many Kensingtonians can remember the Black Horse Hotel, at the intersection of Hanover Street and Frankford Avenue, or the Penn Treaty Tavern, on Beach Street below Marlborough.

It is also within the memory of many, of the Fairhill Mansion, "The Revolution House," which was on a plot extending from York to Cumberland Street, and from Sixth to Seventh Street, with a creek to the north running eastwardly.

Continental Hotel, corner Ninth and Chestnut Streets, was opened for guests on February 16, 1860. For a long number of years this hotel had the patronage of the elite. Opposite to the Continental, at the northeast corner of Ninth and Chestnut Streets, was the Girard House, a house equally as prominent as the Continental.

On Broad Street, west side, below Chestnut, was the commodious and well patronized La Fayette Hotel.

On Chestnut Street above Fifth, the American House.

La Pierre House, Broad Street below Chestnut.

Guy's Hotel, corner Seventh and Chestnut Streets.

The Merchants' House, Fourth Street above Market.

St. Elmo Hotel, Arch Street, north side, above Seventh Street.

LAGER BEER

Philadelphia has the distinction of being the first place in this country where lager beer was brewed. It was brewed by George Manger in 1846, on New Street below Second. It was dispensed at Wolff's saloon, Dilwyn Street below Callowhill.

THE OLD FIRE DEPARTMENT
Fire Companies

Mainly through the efforts of Benjamin Franklin, the Union Fire Company was established on December 7, 1736. Each member agreed to furnish six leather buckets and two stout linen bags, which he was to bring to every fire. The bags were to receive and hold property which was in danger. The headquarters were in Grindstone Alley (now Philip Street) above Market. The membership was limited to thirty.

A second company was formed on January 1, 1738, under the name of the Fellowship Fire Company, with thirty-five members. Headquarters at the Friends' Meeting House on Second Street near Market.

Hand-in-Hand, March 1, 1742, northwest corner Front and Spruce Streets.

Heart-in-Hand, February 22, 1743.

Friendship Fire Company, July 30, 1747.

The Britania Fire Company, 1750.

Sun Fire Company, September 24, 1778. Front and High Streets.

Endeavor Fire Company, February 17, 1785, Key's Alley below Second Street.

Alarm Fire Company, May 1, 1787.

Kensington Fire Company, August, 1791.

Relief Fire Company, December, 1791. Relief Alley near Second Street.

Resolution Fire Company, January 1, 1797.

List of engine and hose companies of Philadelphia arranged according to the date of the institution of each company:

Engine Companies

Hibernia Engine, February 20, 1752, Evelina bel. 3d.

Northern Liberty Engine, May 1, 1756. Front bel. Green.

Vigilant Engine, January 2, 1760, Race bel. 2d.

Delaware Engine, March 21, 1761, South bel. 19th.

Washington Engine, March 4th, 1764. Haines St., Germantown.

Franklin Engine, March 1, 1764. Germantown ab. Franklin.

Harmony Engine, August 24, 1784. Broad ab. Fitzwater.

Reliance Engine, May 10, 1786. N.E. cor. 11th and Anita.

Assistance Engine, December 28, 1789. 6th bel. Coates.

America Engine, April 10, 1790. Buttonwood bel 3d.

Diligent Engine, July 4, 1791. S.W. cor. 10th and Filbert.

Franklin Engine, January 17, 1792. Catharine ab. 3d.

Washington Engine, January 1, 1793. 4612 Main St., Frankford.

Humane Engine, March 1, 1794. S.E. cor. 13th and Oxford Sts.

Washington Engine, January 3, 1796. Lombard bel. 11th.

Friendship Engine, August 18, 1796. S.E. cor. Sepviva and Norris.

Columbia Engine, September 16, 1796. Market ab. 34th.

Hope Engine, November 11, 1796. 6th ab. Fitzwater.

Philadelphia Engine, January 25, 1799. 17th bel. Chestnut.

Weccacoe Engine, May 1, 1800. Queen bel. 2d.

Good Will Engine, March 27, 1802. Race bel. Broad.

Decatur Engine, Feb. 11, 1803. Church Street, Frankford.

Mount Airy Engine, February 9, 1804. Miller Street, Germantown.

Columbia Engine, March 6, 1809. Wistar Street, Germantown.

United States Engine, October 11, 1811. 4th ab. Wood.
Congress Engine, May 11, 1815. Highland Avenue, Chestnut Hill.
Union Engine, March 19, 1819. Germantown Ave. bel. Broad.
Good Intent Engine, April 26, 1819. Allen St. bel. Shackamaxon.
Good Intent Engine, May 8, 1819. Hipple's Lane, Ridge Ave. near eight-mile-stone.
Fellowship Engine, September 3, 1819. Armat St., Germantown.
Globe Engine, May 22, 1820. Germantown ab. 2d Street.
Fairmount Engine, February 22, 1823. Ridge ab. Wood.
Monroe Engine, March 8, 1823. Lancaster Pike, Hestonville.
Hand-in-Hand Engine, May 15, 1823. 9th ab. Poplar.
Southwark Engine, February 5, 1827. 3d ab. Washington.
Manayunk Engine, January 1, 1838. Main St., Manayunk.
Mechanic's Engine, August 4, 1839. Brown bel. 15th Sts.
Western Engine, April 7, 1840. Callowhill ab. 15th.
Liberty Engine, January 1, 1841. Main Street, Holmesburg.
Independence Engine, February 1, 1847. Spring Garden bel. 24th.
Wissahickon Engine, December 27, 1847. Wissahickon Creek.
Franklin Engine, January 8, 1848. Unity Street, Frankford.
Spring Garden Engine, July 12, 1851. 1903 Callowhill.
Kingsessing Engine, October 8, 1857. Darby Road bel. the four-mile-stone.

Hose Companies

Philadelphia Hose, December 15, 1803. S.E. cor 7th and Filbert.
Good Intent Hose, March 8, 1804. 602 Spruce.
Resolution Hose, April 11, 1804. 1936 Germantown Avenue.
Humane Hose, April 10, 1805. Wood bel. 3d.
Perseverance Hose, May 27, 1805. Race bel. 4th.
Neptune Hose, August 6, 1805. 242 Crown Street.
Hope Hose, August 17, 1805. 212-14 Pine Street.
Columbia Hose, May 1, 1806. 806 Race Street.
Southwark Hose, May 6, 1806. 3d bel. Lombard.
Washington Hose, Feb. 22, 1811. 9th ab. Filbert.
Phoenix Hose, August 25, 1817. Filbert ab. 7th.
Fame Hose, January 1, 1818. 20th ab. Lombard.
Diligent Hose, June 3, 1820. 1027 Race St.
United States Hose, July 4, 1826. 423 Buttonwood St.
Niagara Hose, March 28, 1827. Monroe bel. 3d.
Northern Liberty Hose, New Market ab. Coates.
American Hose, September 2, 1828. 619 Jayne.
William Penn Hose, February 3, 1830. Frankford Road bel. Girard.
Robert Morris Hose, March 14, 1831. Lombard ab. 8th.
Independence Hose, July 4, 1831. George bel 3d.
Pennsylvania Hose, August 4, 1831. N.W. cor. 8th and Depot.
Lafayette Hose, October 31, 1831. 4th ab. Brown.
Marion Hose, August 19, 1833. Queen bel. 6th.
Schuylkill Hose, December 9, 1833. Locust bel. 13th.
Good Will Hose, March 1, 1834. Wood bel. 23d.
Moyamensing Hose, July 22, 1837. 8th bel. Fitzwater.
Warren Hose, March 6, 1838. Washington ab. 20th.
Kensington Hose, January 11, 1842. Richmond bel. Otis.

Spring Garden Hose, May 12, 1845. Ridge Ave. bel Jefferson.
Shiffler Hose, January 8, 1846. Moyamensing Ave. ab. Greenwich.
South Penn Hose, March 27, 1846. 10th bel. Thompson.
Fairmount Hose, January 10, 1847. 503 N. 11th St.
Ringgold Hose, March 29, 1847. Randolph ab. Girard Ave.
Taylor Hose, May 1, 1847. Howard and Putnam.
Germantown Hose, May 11, 1848. Washington St., Germantown.
Excelsior Hose, January 28, 1853. Franklin St., Frankford.
Tivoli Hose, June 1, 1855. Brown ab. 22d.
Lincoln Hose, June 5, 1855. Brown bel. 12th.
Union Hose, January 19, 1856. 33d and Grape.
West Philadelphia Hose, May 10, 1856. 37th and Ludlow.

Hook and Ladder Companies

Empire Hook and Ladder, February 6, 1851. Franklin ab. Wood.
Rescue Hook and Ladder, January 27, 1853. Paul St., Frankford.
Mantua Hook and Ladder, March 4, 1855. 40th and Warren Sts.

Fire Alarm Signals

The State House and fire alarm bells in the several districts would strike the number of the fire district twice, and the direction four times; each bell striking the direction from itself. Should the fire be in the vicinity of the State House, the bells in the boxes will ring one, slow and distinct.

In cases of general alarm, requiring the services of the entire department, the bells in the boxes rang 3—2—4, the alarm bells having first signified the district in which the fire was raging. Directions: 1, North; 2, South; 3, East; 4, West; 1-4, N.W.; 1-3, N.E.; 2-4, S.W.; 2-3, S.E. General alarm, first struck direction, then rang incessantly in quick succession.

DISTRICTS

First.—All south of Spruce Street, from Delaware to Schuylkill River. Second.—From Spruce to Race and from Delaware to Schuylkill River. Third.—From Race to Green and from Delaware to Schuylkill River. Fourth.—From Green Street to Allegheny Avenue and from Delaware to Schuylkill River. Fifth.—North of Allegheny Avenue from Delaware River to Broad Street. Sixth.—North of Allegheny Avenue from Broad Street to Schuylkill River. Seventh. —West of the River Schuylkill.

FIREMEN'S PARADES

Triennially the Volunteer Firemen would parade through the city. There was much rivalry among the companies as to which should present the most handsome appearance. Each of their engines and hose carriages glistened with the shine of metals, the glare of bright paintings, together with the elegance of their respective banners of velvet or silk, flowers, and tinsel of gold and silver. The men dressed in dark trousers, bright red shirts, white wool scarves and topped off with heavy firemen's helmets, all "manning the rope" pulling the hose carriage, with its bells ajingling did certainly make a picture.

The largest parade was held in October, 1852. Five thousand and eighty-nine firemen were in line, with their respective apparatus. Eighty-four companies participating. To conduct the parade with discipline and decorum there were two hundred marshals. Every band of music in the city together with many others from outlying points were engaged to take part, embracing about six hundred musicians.

The procession occupied two hours in marching past a given point. The route extended from Kensington through the Northern Liberties, Spring Garden, the city proper, to Southwark.

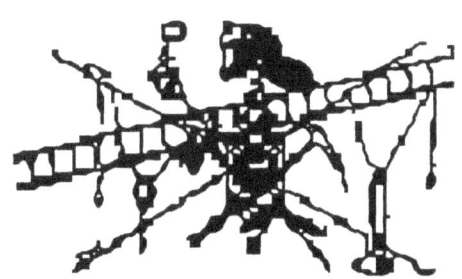

CHANGES IN THE NAMES OF STREAMS
IN AND ABOUT PHILADELPHIA

1860

AMESKA RUN. See Darby Creek.

BEAVER CREEK, flowing through the Almshouse grounds, and emptying into the Schuylkill opposite Pine Street. Called Beaver Creek and Beaver Run in a patent by Penn to Varels Landers in 1692.

BLANSON'S RUN. See Darby Creek.

BOON CREEK OR CHURCH CREEK runs west by south from the junction of Kingsess and Minquas Creek. It received its name from Andreas Boon, one of the original Swedish settlers. It was also one of the routes to the church at Tinicum; hence its name of Church Creek.

BOTANIC CREEK flows into the Schuylkill on the west side, opposite the upper part of Point Breeze and below Bartram's Botanic Garden, from the proximity to which it obtained its name.

BOW CREEK, southern boundary of Philadelphia City, flows from Darby Creek, along the northeastern side of Tinicum Island, and after a short bend nearly due east, enters the Delaware opposite Hog Island.

BRIER CREEK empties into the Schuylkill on the west side in Fairmount Park below Sweet-Brier Mansion.

BYBERRY CREEK. See Poquessing Creek.

COBB'S CREEK. See Darby Creek.

COHOCKSINK CREEK (obliterated) is called in various patents Cococksink, Coxing, Cogogsink, Coxon and Cohocksink or Mill Creek. M. S. Henry, in his Dictionary and Gazetteer of Words and Names in the Delaware Indian Language, defines the name to be Cowehockin "pine lands." The name Mill Creek was given to it from the fact that on this stream, between the present Second and Third Streets, below Girard Avenue, was built the Governor's (Penn's) Mill, and afterward the Globe Mills. One branch of the Cohocksink commenced near the Ford Road, west of the Lamb Tavern, and there was a branch which rose above the present Glenwood Cemetery. The stream flowed generally southwest, crossing Broad Street above Turner's Lane, and crossed the latter about the line of Twelfth Street. It continued to a point between Fifth and Sixth Streets, where it widened into a lake, into which also flowed a stream which rose in the lands of the Gratz estate, probably above Jefferson Street, and flowed eastwardly. The latter was called Coozaliquenaque in the patent to Daniel Pegg in 1684. From the pond or mill-dam it flowed east and south, on the line of the following streets: Randolph Street to Thompson, to Orkney, to Lawrence, to Cambridge, to Bodine, to Laurel, to Allen, thence southeast, emptying into the Delaware at Brown Street.

CHURCH CREEK. See Boon Creek.

CHURCH CREEK. See Darby Creek.

CRESHEIM CREEK. See Wissahickon.

DAM CREEK (obliterated) ran into Hollander's Creek in a direction south by west, and had its source near the Buck Road.

DARBY CREEK empties into the Delaware River opposite the lower end of Tinicum Island. It is the lower portion of a stream which rises in Haverford township, Delaware county, and flows with some irregularities and curves in a southerly direction until it reaches the Blue Bell Tavern, on the Darby Road. The upper portion of this stream was called by the Swedes Kara Rung or Kakaron, Carkoens, Carkons, Carcoens, Carcoon and Chargoes—all supposed to be corruptions of Kara Kung. The name was shortly afterward changed to Cobb's Creek, after William Cobb, an Englishman, who became owner of the old mill. Port Reading Creek rises near Haverford College, in Delaware county, flows through Haverford township, and empties into Cobb's Creek between Haverford Road and Church Road. Indian Run is composed of two branches, one of which rises in Lower Merion, near Ardmore station, and the other north of Elm station, on the Pennsylvania Railroad. They flow south, and unite a short distance before reaching Cobb's Creek, into which they flow. Blanson's Run rises in Darby Township and empties into Cobb's Creek near Paschallville. Naylor's Run rises in Marple Township, and flows south and east into Cobb's Creek. Hermsprota Creek empties into Darby Creek near the intersection of Amesland Road and a road leading to Hog Island, a short distance above Bow Creek. Pusey's Run empties into Darby Creek above the junction with Cobb's Creek, near the borough of Darby. Amesaka Run (patent to Neals Joh, 1684), Ameasaka (patent to Mounce Jones, 1685), rises in Philadelphia and runs into Cobb's Creek near Mount Moriah Cemetery. Below the Blue Bell Tavern a creek joins with Cobb's Creek, which was called the Nyecks (meaning "nasty, muddy"), the Muckruton, and Amesland (after Amas-land, "the land of the nurse"), which was given by the Swedes to the country immediately south of it. Below this junction the creek was called Darby Creek, from the town or village of Darby, near by. It was also called Church Creek, because at one time it was a convenient road to travel to Tinicum Church. Muckinapattus Creek rises in Darby Township, Delaware County, flows southwest, and joins Darby Creek west of the junction with Bow Creek. Muckinapalis means "land that is lower than the surrounding country." Stone Creek rises in Springfield Township, Delaware County, and flowing nearly south enters Darby Creek nor far from its mouth.

DARK WOODS RUN (obliterated) had its source in a spring which rose north of Girard College, and flowed through the western portion of the college grounds until it emptied in a large pond called Dark Woods Pond, in the neighborhood of Brown Street, about Twenty-sixth or Twenty-seventh. The stream ran southwest and emptied into the Schuylkill River not far from the Lincoln monument and a little west of the present steamboat-landing in Fairmount Park.

DELAWARE RIVER was discovered by Henry Hudson, an Englishman in the service of the Dutch East India Company, in the yacht Halve-Maan or Half-Moon, of eighty tons' burden, on the 28th of August, 1609. Various Indian names have been assigned to this stream. Heylin, in his Microcosmos, or description of the world, published in 1622, calls the river Arasapha, which seems to have been derived from Arasaphe, "it goes fine," meaning a river at all times navigable and useful. Poutaxat was another Indian name sometimes applied to the river, but supposed to be more applicable to the bay. It means round or broad, and is applied exclusively to bays. Makerish-kisken and Maris-kitton are corruptions of the name which in early deeds is written Mochijirick-hickon. Mochijirick means "large and great," and hickon "ebb and tide," so that this name meant "a large river in which there were ebbs and tides." Another name was Lenape Whittuck. Lenape means "Indian," and hittuck "a tree." Kit-hanne, meaning "the largest river," was also applied. After Hudson, the first explorer was Captain Cornelius Jacobsen Mey, who, in 1613, entered the river in the yacht Fortune, called the eastern cape Mey and the western Cornelis, another of the western capes being called Hindlop or Hinlopen which latter name was subsequently transferred to Cape Cornelis. The original Cape Hinlopen, near the present town of Lewes, lost its designation as a cape altogether. Mey, on his return to Holland, left behind him a Captain Hendrickson in the yacht Onrust (Restless), who explored the river, it is believed, as far as the mouth of the Schuylkill. On his return to Holland, Hendrickson accompanied his report with a map, on which the river now called the Delaware was designated as the river Van der Vorst Mauritius. But Mey had already chosen as a name the Zuydt or South River, in contradistinction from the Nord or North River. The Dutch also called the stream Nassau River, Prince Hendrick's river and Prince Charles' river. When the Swedes came they called it Swenska Riviere or Swedish River, and it was also called New Swedeland Stream, or the river of New Sweden. The English gave it the name of De la War, which has been modernized into Delaware. This name was given because they supposed that Thomas, Lord de la War, who touched at the bay in his voyage to Virginia in 1610, was the discoverer of the river and as early as 1612 Captain Thomas Argall, of Virginia, speaks of it as the De la War River. The name was therefore given to the river before that which was assigned to it by the Dutch, but the claim that Lord de la War was the discoverer was untenable, inasmuch as Hudson had entered the river in 1609. The bay of the Delaware was called by the Dutch New Port Bay, also Godyn's Bay, after Samuel Godyn, a Dutchman, who made a purchase of land in 1629 from the Indians, extending from Cape Cornelis or Hindlop (Heniopen) inland thirty-two miles and two miles in breadth.

DOCK CREEK (obliterated) was so called by the early settlers because it was the place at which a public dock was situated. It was composed of two branches, one of which commenced between Fourth and Fifth Streets, north of Market, and ran south by east, crossing Market Street west of Fourth, and Chestnut Street about the line of the present Hudson Street, and by the latter south in rear of the property of the Board of Brokers, where it was joined by a branch which began west of Fifth Street, below Walnut, and flowed toward the northeast. It crossed Walnut Street between Fourth and Fifth. These streams, thus united, flowed eastwardly, bearing to the south, and formed the body of Dock Creek, the course of which may be traced by the street of that name. Not far from the Delaware this stream received the water of another branch, which began at about the site of St. Peter's Church, at Third and Pine Streets, and crossed the square bounded by Second, Third, Spruce and Pine Streets until it struck the head of the present Little Dock Street, along which it flowed to the northeast until it reached the main stream. This branch was called Little Dock Creek. The Indian name of Dock Creek was Cooconocon.

DUBLIN CREEK. See Pennypack Creek.

EAGLE CREEK. From the junction of the Kingsess and Mingo creeks a stream runs east for a short distance and empties into the Schuylkill below the first bend in the river. This might seem to be a continuation of Kingsessing Creek, and it has been so called on some of the maps. On Lindstrom's map it is called Ornebo Kyl, La Riviere de Nid des Aigles ("the river of the eagle's nest," or "eagle's nest river"). From this title was obtained the modern name—Eagle Creek.

FALLS CREEK enters the Schuylkill near the Falls, below the mouth of the

HAPPENINGS IN YE OLDE PHILADELPHIA

Wissahickon, and near the Falls tavern.

FLOAT CREEK. See Holt Creek.

FRANKFORD CREEK is formed by the union of three streams. One of these, now known as the Wingohocking, is so called in a patent to Griffith Jones, 1684. It is called Winconico in a patent to John Goodson, 1701, and Wincokoe in a patent to Griffith Jones of the same year. In modern times the Wingohocking has been called Logan's Run, from the fact that it flowed through the grounds of the seat of James Logan, at Stenton. The Wingohocking rises near Mount Airy, curves generally to the south, and passing through Germantown runs eastwardly until it unites with Tacony Creek near Rowland's saw-mill. The Tacony rises in Montgomery county near Shoemakertown (now Ogontz), runs southwest and south, crosses the line of the former Bristol township, and formed the boundary of Bristol and Oxford townships.—Rock Run enters into the Tacony southwest of what was formerly Whitaker's factory.—The Little Tacony rises near the Township Line Road between Dublin and Oxford, runs nearly south through Oxford township and is joined by one or two brooks, and empties into the Frankford Creek east of Frankford. The stream is now called Frankford Creek from the junction of the Tacony and Wingohocking, and enters the Delaware near the U. S. Arsenal. Tacony is called Toaconik in a patent to Robert Adams, 1684; Taoconinck in a patent to Griffith Jones in the same year. Little Tacony is also called Tackawanna. Mr. Henry says Tacony is derived from Tekene and means "woods" or "an uninhabited place." Into Frankford Creek near the Delaware empties a stream called Freaheatah. Frankford Creek derives its name from the village of Frankford, adjoining. A portion of the creek east of the junction of the Little Tacony is called Questionick in a patent to Eric Cock and others, and Quissinuaminck in a patent to Thomas Fairman, 1688.

FREAHEATAH. See Frankford Creek.

GREEN TREE RUN rises in the upper part of the late Roxborough township and runs nearly parallel with Green Tree Lane, and empties into the Schuylkill near the intersection of that lane and the Ridge Road.

GUNNER'S RUN. One branch, called Three-mile Run, rose near Woodpecker Lane and Broad Street, and flowed east by south, crossing above Fairhill, meeting near Germantown Road, having a branch through Harrowgate Garden, and a branch with two forks, one of which runs above and the other below the Norris estate. Pursuing its way southwestwardly until near the Delaware, it makes a sudden bend southeast, and enters the river between the Dyottville glassworks and the Kensington water-works. This stream was called Tumanaramaming in A patent to Thomas Fairman in 1702. It received its name from Gunner Rambo, a Swede who lived near it.

HAY CREEK, the eastern part of Hollander's Creek, extended from Holt or Hell Creek into the Delaware at some distance north of Greenwich Point.

HOLLANDER'S CREEK, according to the map of Lindstrom, made a clear course through from the Delaware to the Schuylkill, making the lower part of the Neck an island, which was further divided by other streams, so that there were three islands at the lower end of what is now considered fast-land in Philadelphia, in addition to League Island. The westernmost was called Manasonk or Manayunk. It was adjoined on the east by Drufwe Island, Isle des Raisins or Grape Island, which was immediately north of League Island, and is now known as Greenwich Island. North of Drufwe Island was another, which has no name. The stream was named after Peter Hollandaer, a Swedish governor, who succeeded Peter Minuit as commandant at Fort Christina in 1639.

HOLT CREEK flowed into Hollander's Creek west of Dam Creek. It was sometimes called Little Hollander's Creek, also Hell Creek. It formed a curious loop in the upper portion, which encircled a piece of ground that might be called an island. The lower part of this loop was called Float Creek.

INCKHORN'S CREEK runs into the Schuylkill River on the west side, near the bend, north of Penrose Ferry. The original name was Andreas Inckooren's Eyl, from the residence of a Swede of that name near it.

INDIAN RUN. See Darby Creek.

KINGSESS OR KINGSESSING CREEK intersects Bow Creek about halfway between Darby Creek and the Delaware. It flows in a northeasterly direction and empties into the Schuylkill nearly opposite Girard Point. This Indian word is derived from Chingessing ("the place where there is a meadow") or Chincessing ("bog meadow").

LAND CREEK empties into the Schuylkill on the west side, between Penrose Ferry and the bend of the river. It bears that name in a patent to Benjamin and Enoch Bonsall in 1705.

LITTLE CREEK was north of Rogue Creek, ran a short course, and emptied into the Schuylkill on the east side in 1750.

LITTLE TACONY CREEK. See Frankford Creek.

LOGAN'S RUN. See Frankford Creek.

MALEBORE'S CREEK emptied in Hollander's Creek east of Ship Brook, and no doubt received that name from Malebore, an Indian chief, whose name is signed to some of the early deeds to Penn. One branch of this creek rose near Fifteenth and Sansom Streets, and ran southwardly to a point south of Pine Street and east of Broad, where it was joined by a branch from Spruce Street between Seventeenth and Eighteenth. Farther down were branches from Eighteenth and South Streets, from Spruce and Twelfth Streets, and from Eleventh Street between Spruce and Pine. The united streams ran southward from Passyunk Road and Eleventh Street, inclining to the west, and bending in the shape of a hook into the marsh-land below Point Breeze until Hollander's Creek was reached. The upper part of this stream after the junction was called Shakhanoning in a patent to Stille and others, 1678; Sheckhaming in a patent, 1695; Shackhemensen; Chickansink Schachachque means "strait," and Schachachque "a strait in a river."

MATS HAY CREEK emptied into the Schuylkill on the east side, above its mouth, and is apparently the same stream which on Lindstrom's map seems to be the western portion of Hollander's Creek. It is on Holmes map, but disappears entirely before the beginning of the present century.

MILL CREEK rises in Montgomery county, runs generally in a southeasterly direction, and empties into the Schuylkill just below the Woodlands. It is called Nanganesey, the original Indian name, in a patent to Yocum; Quarn Creek (Swedish); Monson's Great Mill Fall (Upland records); Mill Creek (Holmes' map); Little Mill Creek (Reed's map).

MILL CREEK. See Cohocksink Creek.

MILL CREEK. See Darby Creek.

MINNOW RUN (obliterated) was composed of two branches, which united in the North-west (now Logan) Square. One branch rose west and south of Bush

Hill and east of Nineteenth Street, flowing south and crossing to the west side of Nineteenth, and entering the square below Vine Street. The other branch rose on the east side of Bush Hill, about the line of Fifteenth Street, and coursed along the east side of that street, and turning westwardly entered Logan Square at Eighteenth Street. These streams then flowed south, and were joined at Nineteenth and Cherry Streets by a stream from Broad and Arch Streets and by two branches from Market Street, one rising near Centre Square and the other at Sixteenth Street. The united streams crossed Twentieth Street at Arch, Filbert Street between Twentieth and Twenty-first, and nearly reached Market Street, but made a curve west of Twenty-first Street, and emptied into the Schuylkill River at Arch Street in a bay of some width.

MINQUAS OF MINGO CREEK intersects Kingsess Creek about halfway between Bow Creek and the Schuylkill, and making a bend around the northern part of Sayamensing Island, now obliterated and subsequently considered a part of Province, afterward State, island, empties into the Schuylkill nearly south of the intersection. It is supposed to derive its name from the tribe of Indians called the Minquas, and was upon their route of travel from the interior of Pennsylvania to the Delaware.

MOYAMENSING KYL which was the southern boundary of Swanson's ground, is frequently spoken of in old deeds and patents, but not marked on old maps. It is believed to have been a stream which entered the Delaware probably between Reed and Dickinson Streets. The word Mayemensin means "a place of meeting or coming together." It is said to have been given to the ground in the lower part of the city in consequence of a meeting of Indians being held there in 1661, to propitiate the English for the murder of an Englishman.

MUCKRUTON CREEK. See Darby Creek.

MULBERRY CREEK flowed into the Minquas or Mingo near the Schuylkill.

PAPER-MILL RUN. See Wissahickon.

PEGG'S RUN (obliterated) ran a course which is now mainly occupied by Willow Street. One branch commenced at Fairmount Avenue west of Fifteenth Street, and then ran southeast nearly to Vine; thence northeast above Callowhill Street and east of Tenth, where it was joined by a branch which rose west of Eleventh Street between Green Street and Fairmount Avenue. The united streams flowed eastwardly to the Delaware. This creek was called Cohoquinoque in a patent to Jurian Hartsfelder for the whole of the Northern Liberties in 1678. It was called Pegg's Run after Daniel Pegg, an Englishman, who was the purchaser of Hartsfelder's Land. On Scull & Heap's map it is call I Cohoquenoque; on Hill's, Cohoquinoque.

PENNYPACK CREEK rises in Montgomery county, crosses the township, enters the Delaware near the town of Holmesburg—Duffield's Run and Ashton Run, uniting with Wooden Bridge Run, enter the Pennypack near Rowland's paint factory.—Sandy Run enters into it north of the Oxford and Dublin poor-house.—Comly's Run and Welsh Run flow into Paul's Run, which joins the Pennypack below Verreeville. On Lindstrom's map this creek is called Pennishpaska, La Riviere de Pennicpacka; by Campanius, Pennishpacha Kyl. In early Swedish patents it is called Pemipacka. Holmes calls it Dublin Creek, whilst in later maps it is called Pennypack and Pennepack. Heckeweider says that Pennypack means "deep, dead water; water without much current."

PERCH CREEK flows into the Schuylkill on the west side, above the Botanic

Garden, and is so called on Hill's map.

PINNEYES CREEK enters the Schuylkill north of the Point Breeze gas-works and is of considerable size. Mr. Henry says that Piney or Pinney in the-Delaware language means "a place to sleep."

POQUESSING CREEK rises in Montgomery county, crosses the northwest line of the late township of Byberry, where it received a branch which flowed mainly through Moreland. It there bends northward into the county of Bucks, again southward when it touches the township line, and flows southeast and southwest, forming the boundary-line of Byberry, and turning to the southeast enters the Delaware. Bloody Run empties into it at Carter's mill, Black Lake Creek at Mechanicsville, and Gilbert's Run about a mile below.—Elwood's Run and Wilson's Run, which rise in Byberry township, unite to form Byberry Creek which enters the Poquessing near the Red Lion tavern.— Colbert's Run and Walton's Run unite and form Walton's Creek, which flows into the Byberry. The latter meets the Poquessing within a mile of where it enters the Delaware River. On Lindstrom's map this stream is called Pouquessinge, La Riviere de Kakimon's. Mr. Henry defines Kakamon's to be a name for the pike, so that this was Pike Creek; but Lindstrom also has upon his map Drake Kylen, La Riviere des Dragons, or Dragon River. Campanius calls it Drake Kylen. In a patent to Nicholas Moore it is called Poetquessingh, and on Holmes' map Potquessin.

RIVER'S CREEK had its rise upon Manasonk Island, at the mouth of the Schuylkill, and emptied into the Delaware west of Hollander's Creek.

ROGUE CREEK empties into the Schuylkill opposite Province Island.

ROSAMOND'S CREEK flows into the Delaware just above the bend of the Horseshoe. It rises in Greenwich Island, formerly Drufwe Island, and derived its name from Martin Rosamond, an Englishman, who resided on the Delaware in the jurisdiction of New Castle court. It was called by the Indians Kikitchimius, meaning the "tree or wood duck," which had its nest in trees.

SCHUYLKILL RIVER is supposed to have been discovered by Captain Hendrickson in the year 1615, in the yacht Onrust (Restless). He belonged to Captain Mey's expedition, and was assigned to the work of exploration of the streams in the neighborhood of the coast. On Hendrickson's map of his discoveries Fort von Nassonene or Fort Nassau is marked, which must have been placed there after Hendrickson's time. There is an island opposite the fort, but nothing like a river such as the Schuylkill is shown. It should be understood that Fort Nassau was built by the Dutch, on the east side of the river, about 1626. It is supposed to have been situated at or near the present Timber Creek, and therefore nearly opposite the mouth of the Schuylkill River. The name Schuylkill is supposed to have been applied by the Dutch, and is said to mean Schuyl ("hidden") and kill ("river")—the "hidden river," because at its mouth the river is not plainly visible to persons coming up the Delaware. Upon a map of the British possessions in North America, engraved in England by Herman Moll in 1715, and upon another of the possessions in New France in 1720, the Schuylkill is called Perquemuck and Perquemuk.

SHIP BROOK OR SHIP RUN rises in the First Ward, nearly north of the bend at the southwestern side of Hollander's Creek, which latter runs into the Back Channel near the western end of League Island.

TACONY CREEK. See Frankford Creek.

THREE CREEK rose south of Hollander's Creek, and flowing nearly north entered the latter almost opposite the mouth of Dam Creek. It was composed of three small creeks, which joined.

TINEY CREEK, which flows into the Schuylkill a short distance above the mouth.

WALTON'S CREEK. See Poquessing Creek.

WINGOHOCKING CREEK. See Frankford Creek.

WISSAHICKON CREEK takes its rise in Montgomery county, flows generally to the south, bearing west, and enters the Schuylkill above the Falls.—Cresheim Creek, which rises in Montgomery county, enters the Wissahickon at Livezey's mill. It received its name from Cresheim, in Germany, from which some of the original settlers of Germantown came.—Paper Mill Run rises near Mount Airy, flows to the southwest, and empties into the Wissahickon near the intersection of Rittenhouse Lane. There was once a paper-mill there. Wissahickon is derived from Wissa mechan ("catfish").

WISSINOMING CREEK rises near the old Wheat Sheaf tavern, on the Bustleton and Wheat Sheaf Turnpike, and flows south by east.

RIVER BOATS
(From the *Evening Bulletin*)

River boats have their place in hearts as well as in history. There is remembrance of many a youthful adventure, when, in the company of their parents, young Philadelphians set out for an excursion up-stream or down-stream on the broad reaches of the river, recollections of delightful days and moonlight nights spent aboard the pleasure craft of the Delaware and, for some, perhaps, romance as well.

The Columbia bears the distinction of being almost the oldest, if not the oldest, boat on the Delaware. Built at Wilmington in 1876, the year of the nation's centennial, it has been one of the busiest of the pleasure craft on the Delaware, figuring in many a famous occasion on the water-front, such as the launching of the cruisers and battleships, sharing in the festivities of the great Peace Jubilee in 1898 and again gaining a place in the naval display coincident with the celebration of Founders' Week, in 1908.

Broad of beam, shallow of draft, sure and steady, the Columbia, along with the old Twilight, another famous boat of the past, was one of the stand-bys of the up-river service in the days when these boats formed a popular service between the city and Riverton, Delanco, Torresdale, Beverly, Burlington and Bristol.

The Columbia was always a popular boat with charter parties because of its spacious decks and at one time carried probably the gayest and most distinguished party that ever sailed on any of these boats when Secretary of the Navy Whitney chartered it, on the occasion of the launching of the Vesuvius and Yorktown, for the transportation of the nation's guests, and when its decks literally dripped with the champagne put on board for the proper toasting of the new Navy.

Another boat, or rather barge, during the centennial and a few years later, was the Creedmoor Cutter, which plied between Philadelphia and a resort at Tacony.

The Twilight, the older boat, was the craft on which many distinguished parties of Philadelphians went down the river to "see off" famous personages, as was the case when a committee accompanied General Grant down the river when he sailed on his trip around the world, or when many local notables went down-stream to witness the departure of the relief ships for Russia, sent out as one of the memorable undertakings of the old Citizens' Permanent Relief Committee.

Another well-known boat was the City of Trenton. It was under that name, shortly after it was built, while it was on its way up the river that a boiler explosion forced its beaching and caused one of the few disasters boats of this type have known on the Delaware. Reconstructed, and renamed the Sagamore, it was put into service between the Battery at New York and Long Island City where it remained until it was brought to this port under the title of the Princeton.

Along with these boats were others some of which have passed. In the days when the old Twilight and the Columbia with the Edwin Forrest were leading the up-river craft, the Major Reybold, the John A. Warner, the Thomas Clyde and the Republic were foremost in down-river service. Of that famous four only the Clyde remains, doing duty as of yore to Woodland Beach and Augustine, although the Republic, which later became the Cape May, and is now the Dreamland, is still active as an excursion boat on the Chesapeake, having gone into the Baltimore Bay service after doing duty for a while between New York and Coney Island. The old Republic, under Captains Lackey and Eldridge, was long one of the sights of the Delaware and so regular was it in its run between the city and the capes that Philadelphians living in the eastern wards could almost set their time-pieces by the blowing of its siren when it approached its dock on the nightly return trip. The Republic was the last of the regular river boats in the Cape May excursion service, although an attempt was made a few years ago to revive a freight line on that run. Before the Republic's day, there had been many famous boats on this route, such as the Richard Stockton, the Lady of the Lake, the Ariel and the Thomas Powell, and it was said the latter had run the distance from the capes to the city in four hours and forty-nine minutes. Were some of the old pilots alive who steered them doubtless many an interesting story could be told of the performances and experiences of these boats.

Then there were smaller craft as The Gazelle, Capt. Theo. Brown, which plied between Otis Street Wharf and Cramer Hill, and the Belmont, which also plied between the Water Works Wharf, Otis Street and Red Mill, N. J. These smaller craft were mostly frequented by the residents of Kensington, who delighted in making trips to Pea Shore.

LATE AND FORMER NAMES OF STREETS
OF THE OLD DISTRICTS OF NORTHERN LIBERTIES, KENSINGTON, PORT RICHMOND AND SPRING GARDEN

Adrian Street, west of Frankford Road, *Ambler Street.*

Amber Street, west of Frankford Road, *Waterloo Street.*

America Street, west of Second Street, *Washington Street.*

Belgrade Street, north of Thompson Street, *West Street.*

Berks Street, from Front to Broad Street, *Chatham Street.*

Berks Street, from the Delaware River to Trenton Avenue, *Vienna Street.*

Bodine Street, east of Third Street, *Adams Street.*

Brooke Street, east of Third Street, *Rose Alley.*

Buttonwood Street, from Second to Third Street, *Tammany Street;* from Third Street to Old York Road, *Buttonwood Street;* from Old York Road to Ridge Avenue, *Logan Street.*

Callowhill Street, from the Delaware River to Fourth Street, *New Street.*

Canal Street, *Cohocksink Creek.*

Columbia Avenue, from the Delaware River to Frankford Road, *Hanover Street.*

Crease Street, below Shackamaxon Street, *Crown Street.*

Dana Street, south of Green Street, *Artillery Lane.*

Darien Street, west of Eighth Street, *Clinton Street.*

Day Street, below Frankford Road, *Dean Street.*

Dilwyn Street, west of Third Street, *Kunkle Street.*

Edgemont Street, north from Gunners' Run, *Brown Street.*

Eighth Street, north of Callowhill Street, *Garden Street.*

Ella Street, from Emerald to Amber Street, *Price Street.*

Fairmount Avenue, from the Delaware River to Old York Road, *Coates Street;* from Old York Road to Ridge Avenue, *Hickory Lane.*

Fifth Street, from Green Street to the Cohocksink Creek (at Thompson Street), *Old York Road.*

Frankford Avenue, *Frankford Road.*

Galloway Street, west of Third Street, *Winter Street.*

Girard Avenue, from Gunners' Run to Frankford Road, Prince Street; from Frankford Road to Sixth Street, *Franklin Avenue.*

Hackley Street, east of Fifth Street, above Berks Street, *Wager Street.*

Hermitage Street, from Green Street to Coates Street, above Third Street, *Smiths Alley.*

Jefferson Street, *Sage Street.*

Julia Street, Coates Street to Brown Street, above Front Street, *Jones Alley.*

Kensington Avenue, northeast from Lehigh Avenue, *Frankford Road.*

Kiehl Street, east of Amber Street, north from Clearfield Street, *Randolph Street.*

Laurel Street, from Delaware Avenue to Second Street, *Maiden Street.*

Lawrence Street, east of Fifth Street, *Apple Street.*

Leithgow Street, west of Fourth Street, north from Poplar Street, *Mechanic Street.*

Lynd Street, north of Green Street, from Fourth to Fifth Street, *Paschall's Alley.*

Mannikin Street, from Norris to Diamond Street, near Fifth Street, *Little Perry Street.*

Manor Street, north of Montgomery Avenue, below Germantown Avenue,

Clymer Street.

Marlborough Street, between Hanover and Shackamaxon Streets, *Crown Street.*

Marshall Street, west of Sixth Street, *John Street.*

Mascher Street, west of Front Street, *Clinton Street.*

Master Street, *Timber Lane.*

Meetler Street, between Fifth and Sixth Streets, *Little Poplar Street.*

Megary Street, east of Hanover Street, above Girard Avenue, *Morris Street.*

Melvale Street, north from William Street, below Richmond Street, *Larch Street.*

Memphis Street, east of Tulip Street, north from Norris Street, *Lemon Street.*

Mercury Street, west of Montgomery Avenue to Palmer Street, *Monroe Street.*

Merino Street, from Second Street to Germantown Avenue, *Little Green Street.*

Minerva Street, north of Spring Garden Street, Seventh to Franklin Street, *Wistar Street.*

Montgomery Avenue is composed of Cherry Street from Richmond Street to Germantown Avenue, and Mud Lane west of Germantown Avenue.

Moyer Street, above East Girard Avenue, *Brown Street.*

Neff Street, above Ann Street, *Maple Street.*

New Market, from Vine to Green Street, Cable Lane; from Green Street to Cohocksink Creek, *Pitt Street.*

Noble Street, from the Delaware River to Ridge Avenue, *Bloody Lane.*

Orkney Street, east of Fifth Street, *Orchard Street.*

Otis Street, from the Delaware River to Belgrade Street, *Wood Street.*

Oxford Street, from Wildey Street to Frankford Avenue, *Savery Street.*

Palethorpe Street, from Girard Avenue to Master Street, east of Second Street, *Perry Street.*

Peel Street, from Van Horn to Lydia Street, below Germantown Avenue, *Rose Alley.*

Percy Street, west of Ninth, north from Poplar Street, *Tyler Street.*

Perth Street, east of Eighth Street, from Thompson to Jefferson Street, *Robinson Street.*

Poplar Street, from the Delaware River to Front Street, *Marsh Street.*

Randolph Street, west of Fifth Street, north from Brown Street, *Elizabeth Street.*

Richmond Street, Point-no-Point Road, *Queen Street.*

Sartain Street, west of Eleventh Street from Poplar Street to Girard Avenue, *Margarette Street.*

Savery Street, east of Marlborough Street, from Wildey Street to Frankford Avenue, *Union Street.*

Sophia Street, from Otter to Edward Street, *William Street.*

St. John Street, west of Second Street, *Ann Street,* from Vine to Willow Street.

Susquehanna Avenue, from the Delaware River to Front Street, *Otis Street.*

Sutton Street, above Master Street, west from Fifth Street, *Summit Street.*

Thompson Street, from E. Norris Street to Frankford Avenue, *Duke Street;* west of Frankford Avenue, *Phoenix Street.*

Toronto Street, from Ann Street west of Larch Street, *Palm Street.*

Twenty-seventh Street, north of Coates Street, *Bush Hill Street.*

Van Horn Street, from Hancock Street to Germantown Avenue, below Girard Avenue, *Rose Alley.*

Warnock Street, north from Poplar Street, west of Tenth Street, *Lewis Street.*

Wildey Street, from Frankford Avenue to Columbia Avenue, *Bedford Street.*

Willow Street, *Pegg's Run.*

Wood Street, west of Second Street, *Brewer's Alley.*

The streets west of Broad Street, running north and south, were numbered from the Schuylkill, which was very confusing to strangers.

On December 8, 1853, Councils gave them new names. Schuylkill Eighth became Fifteenth Street. Schuylkill Seventh became Sixteenth Street. Schuylkill Sixth became Seventeenth Street. Schuylkill Fifth became Eighteenth Street. Schuylkill Fourth became Nineteenth Street. Schuylkill Third became Twentieth Street. Schuylkill Second became Twenty-first Street. Schuylkill Front to Twenty-second, and Ashton Street to Twenty-third Street.

In popular language High Street was always called Market Street, Mulberry was known as Arch Street, Sassafras as Race Street, and Cedar as South Street. In deeds and in ordinances they were invariably designated by the ancient name. After 170 years of attempt to bring the legal titles into common use, Councils abandoned the contest and also gave to those streets their popular names.

DISTANCES IN PHILADELPHIA
MEASUREMENTS WEST FROM DELAWARE AVENUE ON MARKET STREET

NAMES OF STREETS, ETC.	Width of Streets	Length of Streets		Total Distance	
	feet	feet	in.	feet	in.
Delaware Avenue					
Delaware Avenue to Water		136	3	186	3
Water Street	39			225	3
Water to Front		40		265	3
Front Street...	60			325	3
Front to Second..		401		726	3
Second Street	50			776	3
Second to Third...		500		1,276	3
Third Street	50			1,326	3
Third to Fourth		395		1,721	3
Fourth Street	50			1,771	3
Fourth to Fifth		405	2	2,176	5
Fifth Street	50			2,226	5
Fifth to Sixth		396		2,622	· 5
Sixth Street	50			2,672	5
Sixth to Seventh		396		3,068	5
Seventh Street	50			3,118	5
Seventh to Eighth		396		3,514	5
Eighth Street :...	50			3,564	5
Eighth to Ninth		396		3,960	5
Ninth Street	50			4,010	5
Ninth to Tenth		396		4,406	5
Tenth Street	50			4,456	5
Tenth to Eleventh		396		4,852	5
Eleventh Street	50			4,902	5
Eleventh to Twelfth		396		5,298	5
Twelfth Street	50			5,348	5
Twelfth to Thirteenth...................................		396		5,744	5
Thirteenth Street	50			5,794	5
Thirteenth to Broad		528		6,322	5
Broad Street	113			6,435	5
Broad to Fifteenth		396		6,831	5
Fifteenth Street	50			6,881	5
Fifteenth to Sixteenth		396		7,277	5
Sixteenth Street	50			7,327	5
Sixteenth to Seventeenth.............................		396		7,723	5
Seventeenth Street	50			7,773	5
Seventeenth to Eighteenth............................		396		8,169	5
Eighteenth Street	50			8,219	5
Eighteenth to Nineteenth		396		8,615	5
Nineteenth Street	50			8,665	5
Nineteenth to Twentieth		396		9,061	5
Twentieth Street	50			9,111	5
Twentieth to Twenty-first		495		9,606	5
Twenty-first Street.......................................	50			9,656	5
Twenty-first to Twenty-second....................		396		10,052	5

WEST FROM DELAWARE AVENUE ON MARKET STREET

NAMES OF STREETS, ETC.	Width of Streets	Length of Streets		Total Distance	
	feet	feet	in.	feet	in.
Twenty-second Street	60			10,112	5
Twenty-second to Twenty-third		273		10,385	5
Twenty-third Street	50			10,435	5
Twenty-third to River Schuylkill		487		10,922	5
River Schuylkill	438			11,360	5
River Schuylkill to Thirtieth		600		11,960	5
Thirtieth Street	60			12,020	5
Thirtieth to Thirty-first		465	7	12,486	
Thirty-first Street	80			12,566	
Thirty-first to Thirty-second		427	4	12,993	4
Thirty-second Street	60			13,053	4
Thirty-second to Thirty-third		626		13,679	4
Thirty-third Street	60			13,739	4
Thirty-third to Thirty-fourth		500	9	14,240	1
Thirty-fourth Street	60			14,300	1
Thirty-fourth to Thirty-sixth		700		15,000	1
Thirty-sixth Street	60			15,060	1
Thirty-sixth to Thirty-seventh		500		15,560	1
Thirty-seventh Street	60			15,620	1
Thirty-seventh to Thirty-eighth		470	6	16,090	7
Thirty-eighth Street	60			16,150	7
Thirty-eighth to Thirty-ninth		400		16,550	7
Thirty-ninth Street	60			16,610	7
Thirty-ninth to Fortieth		600		17,210	7
Fortieth Street	60			17,270	7
Fortieth to Forty-first		572		17,842	7
Forty-first Street	50			17,892	7
Forty-first to Forty-second		485		18,377	7
Forty-second Street	60			18,437	7
Forty-second to Forty-third		533		18,970	7
Forty-third Street	60			19,030	7
Forty-third to Forty-fourth		332	6	19,363	1
Forty-fourth Street	60			19,423	1
Forty-fourth to Forty-fifth		400		19,823	1
Forty-fifth Street	60			19,883	1
Forty-fifth to Forty-sixth		500		20,383	1
Forty-sixth Street	60			20,443	1
Forty-sixth to Forty-seventh		500		20,943	1
Forty-seventh Street	60			21,003	1
Forty-seventh to Forty-eighth		450		21,453	1
Forty-eighth Street	80			21,533	1
Forty-eighth to Forty-ninth		450		21,983	1
Forty-ninth Street	60			22,043	1
Forty-ninth to Fiftieth		500		22,543	1
Fiftieth Street	60			22,603	1
Fiftieth to Fifty-first		500		23,103	1

WEST FROM DELAWARE AVENUE ON MARKET STREET

NAMES OF STREETS, ETC.	Width of Streets	Length of Streets		Total Distance	
	feet	feet	in.	feet	in.
Fifty-first Street	60			23,163	1
Fifty-first to Fifty-second		500		23,663	1
Fifty-second Street	60			23,723	1
Fifty-second to Fifty-third		500		24,223	1
Fifty-third Street	60			24,283	1
Fifty-third to Fifty-fourth		450		24,733	1
Fifty-fourth Street	60			24,793	1
Fifty-fourth to Fifty-fifth		574		25,367	1
Fifty-fifth Street	80			25,447	1
Fifty-fifth to Fifty-sixth		500		25,947	1
Fifty-sixth Street	60			26,007	1
Fifty-sixth to Fifty-seventh..........................		480		26,487	1
Fifty-seventh Street	80			26,567	1
Fifty-seventh to Fifty-eighth		480		27,047	1
Fifty-eighth Street	60			27,107	1
Fifty-eighth to Fifty-ninth.............................		500		27,607	1
Fifty-ninth Street	60			27,667	1
Fifty-ninth to Sixtieth...................................		500		28,167	1
Sixtieth Street	60			28,227	1
Sixtieth to Sixty-first		500		28,727	1
Sixty-first Street	60			28,787	1
Sixty-first to Sixty-second		500		29,287	1
Sixty-second Street	60			29,347	1
Sixty-second to Sixty-third		500		29,847	1
Sixty-third Street	100			29,947	1

HAPPENINGS IN YE OLDE PHILADELPHIA

NAMES OF STREETS, ETC.	Width of Streets feet	Length of Streets feet in.		Total Distance feet in.	
Market Street	100				
Market to Arch		664		764	
Arch Street	66			830	
Arch to Race		616	5	1,446	5
Race Street	50			1,496	5
Race to Vine...		623	3	2,128	8
Vine Street	50			2,178	8
Vine to Callowhill		498	6	2,677	2
Callowhill Street	70			2,747	2
Callowhill to Pennsylvania		192		2,939	2
Pennsylvania Avenue..................................	80			3,019	2
Pennsylvania to Hamilton...........................		206	6	3,225	8
Hamilton Street	50			3,275	8
Hamilton to Buttonwood.............................		178	11	3,454	7
Buttonwood Street	40			3,494	7
Buttonwood to Spring Garden		207		8,702	3
Spring Garden Street	120			3,822	3
Spring Garden to Green		387	3	4,209	6
Green Street	70			4,279	6
Green to Mount Vernon...............................		191	5	4,470	11
Mount Vernon Street	50			4,520	11
Mount Vernon to Wallace............................		201	5	4,722	4
Wallace Street	50			4,772	4
Wallace to Fairmount.................................		617	6	5,389	10
Fairmount Avenue	80			5,469	10
Fairmount to Brown		259	1	5,728	11
Brown Street	50			5,778	11
Brown to Parrish		356		6,134	11
Parrish Street	50			6,184	11
Parrish to Poplar..		395		6,579	11
Poplar Street	60			6,639	11
Poplar to Girard..		391	2	7,031	1
Girard Avenue	80			7,111	1
Girard to Thompson		578		7,689	1
Thompson Street..	50			7,739	1
Thompson to Master		418		8,157	1
Master Street	50			8,207	1
Master to Jefferson		455	2	8,662	3
Jefferson Street	50			8,712	3
Jefferson to Oxford.....................................		475		9,187	3
Oxford Street	50			9,237	3
Oxford to Columbia		464		9,701	3
Columbia Avenue	60			9,761	3
Columbia to Montgomery		510		10,271	3
Montgomery Avenue.....................................	50			10,321	3
Montgomery to Berks..................................		500		10,821	3

HAPPENINGS IN YE OLDE PHILADELPHIA

NAMES OF STREETS, ETC.	Width of Streets feet	Length of Streets feet in.	Total Distance feet	in.
Berks Street	50		10,871	3
Berks to Norris		500	11,371	3
Norris Street	50		11,421	3
Norris to Diamond		500	11,921	3
Diamond Street	50		11,971	3
Diamond to Susquehanna		530	12,501	3
Susquehanna Avenue	60		12,561	3
Susquehanna to Dauphin		530	13,091	3
Dauphin Street	50		13,141	3
Dauphin to York		500	13,641	3
York Street	50		13,691	3
York to Cumberland		500	14,191	3

FIRST THINGS IN PHILADELPHIA

1681. The first parks or public enclosures laid out in North America for the pleasure and convenience of the people were dedicated at the settlement of Philadelphia, in the Northeastern, Southeastern, Northwestern, South-western and Centre Squares.

1682. First brick house erected in this country (Penn's house).

1685. First almanac printed, "America's Messenger," William Bradford.

1690. The first paper mill established in North America was built upon the Wissahickon, near Germantown, by William Rittenhouse and William Bradford.

1698, February 12th. The first public school in the American Colonies was established at Philadelphia, and a corporation created, entitled "The Overseers of the Publick Schoole founded in Philadelphia." In this school it was ordered by the Governor and Council: "All children and servants, male and female, whose parents, guardians and masters be willing to subject ym to the rules and orders of the said schoole, shall from time to time, with the approbaon of the overseers thereof for the time being, be received or admitted, taught or instructed; the rich at reasonable rates, and the poor to be maintained and schooled for nothing." The first school house was built on the east side of Fourth Street below Chestnut Street. Enoch Flower was the first schoolmaster.

1706. The first Presbytery in the United States was organized at Philadelphia by seven Presbyterian ministers.

1712. The Common Council's resolution, passed this year to the effect that "A Work-house Be Immediately Hired to Employ poor P'sons & Sufficient P'sons appointed to keep them at Work," led, in time, to the erection of the Blockley Hospital, the largest of its, kind.

1718. First American-made printing press, Adam Ramage.

1719. First fire engine bought by any municipality for public purposes.

December 22d. *The American Weekly Mercury*, the first newspaper established in the Middle Colonies, was issued at Philadelphia by William Bradford.

1728. John Bartram commenced on the bank of the Schuylkill the first of America's botanical gardens.

1729. The first botanic garden, for the cultivation of plants having medicinal properties, was established at Bachelor's Hall, Kensington, in the neighborhood of the present Allen and Shackamaxon Streets.

The first treatise against slavery published in any part of the world appeared at Philadelphia, and was written by Ralph Sandiford.

1730. The Mariner's Quadrant was invented by Thomas Godfrey of Germantown, and being taken to England, was introduced into use by one Hadley, who unjustly claimed to be the inventor.

1731, July 31st. The Philadelphia Library, the first public institution of that kind in America, was founded in Philadelphia by Benjamin Franklin, Thomas Hopkinson, Thomas Cadwalader and others.

1732. The Philadelphia Hospital, the oldest in America, was established in connection with the Philadelphia Almshouse.

1735. American type founding made its debut as an art in the shop of Christopher Sauer, in Germantown, and it was first carried on as a regular business in this city immediately after the War of the Revolution by John Baine.

1736, December 7th. The Union Fire Company, the first voluntary association for the extinguishment of fires in the United States, and probably in the world, was founded in Philadelphia by Benjamin Franklin and others.

1743. The American Philosophical Institution, the first institution devoted to science in North America, was founded at Philadelphia by Benjamin Franklin, John Bartram, Dr. Thomas Bond, Thomas Godfrey and others.

The first Bible in a European language printed in North America was published in the German language by Christopher Sauer of Germantown.

1746. The first religious magazine established in North America was published at Germantown, in the German language, by Christopher Sauer.

1749. The first company of American stage players was organized here early in 1749.

First scientific institution in America, founded by Benjamin Franklin.

1751, February 7th. The Pennsylvania Hospital, the first establishment in North America devoted to the relief of the sick and suffering, was chartered by the Assembly of Pennsylvania, at the solicitation of Benjamin Franklin, Dr. Thomas Bond, Rev. Richard Peters and others.

1752. The Philadelphia Contributionship for insurance against losses by fire was established in Philadelphia, being the first fire insurance company established in the American Colonies.

June 15th. The theory that lightning and electricity were the same, which was first suggested by Benjamin Franklin in 1749, was demonstrated by him by drawing lightning from the clouds by means of a kite. The experiment is said to have taken place upon a lot on the east side of Ridge Road, near the present intersection of Buttonwood Street. Franklin was assisted on this occasion by his son, William Franklin, who was then twenty-one years of age.

September. The first lightning-rod used in the world for the protection of a building from danger by lightning was set up by Benjamin Franklin, at his dwelling house, southeast corner of Second and Race Streets.

1753. Pass & Stowe made for the State House the first bell ever cast in this country.

March 4th. The first expedition fitted out in North America for Arctic exploration and the discovery of a northwest passage, sailed from Philadelphia in the schooner Argo, Captain Charles Swaine. The expedition was fitted out by subscriptions in Philadelphia. The vessel proceeded as far as Cape Farewell and Hudson Strait, but being baffled by the ice, was compelled to return to Philadelphia, which port was reached in November of the same year. The same vessel went upon a second voyage in the spring of 1754, but having lost three men, killed by Indians on the Labrador coast, returned in October of the same year without success.

1762, November 26th. The first school of anatomy in North America was opened in Philadelphia by Dr. William Shippen.

1765. Dr. John Morgan's "Discourse Upon the Institution of Medical Schools in America," delivered in the College of Philadelphia, May 30, 1765, constituted the formal opening of the first medical school, and the speaker filled the first medical professorship created in this country. In consequence whereof a "Commencement" was held three years later (in 1768), at which medical honors were conferred, the first in point of time in America.

1766. The first permanent theatre house in America was built here in Southwark.

1768. The first medical society in North America was in existence at Philadelphia.

1769. The first life insurance society, organized for the relief of widows and orphans of the clergymen of the Church of England, was started here.

1773. The American Medical Society was founded in this city by students who came from different parts of the Union to attend the medical lectures here.

1774. Philadelphia philanthropists formed the first Anti-Slavery Society.

The physicians of Philadelphia formed the "Society for Inoculating the Poor," the first benevolent association designed to mitigate the horrors of small-pox founded in the Colonies.

1775. The first pianoforte manufactured in the United States was made by John Behrent, in Third Street below Brown.

In the war against British importations, started in 1775, William Calverly, of this city, set about making American carpets, a local industry destined in time to fulfill the aim of its founder to such an extent that at the present day Philadelphia manufactures more carpets than the whole of Great Britain.

1777. The first United States flag on record, was made here on Arch Street, by Elizabeth Ross.

1780. First American work on medicine by Dr. Benjamin Rush.

The Assembly, in session here, passed the first Abolition Act in America.

The Pennsylvania Bank, the first public bank in the United States, was organized here by Robert Morris.

1781, May 26th. The Bank of North America was established by resolution of Congress, and opened for business in 1783, being the first corporate banking institution established in the United States.

1782. Robert Aitken, of Philadelphia, brought out the first English Bible in this country.

1784. The Pennsylvania Packet or General Advertiser was established as a daily newspaper by John Dunlap and David C. Claypoole, being the first daily paper published in the United States.

1785. The first agricultural society on this continent was "The Philadelphia Society for Promoting Agriculture," formed by Dr. Rush, Robert Morris, Richard Peters and others in 1785.

1786. The Philadelphia Dispensary for the medical relief of the poor, the first institution of the kind in the United States, was established by Dr. Benjamin Rush.

July 20th. The first vessel ever moved by steam was navigated on the Delaware River, at Philadelphia, by John Fitch, being a skiff fitted up for the purpose.

1787, August 22d. A steamboat, forty-five feet long, navigated at Philadelphia, in presence of the delegates to form a Constitution of the United States, by John Fitch, assisted by Henry Voight.

1788, July. Another steamboat, sixty feet long, navigated from Philadelphia to Burlington, New Jersey, by John Fitch.

1789. The first Congress of the United States met here in Congress Mall.

December. A new steamboat navigated at Philadelphia by John Fitch.

1790. The Law School of the University of Pennsylvania, the oldest law school in America, was founded in 1790, with Justice James Wilson of the United States Supreme Court, as professor of law.

Opening of the first Stock Exchange started in America.

Philadelphia was the first capital of the United States.

June, July, August and September. The first steamboat navigated in the world for a passenger and freight-boat ran on the Delaware, between

Philadelphia, Burlington, Bristol, Chester, Wilmington, etc., advertising her trips regularly in the newspapers and passing over three thousand miles in that summer. This was seventeen years before the Clermont, Robert Fulton's first steamboat, navigated the Hudson River.

1791. The Schuylkill and Susquehanna Canal Company, the first public canal company in this country, was chartered here.

First carpet factory started.

1792, June 21. The Philadelphia and Lancaster Turnpike Co. chartered, which made and established the first turnpike-road laid in Pennsylvania.

The Mint of the United States established at Philadelphia, by virtue of act of Congress, being the first Federal mint in the United States.

1794. The Columbianum, the first society for the promotion of the fine arts, in the United States, was established at Philadelphia by Charles Wilson Peale and Joseph Cerrachi, painters, William Rush, sculptor, and others.

1795, September 22d, November 10th. The first voyage ever accomplished by a vessel between Lake Erie and Philadelphia was made by the schooner Whitefish, under command of John Thompson and David Lummis. The vessel was eighteen feet keel, twenty-three feet from stem to stern and six feet beam, without a deck. The route was from Presque Isle, now Erie City, by way of Buffalo harbor; thence by the Niagara River to the mouth of the Chippewa; thence by wagon, on which the schooner was placed, by land to Queenstown, where the boat was launched; thence down the Niagara and along Lake Ontario to Great Sodus and Oswego; thence up the Oswego River to the Falls; around the Falls by land carriage one mile; thence by water to the confluence of the Onondaga and Oneida Rivers; up the latter through Oneida Lake and Wood's Creek to a portage of one mile between the latter and the Mohawk River, over the same by land carriage; thence down the Mohawk to the Little Falls to the same; thence by portage one mile, and down the Mohawk again to Schenectady; then by land carriage to Albany, where the schooner was for the last time launched, thence by the Hudson River, the Narrows along the Jersey coast to Cape May, and up the river Delaware to Philadelphia. The Whitefish after this voyage was taken to Peale's Museum, and for many years remained in the State House yard, until it fell to pieces.

1796. First American type foundry, Binney & Ronaldson.

1799, May 2d. The Philadelphia Water Works, the first of the kind in the country, were commenced, and the water first sent through the pipes January 21, 1801.

1804. The Eruktor Amphibolis, a machine for cleaning docks, invented by Oliver Evans, mounted on a wagon, was propelled by steam along Market Street from Centre Square to the Schuylkill River, being the first land carriage ever propelled by steam in the world. At the Schuylkill River the vessel was launched, a stern wheel attached, and the machine was navigated by steam down the Schuylkill and up the Delaware River to the city of Philadelphia.

First printing ink works, Charles Eneu Johnson.

1805. The Pennsylvania Academy of the Fine Arts, the pioneer of all art institutions in this country, was founded in 1805, and chartered March 28 of the following year.

1807. Joseph Hawkins, of Philadelphia, manufactured the first carbonated water made in America.

1808. The steamboat Phoenix, the first steam vessel which ever navigated the Atlantic Ocean, arrived from Hoboken, New Jersey, where the vessel had been built by John Stevens.

1809, September. The first experimental railroad track laid down in the United States was constructed by Somerville, a Scotch millwright, for Thomas Leiper of Philadelphia, and laid down in a yard adjoining the Bull's Head Tavern, in the Northern Liberties. It was sixty yards in length, and graded an inch and a half to the yard. The gauge was four feet, the sleepers eight feet apart. The experiment with a loaded car was so successful that Leiper had the first practical railroad built in the United States constructed for the transportation of stone from his quarries on Crum Creek to his landing on Ridley Creek, Delaware County, Pennsylvania, a distance of about one mile. It continued in use for nineteen years, and was superseded in 1828 by a canal, which was again superseded in 1852 by a railroad.

A line of telegraphs (semaphore) was set up and operated by Jonathan Grant, between the head of Delaware Bay to Reedy Island and Philadelphia, under patronage of the Philadelphia Chamber of Commerce.

The first insurance corporation was organized in this city.

1810. First Savings Fund Society in America.

1812. Steam works for supplying the city with water were begun in Fairmount Park; and in 1819 Councils erected water power works for the same purpose, which were and for a long time remained the only works of their kind in the States.

1818. Joseph Lancaster started the "Model School" of Philadelphia, the first Normal School in the United States.

1819. The first lithograph executed in America appeared in the June issue of the (Philadelphia) Analectic Magazine.

1821. The Philadelphia College of Pharmacy dates its birth from 1821.

1824. First American Manufacturers' exhibit was held in Carpenters' Hall.

1827. The Pennsylvania Horticultural Society was the first of all such societies in America, having been founded in November, 1827, by a number of Philadelphians under the leadership of Dr. James Meade.

1829. G. A. Shyrock, of this city, earned the distinction of being the first to make paper and boards by machinery from straw and grass.

1830. First penny newspaper, The Cent, published by C. C. Conwell.

First successful women's magazine, *Godey's Lady's Book*, Louis A. Godey, Sixth Street, above Chestnut.

1831. Organizing the first building and loan association, January 31, 1831, The Oxford Provident of Frankford.

Matthias W. Baldwin built an experimental locomotive engine according to his own plans, and differing in many respects from the English engines, which was tested on April 25th on a railroad track laid down in the Philadelphia Museum Arcade, Chestnut Street, and was exhibited there afterward. Subsequently the same engine ran for several months upon a railroad track laid down at Smith's Labyrinth Garden, on the north side of Arch Street, between Schuylkill Seventh and Eighth (Fifteenth and Sixteenth).

In this year Matthias W. Baldwin founded here what has become the largest locomotive building works in the world.

1834. First systematic study of meteorology in aid of agriculture, by Franklin Institute.

1835. First gas pipes in this country were laid here in compliance with an ordinance passed by the two City Chambers.

1848. First issue of the John-Donkey, the first comic paper to be regularly

187

published.

1851. The Spring Garden Institute, for the teaching of useful arts to wage-earning youths, the first of its kind in America, was organized.

1852. For the first time in our history the degree of medicine was conferred upon women at the Female Medical College (now Woman's Medical College) of Philadelphia.

1853. "The Northern Home," founded in this city in 1853, was the first institution in this broad land when the Civil War broke out to open its doors to the children of those who desired to enlist and to build a special home for the orphans of our dead soldiers and sailors.

1854. The Consolidation Act of the City and County of Philadelphia was the first instance of the modern method of making "greater cities."

1857. The Numismatic and Antiquarian Society, whose ranks have since been joined by the most illustrious men of the two hemispheres, and whose scale of measurement for coins and medals is now in general use throughout Europe, was organized by a few Philadelphians on December 27th.

1874. Zoological Garden. First in America. A collection of living animals acknowledged to be by far the best in this country.

1876. Joseph Wharton, of Philadelphia, was the first man in the world to produce pure malleable nickel.

The first World's Fair in this country was held here to celebrate the Centennial anniversary of the Declaration of Independence.

1890. The Company was organized which built the present Philadelphia Bourse, the largest in any country and the only one in this.

1892. Introduction of the pneumatic mailing tube, the first in this country.

Founding of the Wistar Institute of Anatomy, the first of its kind in America.

1897. The first Commercial Museum in America was organized in this city.

1899. National Export Exposition, the first of its nature in the commercial history of the United States.

PETTY'S ISLAND

Petty's Island, or Shackamaxon Island as it was originally known and patented in 1684 by Thomas Fairman, who lived opposite to it at "Pyne Point" (between Cooper's Point and Cooper's Creek). At Friend Fairman's house very frequently meetings of the Society of Friends were held, and in this house William Penn spent his first winter. "Pyne Point," while little known by Philadelphians, is also memorable as the landing place of Benjamin Franklin before he entered Philadelphia. Landing at Burlington by foot, from New York, walking by the shore, a boat came by, on its way to Philadelphia, with several people aboard. As there was no wind they rowed all the way down, and during the night they entered the cove. The tide was the strongest on the New Jersey side. About midnight, not seeing the city, probably obscured by Petty's Island, some of the company were confident that they passed the city of Philadelphia, and would row no further; so they put toward the shore, getting into Cooper's Creek at "Pyne Point." In the morning they weighed anchor and landed at Market Street Wharf on a Sunday morning.

In 1654 Peter Lindestrom, a young Swede, who explored the Delaware from the falls to the capes in the interest of the Royal Commercial College of Sweden, named Petty's Island "Aequikenaska." He pictured the region about Quinkoringh (Cooper's Point) as "beautiful flat and level land, but entirely inconvenient for reaching the shore with vessels on account of the shallow water which is caused by an island which lies about the middle of the river (Petty's) entirely covered with reeds."

The Delaware shad he mentions as "a very fine flavored and excellent tasting fish." Catfish he describes as sweet tasting "like a tench."

Petty's Island was placed under the jurisdiction of New Jersey shortly after the Revolutionary War, when Smith's and Windmill Islands were assigned to Pennsylvania. After Friend Fairman's death the island passed to John Petty, whose name it has retained, although the Mandersons, when they came into possession of the greater portion of the property in 1852, named it Treaty Island, but were unsuccessful in obtaining official recognition of the change, as the Government recognized the old name in authorizing later channel improvements.

The greater part of the island was for a long time owned by the Cooper family, of Camden, who at different times sold or bequeathed portions of it to other parties. The Mandersons, who were in the lumber business in 1852 at Shackamaxon Street Wharf, coming into possession of two large tracts.

The Mandersons owned considerable property in the vicinity of Shackamaxon, Beach and Laurel Streets. On the west side of Beach Street, there were, in the recollection of the writer, stately old-time mansions. The writer frequently called on S. B. Manderson, one of the sons, who latterly resided on Eleventh Street, adjoining the Webster School, above Girard Avenue, who often related to him concerning events in Kensington, notably in the neighborhood of the "Screw-Dock."

William Cramp, the founder of the famous shipbuilding firm, at one time had his shipyard on Petty's Island. He was followed by Henry Simons, the wagon builder, who had a mill there; by Doughty and Kappella, boat builders; John H. Dialogue, shipwright, and Donaghy & Rilat, marine railway.

In 1880, John F. Betz, the brewer, rented that portion between the point (northern) and the thoroughfare, planting numerous willow trees there and calling it "Willow Grove." A resort mainly for dancing and drinking, frequented only by a certain class of sports from Richmond, there were too many brawls there, and the better class of young people stayed away. After a couple of seasons the project was given up, leaving behind a shady grove, used by boating parties as a camp to cook their meals.

About 500 yards west of the point was a low portion of the island, which, when the tide was high, or nearly high, would be used by the numerous gunners and fishermen in "cutting across." This portion was famous for gunning, notably reed and rail birds, ducks, and now and then wild geese, swan, etc. In the fall of the year the gunners who kept their "duckers"—a 12-15 ft. light rowing skiff, very often equipped with a sail—on Miller's Slip, at Shackamaxon Street, Robin's Slip at Marlborough Street, Nixon's, at Hanover Street, Allen's or Faunce's Slip at Otis Street, would "push" through the "mash" and bag numbers of birds, or set out their decoy, or stool ducks in the cove, for "redheads," "butterballs," etc. In the spring these same gunners would go out with their seines and tuns and gill for shad. In the summer they would go out with nets of a smaller mesh, after herring. Up to about 20 years ago, the houses in "Fishtown" that could not boast of a cask of herring in the cellar were few and far between.

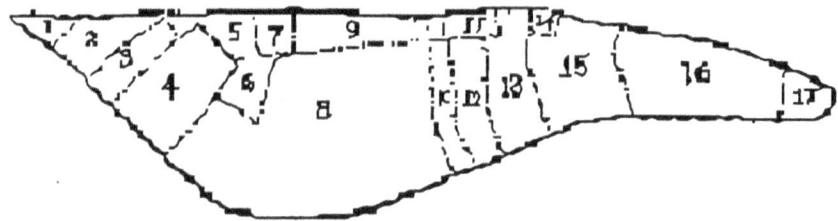

n 1900 the various parcels of land (indicated herewith) were owned by the following:

1	James Manderson	3.50	acres
2	M. C. Cope	15.40	"
3	M. A. C. Morris	30.931	"
4	James Manderson	30.931	"
5	M. A. C. Morris	6.613	"
6	Andrew Manderson	6.981	"
7	Elizabeth Collins	6.184	"
8	Dr. J. Pancoast	118.993	"
9	Andrew Manderson	19.95	"
10	Andrew Manderson	8.199	"
11	J. J. Hatch	3.823	"
12	J. J. Hatch	13.669	"
13	Andrew Manderson	22.9	"
14	J. Rilat	1.167	"
15	American Dredging Co.	29.51	"
16	John Manderson	37.915	"
17	N.Y. Dredging Co.	6.44	"

About 1882 about 23 acres on the western side were cut away and bulkheads inserted, this was done to widen and deepen the ship channel. Subsequently, at the lower end, about 50 acres were cut off.

Previous to the point of the island being improved, i. e., bulkheads inserted, the writer, while a youth, often with companions, would gather calamus there, the whole point a veritable bed of calamus, fed by the tides.

In the winter of 1877 the river was frozen over and numerous persons crossed to New Jersey, or skated, or frolicked on the ice. A number of yachtsmen from Allen's Slip rigged up ice-yachts, sailing around the cove, especially in that part between Cooper's Point and the island. One notorious character of Fishtown, known as "Dad Flick," who kept a saloon at the head of Allen's Slip, opened a booth on the ice, for the sale of liquid refreshments; another "Fishtowner" came up and said jestingly, "Dad, give me a glass of ale."

"Can't do it, Sam, I've got water in the cellar." (Ale was always kept in the cellar).

ATLANTIC CITY, N.J.
Reprinted from *The Evening Bulletin*

Atlantic City has become as familiar to many a Philadelphian in his comings and goings as if it were an active part of his own city. It is now nearer to him in point of time than some localities in the city itself were in the days of horse cars. He may leave his office or his shop at almost any hour of the day and find himself in the midst of ocean breezes sooner than he could have gone, years ago, to Darby or to Manayunk.

Is it to be wondered that today most of us feel that Atlantic City bears to our own city the relation of a sea-washed suburb?

But there are many of us who can readily recollect when a journey to Atlantic City by rail was by no means the promptly agreeable ride which a man may now take in less time than he usually requires for reading his copy of The Bulletin. At that time there was only one railroad to Absecon Island—the Camden and Atlantic; it had no connection with any other road or company, and the major portion of its business by far took place between the end of June and the beginning of September. No one then thought of going to Atlantic City in the winter time; there was no spring or autumn season, and from October to May the small population that lived there the year round was in a state of hibernation. It was shortly before the Fourth of July that the cars usually began to be crowded for the first time in the season, and in September everything would be at a standstill after the day set aside for the "colored excursion" had been duly "observed." The Camden and Atlantic Railroad Company was essentially a summer concern; most of the public never had occasion even to think of it during the other parts of the year, and every hotel on the island was like a tenantless and deserted barn.

A passenger to Atlantic City could go thither on only the Camden and Atlantic, and its only ferry was at the foot of Vine Street—the Cooper's Point Ferry. The average of all the daily receipts of the road for the year round was not more than a thousand dollars. In the summer time there was an early morning excursion scheduled for the majority of July and August days; a morning express, an afternoon express, with an extra one on Saturday afternoons; and one or two accommodation trains. My recollection is that the last boat for the final train down would leave at either 4 or 5 P. M., that the cars were yellow, like those of the Philadelphia, Wilmington and Baltimore and the Reading about the same time, and that the very fastest time that was then regularly made would now be considered ridiculously slow. Indeed, in the late '70s, when it was announced that the Saturday express would go through in an hour and a half, there was great elation over it as an advance in railroading, much doubt being felt, too, whether it would ever be safe to run a train across

191

the sands of New Jersey at a higher rate of speed! Moreover, the ride was usually a very dirty one; how to allay the dust or lessen the quantity of it that spread over the clothes and faces of the passengers was a problem of the day, and many of them would look as begrimed when they reached Atlantic City as if they had been working in a blacksmith shop. The company would announce that everything had been done in using mechanical devices for checking or catching the dust, and at one time, I think, "the ninety-minute train" was preceded by a sprinkler over the entire route.

Few men then thought of going to the shore without a plain linen of mohair duster of either a yellow or gray color, but usually yellow if it were of linen. On a hot afternoon they would be seen rushing to Vine Street Wharf from Front Street, after having jumped from the horse cars, or along Delaware Avenue, with their dusters over their arms, and often with palm leaf fans in their hands. The passengers were nearly all Philadelphians. The very name of Atlantic City was scarcely known in New York, nor was it more known for many years afterwards. The Broad Street Station and the Reading Terminal were not yet dreamed of when the Vine Street Ferry provided the only route from Philadelphia to Atlantic City, and the "Lady of the Lake" on the river and bay was still used by passengers to Cape May who were indifferent to the new railroad of the West Jersey Company or who wanted to go down comfortably with their horses and carriages. If a man or his family from Pittsburgh, or Cincinnati, or Chicago, were seen at Atlantic City, they were regarded in the light of strays or explorers. It was essentially a summer dependency of Philadelphia, and it was not regarded, either, with entire approval by people of fashion, who were inclined to insist that it was rather plebeian as compared with Cape May and its social charms.

The early morning excursion—"the last boat leaves Vine Street Ferry at 6 A. M." was the injunction which was continually impressed upon passengers, most of whom would need to get up before daylight—was peculiarly characteristic of the old Camden and Atlantic. The whole train would be actually special for the lodge, church, association, fire company, musical band or club for which the excursion was organized. During weeks in advance, dead walls and fences would be ornamented with big posters, sometimes in colors, representing a scene in the surf, with men and women in grotesque and highly decent bathing costumes and big straw hats and bonnets; they would be pictured tumbling in the waves, sometimes with their heels up in the air, and on the top of the poster, in startlingly joyous letters, would be printed the words: "Ho! for Old Ocean!" or "A Dip in the Briny!" It might be two hours and a half or more before the train arrived at its destination at the excursion rendezvous, which was a very crude and simple structure, and indeed the Boardwalk itself was scarcely more than a mile of rough planks, often loosely nailed together and also shabby or dilapidated. There were no roller chairs; there were no shops or saloons or hotels directly on it or even adjacent to it; in fact it was raised only a little above the sand, and with the exception of the shanties that were called bath houses, it was, for the most part, disconnected with any sort of business and was largely allowed to take care of itself. The excursionists would swarm over it in bathing clothes, and there were not many persons to be found on it at any time who paid very much attention to "style," outside of the denizens of the "Surf House," a large wooden building situated on Atlantic Avenue, with nothing between it and the ocean but sand dunes. The United States Hotel, another large hotel situated on the upper part of Atlantic

Avenue, in the "residential section," owned by Brown and Woelpper, was one of the "big" hotels. But the most popular hotel at that time was Congress Hall, conducted by "Pop" Hinkel, a beloved and popular boniface. This hotel was situated at Pacific and Massachusetts Avenues.

The first impetus given to Atlantic City was in 1879, when the Camden and Atlantic Railroad wisely used printer's ink in announcing the twenty-fifth anniversary of its coming to Atlantic City.

The Camden and Atlantic Railroad continued to be the only road to Atlantic City until Massey, the Philadelphia ale brewer, who conducted a large ale brewery at the northwest corner of Tenth and Filbert Streets, was persuaded to put a considerable part of his fortune into the construction of a competing one. It was called officially the Philadelphia and Atlantic City Railway, but in popular parlance it was known as the "Narrow Gauge" by reason of its adoption of a standard of contracted width which at that time had some vogue in railroading. There was a good deal of a disposition to welcome it, inasmuch as there was a sentiment that the Camden and Atlantic was a "monopoly," and that fares were too high. But the "Narrow Gauge" proved to be an unfortunate road; from the very day of its opening, when it had an accident, it seemed to have hard luck for some time, and this reputation clung to it during the rest of its existence. Its boats ran from Walnut Street Wharf to Kaighn's Point, and the passengers were often of a cheap or undesirable kind.

The real boom to Atlantic City came when the "Narrow Gauge" introduced 50-cent excursions to Atlantic City. The first few Sundays there was such an exodus of Philadelphians to the "City by the Sea" that they out-eat everything that was on the "island." Food values doubled within an hour; the excursionists were only caught once, for after that they went down laden with shoe and hosiery boxes and packages containing their lunch.

Finally the whole concern was acquired by the Reading; a broad gauge track was laid; first class trains and high speed were introduced; in two or three seasons the good will of the public was obtained, and the Camden and Atlantic, which had passed under the control of the Pennsylvania at a time when the competitive spirit between it and the Reading was still alive, felt the spur of rivalry. There also soon came the third road—that is, the line from Winslow Junction on the West Jersey; Market Street Ferry thus was used for the first time as a starting point for Atlantic City, and indeed the city by the sea became so popular, with three routes, that a rapid transformation from its simplicity to "modern" luxuriousness, and from a Philadelphia to a national resort, began to develop and has been going on ever since in changes which have put it in a class by itself as a great seat of rest and health and pleasure. It has always seemed that the particular impetus to this transformation came from the advent of the Reading as a rival; at least at that time Atlantic City got out of a certain provincial habit of estimating itself and grew along different lines than those which had been followed when it was simply ambitious to get ahead of Cape May and Long Branch.

In later years electricity has become the means of operating still another line in the Pennsylvania system.

How ancient the Vine Street Ferry House now seems with our recollection of it as our one and only Atlantic City gateway.

PENN.

IN CONTRA

HAPPENINGS IN YE OLDE PHILADELPHIA

EASTER SUNDAY AT ATLANTIC CITY

Atlantic City, April 8, 1918.—Atlantic City today staged a wartime Easter extravaganza without parallel for crowds and sartorial splendor. The greatest army of peace and prosperity that ever was assembled at the shore in springtime—typically American in raiment and characteristics, for half of the States and a dozen Canadian provinces were represented—tramped the Boardwalk for hours beside a mirror-like sea, under a burnished canopy of blue and gold.

From the Inlet to Chelsea the phalanxes of fashion moved ceaselessly, bearing upon the common center. From the Garden Pier down to the Marlborough-Blenheim, when the crush was greatest, the wooden way was packed with humanity from the store fronts to the outer rail, a gorgeous flood of marchers, moving sluggishly, eddying in and out about the rolling chairs, crowding the pavilions, the piers and the hotel observation decks.

Thirty thousand persons, the population of a good-sized city, came from Philadelphia to swell the multitude this morning. From shortly after daybreak until noonday train after train rushed them shoreward. Rivers of humanity poured down the streets from the railroad stations and were lost with other streams pouring from the churches, hotels and the cottages to see and be seen in the flood which eddied up and down the sea front.

Ten thousand more came by motor. They parked their machines in the streets, and twenty crosstown avenues from the Boardwalk back to Pacific Avenue were transformed into open-air garages over which policemen stood guard. The police arrangements for Atlantic City's greatest Easter were admirable throughout. Virtually every officer available did Boardwalk duty while the parade was at its height, serving as human guideposts down the center of the jammed promenade.

The day might have been warmer. That was the only drawback to the complete joy of the throngs. A chill wind during the morning caused tens of thousands who had planned to march in the frilliest garb their wardrobes afforded to don wraps and furs instead. But other tens of thousands were not to be deterred from showing their new spring toggery and their gayest millinery, and the spectacle, if not so gorgeous as some of its predecessors, was brilliantly spectacular.

Brilliant colors in wraps no less than in frocks made amends for a pronounced simplicity in the lines of spring styles.

Many of the Boardwalk hotels were compelled to "take down" their registers and refuse to serve hundreds who sought luncheon because the limits of dining room service had been reached. Crowds stood in line to await their turns at tables in all of the Boardwalk restaurants. Thousands of those who came for the day only did not eat at all, because they could not spare the time required to be served.

Scores of moving-picture machines snapped the crowds, while other camera men held up the throngs to catch novelties and crowd effects. One of the unfailing characteristics of an Easter multitude is its enthusiastic willingness to be photographed many times.

The hotels never looked prettier with their gorgeous Easter decorations of roses, azaleas, hydrangeas and other blooms, tastefully massed.

EARLY RAILROAD TRANSPORTATION

Application having been made to the Legislature for a charter for a railroad company to ply between Philadelphia and Norristown, an act was passed on February 17, 1831, incorporating the Philadelphia, Germantown and Norristown Railroad. Eight thousand shares at fifty dollars each were authorized to be issued. The stock was quickly over-subscribed. Rails were laid to Germantown and the road was formally opened on June 6, 1832. The first car drawn by horses left the depot, corner Ninth and Green Streets, at 12.15 P. M., arriving in Germantown three-quarters of an hour later, which was considered great speed. Cars left the depot at intervals of two hours. Fare twenty-five cents. For six months horse-power was used. On November 23, 1832, a great novelty was introduced in the shape of a locomotive engine, which had been built by Matthias W. Baldwin. The engine ran beyond the township line at a speed of about twenty-eight miles per hour. On the following day the locomotive drew four cars loaded with passengers to Germantown, a distance of six miles, in twenty-eight minutes. By act of March 1, 1833, the company was authorized to build a single track on Ninth Street from Spring Garden Street to Vine Street.

In April, 1829, the Delaware and Schuylkill Railroad was incorporated. This railroad was finished and opened on April 23, 1834. The route of same was on Willow Street, from the Delaware River westward to Broad Street to Pennsylvania Avenue, to the Schuylkill River bridge at Peters' Island, there to connect with the Columbia or Pennsylvania Railroad. It was practically the first passenger railroad within the city. The cars were drawn by horses. It was announced that on this date pleasure cars would run at stated periods from the Third Street Hall, northwest corner of Third and Willow Streets. This building was erected to serve a dual purpose—hotel and railroad depot.

Philadelphia and Trenton Railroad was incorporated February 23, 1832, with a capital of six hundred thousand dollars. The depot of the road was established on a lot of ground between Frankford Road and Front Street, north of Harrison (now Palmer Street). The office of the company was at Third Street Hall, Third and Willow Streets. On March 23, 1839, another act of assembly was passed authorizing the company to continue its tracks from the depot in Kensington along the Frankford Road and Maiden Street for one year, until another railroad could be conveniently constructed upon another route from the Kensington depot to the depot at Third and Willow Streets.

The Philadelphia and Reading Railroad Company's charter was passed April 4, 1833. The original object of the company was to construct a railroad from Peters' Island, four miles from Philadelphia, where connection was made with the Philadelphia and Columbia Railroad to Reading, a distance of fifty-four miles. Portions of the road were opened for travel in 1835. The Port Richmond branch, five miles long, from Port Richmond on the Delaware to the Falls of Schuylkill was completed in 1842. After the State Railroad was relocated, in 1850, the old line from Thirteenth and Callowhill Streets, Philadelphia, to Peters' Island, was purchased by the Philadelphia and Reading Railroad Company.

A subsidiary company was The Laurel Run Improvement Company, chartered May 18, 1871, and changed by act of December 12, 1871, to the Philadelphia and Reading Coal and Iron Company.

North Pennsylvania Railroad. In 1851 considerable interest was manifest for the construction of a railroad connecting Philadelphia with the Lehigh coal region. This resulted in the incorporation on April 8, 1852, of the Philadelphia, Easton and Water Gap Railroad Company. The title of the company was changed by act of April 18, 1853, to the North Pennsylvania Railroad Company. It was formally opened on Monday, July 2, 1855, by an excursion from the Cohoquinoque Station, at Front and Willow Streets, to Fort Washington. The road was opened through to Bethlehem in 1857. The passenger depot remained at Front and Willow Streets until 1864, when it was removed to Germantown Road, above Thompson Street (later used as the Milk Depot). Subsequently a depot was built at Third and Berks Streets. The North Pennsylvania Railroad is now a part of the Reading Railway system.

The Pennsylvania Railroad. This road grew out of the mixed railroad and canal system constructed by the State between Philadelphia and Pittsburgh. On the 13th of April, 1846, an act to incorporate the Pennsylvania Railroad was passed. The capital stock of the company was fixed at $7,500,000 with the privilege of increasing same to $10,000,000. During the year of 1847 the city of Philadelphia subscribed $2,500,000 to the stock of the company. The next year the county of Allegheny subscribed $1,000,000. Much of the success attending the Pennsylvania Railroad is due to the almost military rigidity with which its workings were arranged under the inspiration of its chief engineer and first president, J. Edgar Thomson. For twenty years he marked out and reiterated in his annual reports the plan for the future of the Pennsylvania Railroad, and he never deviated from that plan, pursuing it persistently, patiently and faithfully.

TRACTION NOTES

A stage coach drawn by two horses was the beginning of Philadelphia's present transit system.

It made hourly trips from "Schuylkill Seventh and Chestnut Streets down to the Merchants' Coffee House in Second Street." That was in December, 1831.

James Boxall was the genius who inaugurated its hourly trips. He was proprietor, driver, conductor and ticket agent. The fare was ten cents single, or a dozen tickets for a dollar.

Philadelphia, with its suburbs, had at this time about 175,000 inhabitants. James Boxall was the only man among these thousands who possessed brains enough to perceive the possibilities of his scheme.

Within two years another bus line was put in operation. It ran the length of the city north and south. Starting down at the Navy Yard, it led out Second Street to Kensington. The fare was a "levy," or twelve and one-half cents. Its time schedule was one trip per hour.

Not until twenty-five years later (1858), was the first horse or street car line established in the city.

City Councils as early as 1855 had appointed a special committee to report on street railways. They were then in operation in New York and Boston. The committee favored the innovation.

Meanwhile, capitalists were at work in Harrisburg endeavoring to secure a charter for a proposed railway line, to be operated by horse power, on Fifth and Sixth Streets.

Instantly there were intimations of corruption. The most violent opposition to the project was aroused. Mass-meetings were held in protest. Fiery orators harangued the crowds. Unique objections were urged against Philadelphia's premier horse-car line.

A protest signed by 1,200 persons living on Fifth and Sixth Streets was presented to the Legislature. The Legislature brushed all these complaints aside and granted the charter prayed for.

1858

In May, 1857, the Philadelphia and Delaware River Railroad was chartered, giving the right to build a road from Philadelphia to Frankford, upon which cars drawn by horses could be used. Horse cars were in use from January 8, 1858, to November 17, 1863, when the Frankford and Southwark Passenger Railway introduced "dummies" which ran from the depot, Fourth and Berks Streets, to Frankford. The first was called the Alpha, and the second the Sea Gull. As other cars were added, they were called No. 1, 2, etc. The engine was on one side, and the boiler, an upright one, was on the other side, with the engineer sitting between them, not a choice seat in midsummer. These "dummies" with trailer attached seated 64 passengers. The trailers (old horse cars) had additional seats on the roof. A spiral ladder made of light iron was hooked on the rear of the car.

The old depot at Fourth and Berks Streets was abandoned in January, 1872, the company having erected a new depot at Kensington Avenue and Cumberland Street.

1859

March 24. Chestnut and Walnut Street Railway, act of legislature, approved by Council. Company agreed to pay $100,000 towards bridge over the Schuylkill.

May 30. Sunday cars run on Green and Coates Street Railway.

June 23. Arch Street Railway to Fairmount commences operation.

July 17. Green and Coates Street Railway cars stopped running on Sunday, by order of the Mayor.

July 21-23. Sunday car case argument before Supreme Court.

July 23. Indignation meeting in Independence Square on Sunday cars.

October 24. Chestnut and Walnut Street cars commence running to Twenty-second Street.

1860

May 24. Fire, Richmond and Schuylkill River Railway (Girard Avenue Line—Palmer to Thirty-first Street.) Depot, Girard Avenue above Twenty-sixth Street.

1865

February 1. Passenger railway fares raised to 7 cents.

1866

May 13. Chestnut and Walnut Street Railway commenced west of new Chestnut Street bridge.

December 30. Depot of Second and Third Street Railway destroyed by fire.

1877

March 21. Trial of steam passenger cars on the West Philadelphia (Market Street) P. R. W. Co. Seven dummy engines were in use.

September 22. Great excitement among brokers and bankers in consequence of the discovery of an over-issue of stock of the Market Street Railway Company, which it was subsequently ascertained amounted to about 11,000 shares.

1878

April 13. Steam dummy cars, after a year's trial by the Market Street Railway Company, withdrawn from service. Too expensive.

1879

July 31. Seventeenth and Nineteenth Streets Passenger Railway formally opened as a portion of the Continental Passenger Railway.

December 4. The controlling interest in the Union Passenger Railway Company, 12,600 shares, purchased by a combination, principally composed of officers and stockholders of the Continental Passenger Railway Company, at

$100.00 a share. (This was the nucleus to the formation of combinations, eventually forming the Philadelphia Rapid Transit Company).

Ridge Avenue Passenger Railway Company commenced to sell five tickets for the conveyance of passengers for 25 cents. Single fares remained at 6 cents.

1880
March 25. Stable of the Richmond branch of the Union Passenger Railway Company, Thompson and Norris Streets, burned. Loss, $20,000.

1881
June 24. Fifteen thousand three hundred and nine shares of stock in the Germantown City Passenger Railway Company (Fourth and Eighth Streets) being a controlling interest, sold to a syndicate represented by the People's (Callowhill Street) Railway Company.

July 27. The Lombard and South Street Passenger Railway leased to the West End and Angora Passenger Railway Company.

October 18. By vote of 18,463 shares in favor, to 3,501 against the proposition, the stockholders of Germantown Passenger Railway (Fourth and Eighth Streets) resolved to lease their road and franchises to the People's Passenger Railway (Callowhill Street) for 999 years at a maximum rental of $4.50 per share, or nine per cent. on the capital stock.

1882
March 18. Directors of the Union Passenger Railway Company resolved to adopt the cable-motor system for propulsion of their cars on Columbia Avenue branch from Twenty-third Street to East Park entrance.

June 6. Spruce and Pine Streets Passenger Railway cars commenced to run for five-cent fares to Fairmount and Gray's Ferry, from Delaware Avenue.

June 20. Lombard and South Street, and Spruce and Pine Streets Passenger Railway Companies (five-cent fare roads) began a system of exchanges for six cents over both roads.

July 26. Stockholders of the West End Passenger Railway Company, by a vote of over 6,000 shares to 3,300 agree to consolidate their company with Lombard and South Streets Passenger Railway Company. .

October 4. The President and Directors of the People's Passenger Railway Company (Callowhill Street) which also controlled the Germantown, Fourth and Eighth, Girard Avenue and Green and Coates Street lines resigned, and Charles J. Harrah, who had obtained the controlling interest of the stock, was elected President, with a new board of managers.

"Tinkle, tinkle, little bell, when you'll come no one can tell! Remember the old horse car? Apathetic in motion and rich in atmosphere, for decades these snappy roadsters rambled tediously over their tortuous tracks, propelled by decadent equine energy and guided by hands that spared not the lash lest they hold a slack rein. Remember their aromatic summer torridity? Remember the four and six horse hitches on snowy winter nights—the endless blockades—the exciting moments when the driver would run the car off the track and then bounce it boldly on again? And last, but far from least, remember the straw that "warmed" your feet in winter, and by its absence, invariably on the first day of April, It reminded you that it was April Fool's Day? In the "good old days," a few hours one way or the other meant nothing. Now the cry is "Step on it!"

October 4. The President and Directors of the People's Passenger Railway Company (Callowhill Street) which also controlled the Germantown, Fourth and Eighth, Girard Avenue and Green and Coates Street lines resigned, and Charles J. Harrah, who had obtained the controlling interest of the stock, was elected President, with a new board of managers.

1883

April 7. Cable-motor branch of Union Passenger Railway, Columbia Avenue, from Twenty-third Street to the Park, commenced regular operations.

July 23. The direction taken by the cars on the Thirteenth and Fifteenth Streets Passenger Railway reversed, running up Thirteenth Street and down Fifteenth.

September 19. Workmen commenced laying the cable road of the Union Passenger Railway Company on Columbia Avenue east of Twenty-third Street.

1884

May 12. Stockholders of the West Philadelphia Passenger Railway Company ratified a lease of their road to the Philadelphia Traction Company for nine hundred and ninety-nine years, on a contract to pay each stockholder ten dollars per share annually, in half-yearly payments.

June 30. Stockholders of the Union Passenger Railway Company at a special meeting agreed to lease their road to the Philadelphia Traction Company for nine hundred and ninety-nine years.

November 24. New line of People's Passenger Railway Company, via Susquehanna Avenue from Eighth to Twenty-second Street, and by way of Islington Lane (now Diamond Street) and Twenty-third to Norris Street and east on Norris to Germantown Avenue, on Fourth Street to Walnut, and Eighth Street to Susquehanna Avenue, opened for travel.

1885

January 26. Cable passenger railway of the Philadelphia Traction Company went into operation on Columbia Avenue and Master Street.

June 13. New cable of the Traction Company on Columbia Avenue, between Twenty-third Street and East Park, put into operation.

1886

January 16. A majority of the stock in the People's Passenger Railway (Callowhill Street) Company, which was the lessee of the Germantown, Fourth and Eighth, Green and Coates, Girard Avenue and Norris and Susquehanna roads, sold to a syndicate composed principally of stockholders of the Lombard and South Streets P. R. W. Company, and reorganized by the latter.

March 3. Fire at the stable of People's Passenger R. W. Company, at Eighth and Dauphin Streets. Loss, $5,000. It contained 128 horses, which were rescued.

April 2. The traction company withdrew the night cars running on the Richmond, Columbia Avenue, Seventeenth and Nineteenth Streets, and Chestnut and Walnut Streets branches.

April 14. New line of night cars commenced on the Hestonville, Mantua and Fairmount (Arch Street) Railway from Second and Arch Streets to Forty-third Street and Lancaster Avenue.

Night cars resumed running on the railways formerly furnished with that service by the traction company.

October 10. Cable cars commenced running on the Columbia Avenue branch of the Union Passenger Railway.

1887

February 25. The Philadelphia Traction Company gave notice that on and after the first of April the fare on all lines controlled by the company would be five cents for a single ride, with privilege of transfer at certain points and additional charge of two cents for transfer at other points formerly freely given.

March 1. The Traction Company announced a reduction of fare to five cents, and transfers without extra charge.

March 4. The People's Passenger Railway Company reduced fare for all passengers, except infants in arms, to five cents, including all existing transfer privileges.

March 7. The Traction Company and all the other passenger railway companies commenced carrying passengers at five cent fares. Exchange tickets between other roads than the Traction, Ridge Avenue and People's Passenger

Railway systems, seven cents.

March 21. Stable and hayloft of the Thirteenth and Fifteenth Streets Passenger Railway Company, at Carlisle and Cumberland Streets, burned. Loss, $8,000.

August 4. An electric car built by Wm. Wharton, Jr., & Co., and run with the electric power and energy of storage batteries on the car, was run from Gray's Ferry over the Spruce and Pine Streets Passenger Railway to Dock and Walnut Streets with passengers, making two trips.

November 2. Lease of the Lombard and South Streets Passenger Railway lines by the People's Passenger Railway Company rescinded.

1888

January 10. Cable cars of the Traction Company began running on Seventh and Ninth Streets between Columbia Avenue and McKean Street.

June 14. New system of attaching the cars of the Fairmount branch of the Philadelphia Traction Company to the cable motor cars at Franklin and Wallace Streets went into effect.

August 10. Eight cent exchanges inaugurated on the Traction Company's system.

1890

March 1. Cars began running on the Catharine and Bainbridge Streets branch of the Philadelphia Traction Company.

Coaches of the Omnibus Company General began running on Broad Street.

May 1. Lehigh Avenue electric cars began regular service with six cars.

July 2. The Fairmount Park Motor Company formed to build and operate a gravity railroad in the Park.

1892

April 1. The Frankford and Southwark (Fifth and Sixth) Passenger Railway Company took possession of the Tenth and Eleventh (Citizens Line) Passenger Railway Company.

August 15. The construction of the Traction Company's first electric trolley line was commenced on Catharine and Bainbridge Streets.

August 18. Stockholders of the Ridge Avenue Passenger Railway Company leased the line to the Traction Company, the lease to go into effect September 1st.

December 14. First trolley cars operated in the city on Catharine and Bainbridge Streets.

1894

August 12. Trolley cars of the People's Traction Company began running to Mt. Airy.

November 9. The People's Passenger Railway Company reduced the fare to Germantown from ten to five cents.

December 9. The agreement between the People's and Electric Traction Companies, under which free transfers are made at nearly every point where lines intersect, went into effect.

1895

July 22. Leading stockholders of the People's and Electric and the Philadelphia Traction Companies agreed to consolidate and form a company with a capital of $30,000,000, a charter for which was afterwards obtained and consolidation effected, dating from October first.

October 6. The lease of the Philadelphia Traction Company to the Union Traction Company was signed, and the consolidation of the Philadelphia, People's and Electric Traction systems was consummated, the Union Traction Company taking control. John R. Beetem, General Manager of the People's Traction Company, was appointed General Manager of the Union Traction Company.

October 16. Directors of the Union Traction Company decided to fix the rate of fares on all lines at five cents for a straight ride, except to certain suburban points, with eight cents for exchange tickets, abolishing free transfers.

December 17. The strike declared against the Union Traction Company by the Amalgamated Association of Street Railway Employes was inaugurated. Cars were run during the morning on most of the company's lines, especially the lines of the People's division, where almost the regular service was maintained. Disorder and rioting prevailed.

December 25. There was a tie-up on the Girard Avenue line. Cars were attacked by rioters. Ten men charged with inciting to riot were arrested at Second Street and Girard Avenue.

1896

November 10. The Fairmount Park trolley road formally opened.

December 20. George D. Widener elected President of the Philadelphia Traction Company to succeed the late D. W. Dickson.

1897

March 3. The power house of the Union Traction Company at Thirteenth and Mount Vernon Streets was destroyed by fire. Loss, $400,000. Two killed and about a score injured.

1898

February 1. The Union Traction Company took possession of the property of the Hestonville, Mantua and Fairmount Passenger Railway Company.

1899

June 19. Eight or ten masked men entered the office of the Fairmount Park Transportation Company, near Belmont, after the cars had ceased running for the night, and after overpowering the receiver and five other employes, forced the safe and abstracted $3,355.57.

PASSENGER RAILWAYS

1876

Single fare 7 cents, 4 tickets 25 cents. Children under ten years, 4 cents.

CITIZENS P. R. W. CO. Tenth and Eleventh Streets. Down Tenth Street to Reed Street, to Eleventh Street, up Eleventh Street to Diamond Street, to Tenth Street, to depot, corner Montgomery Avenue.

Main Street Branch. Down Tenth Street, up Twelfth Street, Wharton Street to Mifflin Street.

CONTINENTAL P. R. W. CO. From Montgomery Avenue and Eighteenth Street, up Montgomery Avenue to Twentieth Street, to Ridge Avenue, to South College Avenue, to Twentieth Street, to Federal Street, to Eighteenth Street, to Francis Street, to Perkiomen Street, to Vineyard Street, to Ridge Avenue, to Eighteenth Street, to Montgomery Avenue.

EMPIRE P. R. W. CO. Twelfth and Sixteenth Streets. Down Twelfth Street to Wharton Street, to Seventeenth Street, to Carpenter Street, to Sixteenth Street, up Sixteenth Street, to Montgomery Avenue, to depot, corner Twelfth Street.

FRANKFORD & SOUTHWARK P. R. W. CO. Fifth and Sixth Streets. Down Kensington Avenue to Front Street, to Berks Street, to Sixth Street, to Jackson Street, to Fifth Street, up Fifth Street to Berks, to Front Street, to Kensington Avenue, to depot, corner Cumberland Street.

Lehigh Avenue and Powell Street Branch. Up Kensington Avenue to Lehigh Avenue, to Sixth Street, down Sixth Street to Powell Street, to Fifth Street, up Fifth Street to Lehigh Avenue, to Kensington Avenue, to depot.

Frankford Steam (dummy) Line Branch. Up Kensington Avenue to Adams Street, to Main Street, to Margaretta Street and return over same route.

GERMANTOWN P. R. W. CO. Fourth and Eighth Streets. Down Dauphin Street to Germantown Avenue, to Fourth Street, to Dickinson Street, to Eighth Street, up Eighth Street to Columbia Avenue, to Seventh Street, to depot, Dauphin Street. Each alternate car turning up Walnut Street to Eighth Street.

Germantown Branch. From Dauphin Street up Eighth Street to Germantown Avenue, to Germantown and return.

Girard Avenue Branch. From Twenty-sixth Street on Girard Avenue to Palmer Street, to Beach Street, to Shackamaxon Street, to Girard Avenue, to Elm Avenue (now Parkside Avenue) to Belmont, returning over same route.

GREEN & COATES P. R. W. CO. From entrance of Park, down Fairmount Avenue to Twenty-second Street, to Green Street, to Fourth Street, to Dickinson Street, to Eighth Street, up Eighth Street to Fairmount Avenue to Park. Each alternate car turning into Walnut Street to Eighth Street.

Delaware River Branch (one horse). Up Beach Street to Fairmount Avenue, to Eighth Street, returning down Fairmount Avenue to Fourth Street, to Green Street, to Beach Street.

HESTONVILLE, MANTUA & FAIRMOUNT P. R. W. CO. Down Lancaster Avenue to Haverford Avenue, to lower deck of Fairmount Bridge, to Callowhill, to Twenty-second Street, to Race Street, to Second Street, to Walnut Street, to Dock Street, to Third Street, to Vine Street, to Twenty-third Street, to Spring Garden Street, to upper deck of Fairmount Bridge, to Spring Garden Street, to Lancaster Avenue, to Belmont Avenue depot, Forty-third Street and Lancaster

Avenue.

Hestonville Branch Out Lancaster Avenue to Fifty-second Street and return over same route.

Arch Street Branch. Down Hamilton Street to Twenty-fifth Street, to Spring Garden Street, to Twentieth Street, to Arch Street, to Second Street, returning up Arch Street to Twenty-first Street, to Callowhill Street, to depot.

Lombard & South Streets Branch. Down Lombard Street to Front Street, to Dock Street, to Delaware Avenue, returning up Dock Street, to Front Street, to South Street, to depot, corner Twenty-fifth Street and South Street.

Southern Branch. From depot, Thirteenth Street and Snyder Avenue, down Snyder Avenue, to Twelfth Street, to Dickinson Street, to Eighth Street, to Christian Street, to Fifth Street, to Lombard Street, to Fourth Street, to South Street, to Passyunk Avenue, to Mifflin Street, to Twelfth Street, to Snyder Avenue, to Broad Street.

MANAYUNK & ROXBOROUGH INCLINED PLANE P. R. W. CO. RIDGE Avenue, from Barren Hill to Wissahickon Station, Reading B. R., and return.

PHILADELPHIA CITY P. R. W. CO. Chestnut and Walnut Streets, from depot to Forty-second Street, down Chestnut Street to Front, to Walnut Street, to Twenty-second Street, to Chestnut Street, to Forty-second Street.

Fairmount Park Branch. Down Belmont Avenue to Lancaster Avenue, to Thirty-second Street, to Chestnut Street, to Front, to Walnut, to Twenty-second Street, to Chestnut Street, to Thirty-second Street, to Lancaster Avenue, to Belmont Avenue.

Darby Branch. Down Darby Road to Woodland Avenue, to Chestnut Street, to Front Street, to Walnut Street, to Twenty-second Street, to Chestnut Street, to Woodland Avenue, to Darby Road.

Mount Moriah Branch. Same as Darby Branch, as far as Mount Moriah.

PHILADELPHIA & GRAYS FERRY P. R. W. CO. Spruce and Pine Streets.

Grays Ferry Branch. Third and Dock Street, to Second Street, to Pine Street, to Twenty-third Street, to Grays Ferry Road, to Grays Ferry Bridge, return by Grays Ferry Road to Christian Street, to Twenty-second Street, to Spruce Street, to Third Street, to Dock Street.

Fairmount Park Branch. Same as above to Twenty-third Street, to Callowhill Street, to Twenty-fifth Street, to Green Street, entrance to Park.

PEOPLE'S P. R. W. CO. Callowhill Street. Park entrance to Biddle Street, to Twenty-fourth Street, to Callowhill Street, to Front Street, to Vine Street, to Delaware Avenue. Returning up Vine Street to York Avenue, to Callowhill Street, to Schuylkill River.

RIDGE AVENUE P. R. W. CO. Down Ridge Avenue to Tenth Street, to Arch Street, to Second Street. Returning up Arch Street to Ninth Street, to Ridge Avenue, to depot, Thirty-second and Ridge Avenue.

Manayunk Branch. Up Ridge Avenue to Manayunk and returning by same route.

SECOND & THIRD STREETS P. R. W. CO. Down Frankford Avenue to Jefferson Street, to Second Street, to Mifflin Street, to Third Street, to Germantown Avenue, to Oxford Street, to Front Street, to Amber Street, to depot.

Frankford Branch Up Frankford Avenue to Paul Street, to Main Street, to Arrott Street. Returning over same route.

North Penn Branch. Down Frankford Avenue to Huntingdon Street, to Coral Street, to Cumberland Street, to Emerald Street, to Dauphin Street, to Third Street, to Berks Street, to Second Street, to Dock Street, to Third Street, to

Germantown Avenue, to Oxford Street, to Third Street, to Berks Street, to Second Street, to York Street, to Coral Street, to Cumberland Street, to Amber Street, to

Richmond Branch. Up Lehigh Avenue to Richmond Street, to Frankford Avenue, to Manderson Street, to Beach Street, to Laurel Street, to Delaware Avenue, to Fairmount Avenue, to Second Street, to Dock Street, to Third Street, to Brown Street, to Beach Street, to Manderson Street, to Frankford Avenue, to Girard Avenue, to Norris Street, to Richmond Skeet, to Lehigh Avenue.

Bridesburg Branch Up Lehigh Avenue to Richmond Street, to Bridge Street, to Washington Street. Returning by same route.

SEVENTEENTH & NINETEENTH STREETS P. R. W. CO. Up Nineteenth Street to Norris Street, to Seventeenth Street, to Ridge Avenue, to Francis Street, to Seventeenth Street, to Carpenter Skeet, to Nineteenth Street, to depot at Master Street.

THIRTEENTH & FIFTEENTH STREETS P. R. W. Co. Up Carpenter Street to Fifteenth Street, to Master Street, to Ridge Avenue, to Columbia Avenue, to Thirteenth Street, to Carpenter Street, to Broad Street, to depot, above Washington Avenue.

Norris Street Branch. Up Carpenter Skeet to Fifteenth Street, to Columbia Avenue, to Broad Street, to Norris Skeet, to Thirteenth Street, to Carpenter Street, to Broad Street, to depot.

South Broad Street Branch. From depot, down Broad Street to Wolf Street, and returning by same route.

North Broad Street Branch. From Norris Street up Broad Street to Cambria Street. Returning over same route.

UNION P. R. W. CO. Down Brown Street to Twenty-third Street, to Wallace Street, to Franklin Street, to Race Street, to Seventh Street, to Federal Street, to Front Street, to Wharton Street, to Ninth Street, to Spring Garden Street, to Twenty-third Street, to Brown Street, to Park entrance.

Richmond Branch. Down Thompson Street to Marlborough Street, to Belgrade Street, to Frankford Avenue, to Master Street, to Franklin Street, to Race Street, to Seventh Street, to Passyunk Avenue, to Ellsworth Street, to Broad Street, up to Christian Street, to Ninth Street, to Spring Garden Street, to Seventh Street, to Oxford Street, to Fourth Street, to Norris Street, to Memphis Street, to York Street, to Thompson Street, to depot, corner Norris Street.

Columbia Avenue Branch. Down Columbia Avenue to Franklin Street, to Race Street, to Seventh Street, to Market Street, to Front Street. Returning, up Market Street to Ninth Street, to Spring Garden Street, to Seventh Street, to Columbia Avenue, to depot at Twenty-third Street.

Spring Garden and Poplar Street Branch. (One horse.) Down Brown Street to Twenty-third, to Wallace, to Twenty-second, to Spring Garden Street, to Seventh Street, to Poplar Street, to Twenty-ninth Street, to Park entrance.

Cedar Street Branch. From York Street up Cedar Street to Somerset Street, to Richmond Street. Returning by same route.

Christian Street Branch. Up McKean Street to Ninth Street, to Ellsworth Street, to Twenty-third Street, to Christian Street, to Seventh Street, to depot at corner McKean Street.

Jefferson Street Branch. From Twenty-fourth Street down Jefferson Street, to Franklin Street, to Thompson Street, to Front Street, to Columbia Avenue, to Franklin Street, to Master Street, to Twenty-fourth Street, to Columbia Avenue, to depot at Twenty-third Street.

WEST END P. R. W. CO. From Woodlands Cemetery on Baltimore Avenue, to Fortieth Street, to Locust Street, to Thirty-sixth Street, to Powelton Avenue, to Thirty-fifth Street, to Zoological Garden. Returning on Thirty-fifth Street to Eadline Street, to Thirty-third Street, to Walnut Street, to Thirty-sixth Street, to Locust Street, to Thirty-eighth Street, to Woodland Avenue, to Baltimore Avenue.

Fairmount Park Line. From South Street Bridge, to Thirty-fourth and Spruce Streets, on Spruce Street to Thirty-eighth Street, to Lancaster Avenue, to Forty-first Street, to Elm Avenue, to George's Hill. Returning to Fortieth Street, to Locust Street, to Thirty-sixth Street, to Spruce Street.

WEST PHILADELPHIA P. R. W. CO. Market Street from depot, Forty-first and Haverford Avenue, down Forty-first Street to Market, to Front. Returning over same route.

Haddington Branch. Out Market Street, from Front Street, to Forty-first Street, to Haverford Avenue, to Sixty-seventh Street. Returning to Sixty-fifth Street, to Vine Street, to Haverford Avenue, to Forty-first Street, to Market Street, to Front Street.

www.ingramcontent.com/pod-product-compliance
Lightning Source LLC
Chambersburg PA
CBHW080409290526
45791CB00008BA/2207